Farmlands, Forts, and Country Life

The Story of Southwest Denver

Sharon R. Catlett

Hope you enjoy the book! *Sharon R. Catlett*

WESTCLIFFE PUBLISHERS

ISBN-13: 978-1-56579-545-7

Editor: Kelly Kordes Anton
Designer: Barrett Webb / Rebecca Finkel
Production Manager: Craig Keyzer / Rebecca Finkel

Published by:
Big Earth Publishing
3005 Center Green Drive
Boulder, CO 80301

Printed in U.S.A. by Sheridan Books

Library of Congress Cataloging-in-Publication Data on file

For information about other fine books and calendars from
Big Earth Publishing, please contact your local bookstore, call us at
1-800-523-3692, or visit us on the Web at bigearthpublishing.com.

COVER PHOTO: Left: Mullen students milking cows; Center: Grant
family cow herd at National Western Stock Show; Right: 2 boys with
Perchon horses at J. K. Mullen Home for Boys.

TITLE PAGE PHOTO: The 1864 flood of Cherry Creek and the South
Platte River surprised Denver's early residents who had built homes
and businesses in the dry creek bed or near the river.

The author and publisher of this book have made every effort to
ensure the accuracy and currency of its information. Nevertheless,
books can require revisions. Please feel free to let us know if you
find information in this book that needs to be updated, and we will
be glad to correct it for the next printing. Your comments and suggestions are always welcome.

Acknowledgments

I am indebted to numerous people who have enabled me to present some of the struggles and triumphs of the working people who developed the southwest Denver neighborhoods. A huge thank-you goes to my friend and mentor, Millie Van Wyke, who suggested this project after writing her book, *The Town of South Denver,* and assisted me along the way. A big thank-you, also, to another friend and writer, Marie Stearns, for many helpful critiques and encouragement. My thanks to all who graciously granted me interviews and reviewed portions of my manuscript, gave me references for further information, and loaned me photos and books; to staff members at the Denver Public Library, Western History Department, the Colorado History Library, and the Colorado Office of Archaeology and Historic Preservation; and to contacts made through the Colorado Independent Publishers Association.

Thanks also to editor Kelly Kordes Anton and graphic designers Rebecca Finkel and Barrett Webb and to Bev and Elroy Adams, Glenn Adams, Trish Amole, Jan Marie Belle, Mark Bernstein, Jan Burns, Jimmie Butler, Carole E. Campbell, Thelma Cottier, Linda Doyle, Jerry Esparsa, Janell Flaig, Diane Franson, Newell Grant, Peggy Hildmann, Duane Howell, Joanna McCaig, Barbara Munson, Dr. Tom Noel, Janice Pelster, Bonnie Perez, Karen Scharf, Mary Rose (Momo) Shearer, Carol Steele, Janet Merrifield Steele, Ann Student, Tim Summers, Mary Ullmer, Bud Wells, Karen Woodward, and Christy Ziemba for their extra efforts to help me. Finally, special thanks to my husband and best friend, Lindell, for his backing, and to my family and friends for their continued interest during this 10-year project.

I have striven for accuracy in my research and interviews, and I apologize for any inadvertent errors I may have made. I regret that space does not allow me to relate all the intriguing stories that abound in southwest Denver. Perhaps my efforts will inspire other authors to write more about this part of town.

—*Sharon Catlett*

For my husband, Lindell,

my children, Rick, Randy, & Pam,

and all others who grew up in southwest Denver

and acquired a strong work ethic.

Southwest Denver

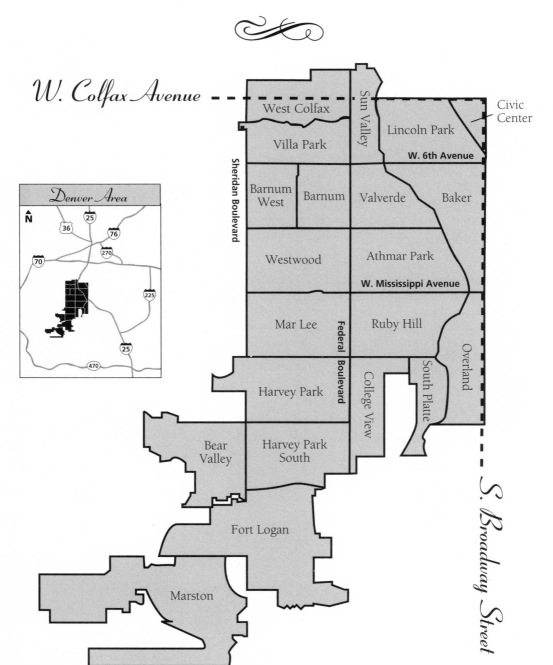

W. Colfax Avenue

West Colfax

Villa Park

Sun Valley

Lincoln Park

Civic Center

W. 6th Avenue

Sheridan Boulevard

Barnum West

Barnum

Valverde

Baker

Westwood

Athmar Park

W. Mississippi Avenue

Mar Lee

Federal Boulevard

Ruby Hill

Overland

Harvey Park

College View

South Platte

Bear Valley

Harvey Park South

Fort Logan

Marston

S. Broadway Street

Denver Area

N

36
25
76
70
270
225
70
25
470

Contents

Introduction

Numerous Denver history books focus on the prominent families east of Broadway and their contributions to the city, largely ignoring southwest Denver, a significant part of the city south of Colfax Avenue and west of Broadway. This may be because, from their beginnings in 1858, a rivalry existed between west Denver (originally called Auraria) and east Denver (known as Denver City). After a flood in 1864, many city leaders headed east for higher ground while persons of lesser means remained on the west side of Cherry Creek. Possibly as a result, history gives little mention to the blue-collar workers and the professional men and women who shaped the city's southwest quadrant. My purpose in writing this book is to give long-overdue recognition to people and places many current residents may not know about.

Beginning in Auraria, at the confluence of Cherry Creek and the South Platte River, Denver, the Queen City of the Plains, spread south and west, annexing portions of Arapahoe and Jefferson counties until December 1973. After passage of the Poundstone Amendment in 1974, these annexations ceased. The 21 neighborhood names and boundaries listed in this book were defined by the Denver Community Planning and Development Agency after a systematic survey in 1971–1972.

To bring this part of the city to life, this book tells about early forts and country estates of the wealthy, now surrounded by the neighborhoods that developed west of Broadway. It focuses on Denver's working class—the farmers, teachers, government employees, engineers, small-business owners, and industry workers who helped shape southwest Denver. This is the story of people who eked out a living during tough times, people who grew up poor and wanted something better for their children, and people who worked for the improvement of their community and still made time for worship and recreation. This is also the story of people of means who established summer homes in the country, which are bordered today by houses of middle-income families. Denver natives and transplants alike will recognize names and learn the histories of many interesting places.

For starters, in the latter part of the 19th century, Union soldiers marched at Camp Weld, famed circus-promoter P. T. Barnum purchased hilltop land west of Denver, and pioneers replaced their log houses with Victorian homes in the Baker neighborhood. South of the city, officers and infantrymen paraded at Fort Logan while Catholic girls studied at Loretto Academy.

When it comes to name-dropping, this part of the city cannot be beat. During the early 1900s, Margaret (Molly) Brown entertained socialites at her summer home overlooking Bear Creek. Paul Whiteman, the "King of Jazz," established the "Black and White Farm" for his renowned parents, Wilberforce and Elfrida Whiteman. John and Catherine Mullen founded an orphanage for boys that evolved into J. K. Mullen High School, and West High graduate Mary Coyle Chase wrote the Pulitzer Prize–winning play *Harvey*.

In reading this book, you will see the transition from agricultural community to city. Old-timers in Valverde and Westwood recall growing strawberries for the local creamery, raising alfalfa and nationally known celery, and milking cows before school. Goats munched on the grassy hills of College View and pigs grew fat in Bear Valley during the country farm era before World War II. When GIs returned from military service, construction boomed as houses went up almost overnight. Shopping centers were born. Schools and parks dotted the streets, forever changing the countryside. Churches outgrew their basement beginnings, and civic organizations, PTAs, Scout troops, and sports teams flourished.

This is not an all-work-and-no-play part of town, even though many favorite recreational spots remain only in memory and photographs. Older residents fondly recall walking or riding the trolley to the Comet Theater, donning roller skates for carefree hours at the Westwood Skating

A horse-drawn rail car travels west of the South Platte River along Hampden Avenue, near Fort Logan, late 1800s.

Rink, or frolicking at Progress Plunge Swimming Pool. Some remember ice skating at Frenchies Lake or Anderson Lake (now Huston Lake and Garfield Lake) or attending classes at Garden Home School before it became Westwood School (now Castro Elementary School).

The following pages contain stories of southwest Denver pioneers—stories that need to be celebrated that we might give a more complete picture of Denver's history. The diverse people and places of southwest Denver, from the Overland Cotton Mills to Pinehurst Country Club, weave a rich historical tapestry.

CHAPTER ONE

Westside Beginnings

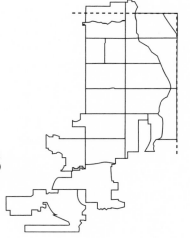

*I*n the first 50 years of its history, from approximately 1850 through 1900, Denver grew from a small mining town into a populous city. Not only did the city grow from about 6 miles to 60 miles square, but the population catapulted from around 1,000 to more than 130,000. The time was marked by rivalry between the city dwellers on either side of Cherry Creek, military presence in the form of Camp Weld, and the introduction of the railroad, which brought an influx of people. During this time, two significant Denver neighborhoods developed in what was called the Westside: Lincoln Park and Baker. For various reasons, including lower land costs due to the propensity for flooding and the rich farmland, the working class tended to settle in this area.

Rivalry between Auraria and Denver

Denver's early appearance was rough and raucous, scrubby and plain, not one that would draw people of refinement. The early settlers came in their work clothes, leading packhorses and mules loaded with gold-mining equipment. Hearing of lucky strikes in mountains to the west, many miners headed from the plains to find their fortunes in Central City or Leadville. During the lonely winter of 1858 to 1859, the settlements of Auraria and Denver City, located near the confluence of Cherry Creek and the South Platte River, had a deep-seated rivalry as they competed for business. "The proselytizing of Aurarians and aggressive manners of Denver City men brought on a feeling of competition that soon developed into one of great animosity, encroaching upon social, business and political relations," said Jerome Smiley, an early historian.[1]

Gen. James Denver

Auraria took its name from a village in the gold district of northern Georgia, while Denver City adopted the name of Gen. James Denver, a lawyer, statesman, explorer, and military commander who headed troops in the Kansas Territory, which extended west to the Rocky Mountains and included the settlements of Auraria and Denver City.

By the middle of June 1859, many new buildings had been added to both towns. Auraria was ahead of Denver City, both in the number of structures and in population, with more than 250 buildings compared to the 150 of its rival. The two places contained approximately 1,000 permanent inhabitants, and an active rivalry for trade persisted between merchants during the summer. The *Rocky Mountain News*, the first newspaper in the area, delighted Aurarians with its location on the west side of the creek at Market Street.

Animosity between the two towns lessened through the autumn as people discussed consolidation to provide a stable city government capable of maintaining law and order and protecting life and property. Before the end of 1859, citizens of Denver City and Auraria agreed to call the consolidated municipality (along with Highland) the City of Denver. During a mass meeting in 1860, Aurarians proposed that "Auraria proper shall be known as Denver City, West Division." The proposal passed in an election and citizens of both towns celebrated by moonlight on the first bridge built across Cherry Creek directly uniting the two settlements. From then on Auraria was known as Denver West or West Denver.[2]

Five years later, in 1864, a flood swept away the crude offices of the *Rocky Mountain News* along with City Hall, stables, warehouses, and other businesses along the banks of Cherry Creek. Because of its lower elevation, the community on the west side sustained more damage than the higher east side. As a result, some residents and businesses from the west side moved to higher ground across the creek. By the close of the year, new buildings advanced the metropolitan appearance of east Denver. The *Rocky Mountain News* rebuilt on the west side, but the old Auraria district did not begin to recover its prestige until the arrival of the railroad in 1870.

Camp Weld

Military bases helped shape the character of parts of southwest Denver. Camp Weld opened 2 miles west of Denver in 1861, training Colorado's first regiment of volunteers to fight in the Union army to stop a Confederate invasion of the West. Its soldiers were a tough and hardy bunch, drawn mostly from mountain mining camps. Started by Territorial Governor William Gilpin, the

40-acre post near West 8th Avenue and South Vallejo Street consisted of hospital, mess hall, stockade, officers' quarters, and barracks for enlisted men. Gilpin financed the fort by printing counterfeit money to pay for construction and salaries. He hoped federal officials would overlook the illicit financing because of his good intentions to strengthen the Union army and provide protection against Indian raids.

Named for the first territorial secretary, Lewis Weld, the fort was not designed to withstand hostile attacks, but it did attract large crowds from the city for social events. To relieve the boredom of garrison life, soldiers staged plays and musicals. Beginning in 1861, people traveled the 2-mile distance to watch the troops' evening parade as well as the entertaining programs.

Denver's enchantment with the fort faded when discontented soldiers found their way to town, visited saloons, and fought with residents. Bored and unhappy because they were paid in worthless "Gilpin dollars," they caused a ruckus and disturbed polite society. Gilpin was removed from office for financing the army post with counterfeit money, but he never faced prosecution.

When called to action, soldiers from Camp Weld won a decisive victory over the Confederate army in 1862 at Glorieta Pass, New Mexico, ending the South's

Camp Weld, a 40-acre army post, where Colorado's first regiment of volunteers trained during the Civil War. A marker commemorating Camp Weld stands at the southwest end of West 8th Avenue viaduct near South Vallejo Street.

dream of controlling goldfields in the West. In 1864, regular army troops were sent to fight battles in the East, leaving the plains unpatrolled. Indians isolated the city by cutting telegraph lines and stopping traffic in and out of Denver. Even though newsprint was unavailable, the *Rocky Mountain News* continued printing, using paper bags or any paper scraps the publisher could find.

In the fall of 1864, Cheyenne and Arapaho leaders met with Governor John Evans and Col. John Chivington at Camp Weld to talk about war and peace. Peace did not prevail, however, as Governor Evans called for volunteers to fight the tribes. In December, the Third Colorado Volunteers, led by Chivington, fought in the Battle of Sand Creek, Colorado, which resulted in the deaths of hundreds of Indians. Known today as the Sand Creek Massacre, this "battle" included the deaths of mostly women and children.

Camp Weld closed in 1865 after two major fires destroyed most of the buildings. A granite monument located at South Vallejo Street on the western approach to the West 8th Avenue viaduct commemorates Camp Weld.[3]

Railroads Bring in the People

The railroad arrived in 1870, ending Denver's pioneer era. The population soared to nearly 5,000 as new arrivals poured in. Throughout the 1870s, Denver's role as a supplier and market for mountain mining areas spurred the growth of the neighborhood on the west side of the city as permanent homes and businesses began dotting its streets.

Isabella Bird, an Englishwoman living in Estes Park, described the great Queen City of the Plains as "a busy place, the distributing point for an immense district, with good shops, some factories, fair hotels. . . . Peltry shops abound, and sportsman, hunter, miner, teamster, emigrant can be completely rigged out at fifty different stores."[4]

Many people came to Denver for health reasons. The common disease, tuberculosis, along with asthma and consumption, was rumored to be cured by the high altitude and clean, dry air in Colorado. As Bird observed, "Asthmatic people are there in such numbers as to warrant the holding of an 'asthmatic convention' of patients cured and benefited."

The Westside

Two present-day neighborhoods, Lincoln Park and Baker, were commonly referred to as Denver's Westside because of their origin as Auraria on the west side of Cherry Creek.

Lincoln Park is bounded by West Colfax Avenue, Speer Boulevard, West 6th Avenue, and the South Platte River. Immediately south is the Baker neighborhood, extending between West 6th Avenue, Broadway, West Mississippi Avenue, and the South Platte River.

Auraria's settlers laid out roads parallel to Cherry Creek, while Denver's streets followed the South Platte River, creating the diagonal street pattern of modern Denver's downtown area. The 1864 Congressional Land Grant gave Denver 960 acres (1.5 square miles) and established Denver's boundaries with Broadway on the east, West Colfax Avenue on the south, Zuni Street on the west, and the equivalent of West 26th Avenue on the north. Street systems changed when developers laid out streets south of Colfax. They used an east-west/north-south grid that followed the ordinal points of the compass as dictated by federal land policies.[5]

Denver grew from 6 square miles in 1874 to about 60 square miles by 1900, with a population of more than 130,000. After Cherry Creek flooded several times, the power elite—including bankers, politicians, and silver and cattle barons—built mansions on high land east of Cherry Creek and east of Broadway, forming the fashionable and exclusive Capitol Hill area.

Men and women of more meager assets settled on lower, less costly land west of Cherry Creek. When railroad tracks were routed near the South Platte River, many residents found themselves literally "across the tracks" from Denver's power elite as the city spread south and west toward the mountains. Although they

A Denver Tramway trolley heads south along Bannock Street about 1900. The smokestack of Arapahoe County Hospital (now Denver Health) is in the background.

generally possessed less wealth and prestige, Westside residents were strong, industrious people of integrity and perseverance. They knew how to grow crops, build houses, make repairs, and survive tough times. They worked as farmers, schoolteachers, electricians, plumbers, engineers, small-business owners, and factory and government employees. Westside residents, as you will discover in these pages, contributed significantly to the city's progress.

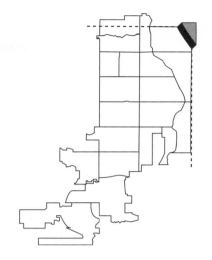

CHAPTER TWO

Civic Center

*I*n the heart of downtown Denver is the Civic Center neighborhood, bounded by West Colfax Avenue, Broadway, and Speer Boulevard. Elegant homes were in the area as early as the 1880s, including the impressive Byers-Evans House. Early in the 20th century, the City Beautiful movement affected the area, producing monuments such as the Voorhies Memorial Entrance and the City and County Building and creating a public space for celebrations. The Denver Mint, Denver Public Library, and Denver Art Museum continue to define the area along with the Colorado History Museum and the Colorado Judicial Building. Surrounded by arts, culture, and government, the neighborhood, now called the Golden Triangle district, is bringing residential living back to the area with new high-rises.

Denver citizens celebrate the Festival of Mountain and Plain in the 1890s.

Byers and Evans

Following the Silver Panic of 1893, city leaders looked for a way to lift residents' spirits and boost business. United by newspaperman William N. Byers, leaders organized the Festival of Mountain and Plain, first held in October 1895 at

Colfax Avenue and Broadway. They invited people from across the nation to view exhibits of Colorado's agricultural, mining, and mercantile enterprises. The festive occasion, staged over three days, also featured marching bands, military reviews, and parades with floats, much like the Mardi Gras celebrations in New Orleans.

Workers were still adding finishing touches to the Colorado State Capitol Building on the hill overlooking the festival, although legislators had moved into the impressive structure in January. Work was not completed until about 1908. The Festival of Mountain and Plain delighted Denverites and tourists nearly every year through 1915, and it returned in the 1980s with the premiere of A Taste of Colorado, which runs every Labor Day weekend.[1]

While Byers was Denver's biggest promoter, John Evans was the city's leading builder. The two men worked well together and did more than any others to organize the rough frontier town into a major metropolis. Evans, born in Ohio to Quaker parents, was appointed governor of Colorado Territory by President Abraham Lincoln in 1862. Unlike many gold seekers who came west, Evans was educated. He arrived in Denver with a degree in medicine and accomplishments in the fields of education and government as well. The wealthy 48-year-old possessed the money and background to help build Evans a university, churches, and railroads. He erected a neat brick home with white trim and an iron fence at 1102 14th Street, Denver's first ritzy residential street. Since most Denver dwellers lived in small log homes in the 1860s, Evans' large home attracted much attention and became the headquarters for civic and social activities.[2]

As Byers and Evans dealt with the city's economic problems, their wives sought ways to aid poor and destitute citizens. Elizabeth Byers, an attractive woman still in her 20s, founded the Ladies United Aid Society in 1860. With the help of Margaret Gray Evans she reorganized the group in 1872 as the Ladies Relief Society. Together, they started the Old Ladies Home in 1873. The home was restored years later and renamed The Argyle. Other private and church charities combined in 1887 as the Charity Organization Society, which evolved into the United Way. Elizabeth Byers also started the Home of the Good Shepherd for homeless girls in 1885. The home, originally on the southwest corner of West Cedar Avenue and Cherokee Street, moved to a larger space on South Colorado Boulevard and Louisiana Avenue in 1912.[3]

In 1878, John Evans erected a sandstone chapel at West 13th Avenue and Bannock Street in memory of Josephine Evans Elbert, a daughter from his first marriage. The chapel was relocated in 1960 to the University of Denver campus; Evans was one of the university's founders. He died in 1897 at age 83.

Byers-Evans House

The Evans son, William Gray Evans, carried on the family's enterprises. In 1889, he and his wife, Cornelia, bought a house built six years earlier by William N. Byers. Located in the Evans subdivision near the chapel, the two-story Italianate house was the former home of the Byers family and became known as the Byers-Evans House. William completed an addition to the home for his widowed mother and younger sister. The house remained in the Evans family until 1981, when it was donated to the Colorado Historical Society (CHS). Listed on the National Register

The William Byers family built this house on Bannock Street in the 1880s.

of Historical Places, the house at 1310 Bannock Street was restored in 1989. It is open to the public for tours and special events such as lectures and Mother's Day teas hosted by the CHS. Interactive video displays and exhibits showing Denver's development are featured in the former servants' quarters and garage.[4]

The City Beautiful Movement and Civic Center

As the city recovered from the Silver Panic of 1893, Denverites wanted to improve their young city. Inspired by the City Beautiful movement springing up from the 1893 Columbian Exposition in Chicago, Mayor Robert W. Speer initiated programs to create parks, boulevards, and a civic center. Each spring the city distributed free maple and elm trees to beautify the drab city of the plains.[5]

The newly formed Municipal Art Commission hired Charles M. Robinson to draft a plan featuring a landscaped civic center. After voters defeated a bond issue for the 1906 plan, Speer appointed an independent commission to pursue the idea. An area bounded by Colfax Avenue, West 14th Avenue, Broadway, and Bannock Street was cleared of buildings except for the library. The lawn was planted by 1915.

In 1916, Speer hired Edward H. Bennett, a Chicago architect, to design a plan incorporating ideas of previous planners and new ideas Speer had acquired in

Europe. The new plan included a large meeting place for civic events, a strong north–south axis bisecting the east–west axis, and a monument to honor people who gave money and other gifts to beautify the city. Meanwhile, Mayor Speer urged wealthy citizens to give some of their riches back to the community where they had prospered. His speech, "Give While You Live," generated only a moderate response, raising a little more than $500,000.

Work on the structures began in 1917, with construction of four decorative pylons and a line of balusters. Speer died unexpectedly in 1918, before the realization of his dream. His influence, however, remained, as the public gathering space took shape.

Bennett's plan included a triangle of land to the north of Colfax Avenue and a corresponding triangle to the south of West 14th Avenue, causing curves in the two streets as they were rerouted to skirt structures in the triangles. The south triangle contained the Court of Honor, with names of civic benefactors inscribed on the wall. The curved structure, completed in 1919, surrounded a Greek theater—a terraced, semicircular, open arena—seating 1,200. To the north, the Voorhies Memorial Entrance was finished in 1920. Bequeathed by banker John H. P. Voorhies, the main entry at Acoma Street drew citizens from downtown through an arched opening anchored by a colonnade of Ionic columns constructed of Turkey Creek sandstone. A pool was added two years later, graced by two cherub-on-dolphin fountains fashioned by Denver sculptor Robert Garrison.

Initially, the Municipal Band gave concerts at the Greek theater, which was designed with a "glass curtain" that could be lowered behind the band to improve acoustics. Paintings by local artist Allen True depicted two scenes of pioneer life—the trapper and the prospector—on both sides of the stage. John K. Mullen donated the *Bucking Bronco* statue, and Stephen Knight funded the *On the War Trail* statue of an American Indian brandishing a spear in defiance of the conquering white man.[6]

Drug dealers and transients congregated in the Civic Center during the 1970s, among the deteriorating monuments and fountains. When voters passed a bond issue in 1982, the Peña administration started restoring the park's former beauty. Funds from another bond issue in 1989 went to improve the flower gardens and street lamps. The area continues to see improvement at the beginning of the 21st century as agencies band together to ease the homeless situation in Denver.

The Denver Public Library

In 1903, the Denver Public Library occupied a dilapidated building on the southeast corner of Colfax Avenue and Bannock Street. The structure was originally

A modern $3.3 million central library opened in 1955 at W. 14th Avenue & Broadway.

built as La Veta Place, a luxury suburban townhouse complex financed by businessman David Moffat in the early 1880s. At one time, La Veta Place belonged to Augusta Tabor, the first wife of silver baron Horace Tabor, who rented the fancy apartments to Denver's socialites. The townhouse deteriorated after the Silver Panic of 1893 and the matron's death in 1895 and was demolished to make way for a new library.[7]

The city opened the new library in 1910—a stately $430,000 Greek Revival structure fronted by huge Corinthian columns. A grant from the Andrew Carnegie Foundation provided nearly half the funds. Several branch libraries sprang up in 1912, allowing the central library to emerge as a reference facility containing rare books, artwork, and a collection of newspaper clippings and documents that made up the Colorado Collection.

The Denver Public Library (DPL) continued to grow. Combined items from the Colorado Collection and Western Americana departments formed the nucleus of the Western History Department in 1935. Concerned about overcrowded conditions, the Library Commission selected a location at the southwest corner of West 14th Avenue and Broadway for a new central library. Architect Burnham Hoyt designed the modern $3.3 million library in conjunction with the firm of Fisher & Fisher. DPL converted a remaining portion of the O'Meara Ford Showroom into a children's wing of the new library, which opened in 1955. A basement auditorium, named for Malcolm Glenn Wyer, seated 372 people for public hearings, concerts, movies, lectures, and library-sponsored programs. Wyer headed the library from 1924 to 1951.[8]

The central library struggled during the 1970s and early 1980s due to lack of funding for staff and maintenance. Dr. Rick Ashton was appointed to the top position in July 1985. Five years later, voters passed a bond issue that included allotments for new libraries and renovations to existing facilities. Architect Michael Graves designed a seven-story addition to the central library, which tripled its size. While the exterior represents a village with structures of different colors and shapes, the interior features walls, tables, and lamps of golden maple. The new facility opened in 1995, with an innovative great hall, western history reading room, and art gallery.

The old Carnegie Library building, at 144 West Colfax Avenue, was remodeled for city offices and became known as City and County Building Annex No. 2.[9]

The City and County Building

Work on the City and County Building at the west edge of Civic Center Park began in 1924 and was completed in 1932, providing a dominant structure to balance the capitol building directly east. Designed with a Beaux-Arts Neoclassical façade, the majestic structure sat on a base of dressed Cotopaxi granite, with Doric columns curving toward the capitol. Granite from Stone Mountain, Georgia, formed the upper walls and entry columns. The grand staircase led to an impressive three-story Corinthian entry with enormous bronze doors, the largest bronze doors in America. The interior incorporated 11 varieties of marble.

Denver's traditional holiday lighting display started in the 1920s with a simple lighted tree in Civic Center.

First conceived in Mayor Speer's 1906 City Beautiful plan, the splendid city hall was adorned with a carillon clock tower and chimes donated in Speer's memory by his wife, Kate. The slender bell tower and the building's fairly low profile protected a panoramic view of the mountains from Capitol Hill. Located at 1437 Bannock Street, Denver's City and County Building stretches over a full city block.[10]

Denver's traditional holiday lighting display started in the 1920s when the city granted electrician John Malpeide permission to put up a lighted tree in Civic Center. The display grew more elaborate, beginning with a few hundred lights on the City and County Building, and soon used more than 30,000 lights. Requiring a large budget by the 1950s, the popular spectacle was in jeopardy until 1985, when permanent funding was ensured through private and corporate donations to the Keep the Lights Foundation.[11]

The Denver Mint

The Denver Mint went in at 320 West Colfax Avenue, between Cherokee Street and Delaware Street, in 1909. Built of pink Pikes Peak granite and Colorado gray granite, the two-story citadel was inspired by the Palazzo Medici-Riccardi in Florence, Italy, although several additions have altered the original rectangular shape. Free public tours made it a popular Denver attraction until tight restrictions were imposed after the terrorist acts of September 11, 2001. Tours resumed again by reservation in May 2004. One of only two full-service mints in the nation, the facility is the largest coin producer in the world.[12]

On the Northern Fringe

The Pioneer Monument Fountain, at the northwest corner of Colfax Avenue and Broadway, replaced the old city fire station that once contained two horse-drawn wagons. Erected in 1911, statues honor a prospector, a mountain man, and a pioneer mother (holding a baby in one arm and a rifle in the other). In the center is a replica of frontiersman Kit Carson on his horse. The figures sit on a hexagonal granite base, supporting a fountain with horse troughs on each side where travelers could water their horses.[13]

North of Civic Center, the City Hall Annex No. 1, at Colfax Avenue and Bannock Street, was built in 1949 as classrooms for the University of Denver Business School. In 2002, the International-style edifice was renovated and consolidated into an addition. Designed by David Owen Tryba, the addition is called the Wellington E. Webb Municipal Office Building after the Denver mayor who served from 1991 to 2003.[14]

The Evans Addition

The Evans Addition neighborhood, named after developer and governor John Evans, extended roughly from Broadway to the alley of Cherokee and Delaware

Streets between Colfax and West 11th Avenues. The once-elite neighborhood struggled after the economic panic of 1893 and the departure of the rich who settled in Capitol Hill. Working-class blacks and Mexican-Americans moved in next to longtime residents of German and Scandinavian descent.

The area filled with apartments, single-family homes, duplexes, offices, industrial enterprises, and car dealerships. Robert R. Hall Cadillac occupied the northeast corner of West 11th Avenue and Cherokee Street. The Denver Coca-Cola Bottling Plant operated at 1025 Cherokee Street from 1925 to 1948. Rocky Mountain Bank Notes built its striking headquarters at West 11th Avenue and Delaware Street.

In 1964, the Denver Wax Museum opened at West 9th Avenue and Bannock Street. The Museum for Children started on Bannock Street in 1975, about the time the Denver Catholic Archdiocese moved from Bannock Street to offices at 2nd Avenue and Josephine Street. Plans to rebuild sections of the Evans Addition near Speer Boulevard for the 1976 Olympics were scrapped after voters defeated a 1972 ballot proposal to help fund improvements for the Games.[15]

By the early 1970s, hippies and counterculture institutions occupied many of the neighborhood structures, in addition to low-income immigrants and transitory college students who attended Metropolitan State College or Community College of Denver at West 12th Avenue and Acoma Street.

Evans School

Evans School stood at West 11th Avenue and Acoma Street, on land once donated by Territorial Governor John Evans as a possible site for Colorado's state capitol. After an elevated site was chosen for the capitol instead, Denver Public Schools acquired the plot and erected a $130,000 structure first known as the New Broadway School. The school opened in 1905 with a capacity for 750 students.

Enrollment declined in the late 1920s as industry began to displace residents from the Evans Addition. In 1928, the school served deaf elementary students from across the city; two years later it added a program for blind children. Evans School closed in 1972, due to a waning number of children, low academic performance, and antiquated facilities.

The school, which sold for $650,000 in 1974, was listed on the National Register of Historic Places in 1980. The new owners, Alan and Robert Eber, opened the abandoned building occasionally as a Halloween haunted house, owing to rumors about ghosts roaming the halls. The vacant house is on Colorado's Most Endangered Places List and now awaits its fate.[16]

The Denver Art Museum

The Byers-Evans House was spared as the sole survivor of the elite residential Evans Addition neighborhood when the city cleared land for a new art museum. Tracing its origin to the Denver Artists Club of 1893, the Denver Art Museum once exhibited its treasures at Chappell House, which was donated to the city in 1922 by Mrs. George Cranmer, wife of Denver's park planner, and her brother, Delos Chappell. Later, the museum took its expanded collection to the newly constructed City and County Building.[17]

The new Denver Art Museum, designed by Italian architect Gio Ponti and local architect James Sudler, featured a Corning glass tile exterior with narrow window slits, some in protruding surrounds. Situated at 100 West 14th Street, next to the Byers-Evans House, the art gallery opened in 1971 as patrons passed through a dramatic oval entrance into an airy lobby and stacked vertical galleries.

The Frederic C. Hamilton Building, a modern landmark expansion that opened in October 2006, was designed by Daniel Libeskind, who was involved in the new World Trade Center project in New York City. The added space nearly doubled the size of the museum, providing three new state-of-the-art galleries to display permanent exhibits.[18]

The Golden Triangle

In the mid-1970s, the Auraria urban renewal project north of Colfax Avenue incorporated three colleges into the Auraria Higher Education Center, leaving the old Evans neighborhood with few residences and blocks of parking lots. As the oil boom financed downtown skyscrapers, developers began to look at the Evans Addition area as a promising extension of the central business district. Newspapers and planners referred to the former residential area as the Golden Triangle, most likely after a similar sector of Pittsburgh praised as a successful real estate venture. Speculators drove up property prices, and the wax museum and children's museum could not afford to stay in the neighborhood.[19]

Bail bondsmen converted houses into offices, especially along the west side of Delaware Street near the new Denver city jail and police headquarters, which opened in 1978 on the block bounded by West 14th Avenue, Cherokee Street, West 13th Avenue, and Delaware Street. Lawyers established offices in the area, art galleries went in along parts of Broadway, and politicians often set up campaign headquarters in the Golden Triangle.

Property owners reacted to an effort by the Denver Urban Renewal Authority (DURA) to clear about eight blocks east of Speer Boulevard between West 11th

Avenue and West 13th Avenue and persuaded city council to delay the action. They organized the Golden Triangle Association to raise private money for redeveloping the area. But as the oil boom collapsed, buyers who had paid exorbitant prices for the properties lacked resources for development and could not pay off their debts. Banks foreclosed on loans and razed buildings, including historic homes designed by noted architect Robert S. Roeschlaub, to reduce maintenance costs and taxes.[20]

The area was touted as the preferred site for the Colorado Convention Center until a dispute surfaced with other speculative interests. The city finally called in the Urban Land Institute to decide on a location for the new convention center. The arbitrating body chose a site at 700 14th Street, next to the old Currigan Exhibition Hall.

After the millennium, the neighborhood's personality changed as elaborate, luxury, high-rise condominiums added to the mix of historic homes, commercial buildings, and mid-rise condos. The 15-story Belvedere at 475 West 12th Avenue opened in 2001 with 74 units, and the 18-story Prado at 300 West 11th Avenue opened a year later. Developer Craig Nassi, a former Aurora schoolteacher, said his projects appealed to athletes, young professionals, and high-profile lawyers.[21]

Another developer, Mickey Zeppelin, a former president of the Golden Triangle Neighborhood Association, said Nassi's developments redefined the paradigm of the Triangle, since others had thought in terms of six- to eight-story buildings. Some residents, irritated by the condos' height and scale, felt the European architectural design did not fit with the neighborhood's character.[22]

Nassi's third high-rise, the Beauvallon, went in across Broadway, at 925–975 Lincoln Street, in 2004. Its 14 stories included 210 units, four restaurants, a 12,000-square-foot spa and health club, and a rooftop pool with a swim-up bar.

Acoma Street, connecting the Golden Triangle to Civic Center and downtown, has become "The Avenue of the Arts" with its art studios, galleries, and cafes. The Acoma Center, 1080 Acoma Street, provides a place for civic functions in the Golden Triangle and hosts performing and visual arts programs for patrons from the entire metro area.

The Colorado History Museum and Colorado Judicial Building

Since its eastern boundary extends to Lincoln Street, the Golden Triangle also claims the Colorado History Museum and Colorado Judicial Building, which share a square block. Outgrowing its classical Greek Revival edifice on the corner of East 14th Avenue and Sherman Street, the Colorado History Museum moved to the three-story gray brick building at 1300 Broadway in 1977. A colorful mural depicting Colorado's history was painted across the façade, which was originally designed as the back of the building. Three north terraces descended to an open courtyard between the two state buildings.[23]

At the north end of the block, the five-story white Colorado Judicial Building was constructed on two legs straddling the first floor. Although Otto and Helen Friedrichs provided a large donation for a fountain, the plan was modified to feature an outdoor overhead mural picturing the evolution of law instead.

Downtown Celebrations

Civic Center, west of Broadway at Colfax Avenue, continues to serve as the central hub and gathering place for Denver-area residents, as it has since the first Festival of Mountain and Plain in 1895. Civic Center has hosted citywide events

A large crowd attends a municipal band concert in Civic Center's Greek theater in 1920.

such as the People's Fair, Cinco de Mayo festivities, and dramatic presentations in the Greek theater.

The Denver Partnership, a group of downtown business owners, sponsored A Taste of Colorado on Labor Day in 1984 as a morale booster following the economic decline of the 1970s. Reminiscent of the long-ago Festival of Mountain and Plain, the free celebration has gained in popularity each year. In 2005, nearly 500,000 adults and children enjoyed a variety of bands and entertainers plus 250 booths offering food, clothing, and wares.[24]

The Civic Center Conservancy

The Civic Center Conservancy formed in 2004 to raise funds to restore and revitalize Denver's central park. In partnership with the Denver Parks and Recreation Department, the conservancy's first job was to replace crumbling concrete in the Greek theater. In 2006, the organization started a farmers' market featuring Colorado produce, gourmet food products, and lunchtime restaurant delicacies for downtown visitors and businesspeople. The conservancy is currently reviewing new ideas from Daniel Libeskind, architect of the Denver Art Museum's Frederic C. Hamilton Building.

A man hauls a load of snow past the pioneer monument at Civic Center following a record snowstorm, December 1913.

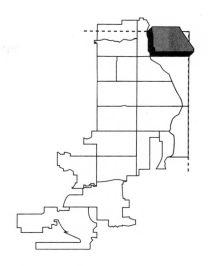

CHAPTER THREE

Lincoln Park

The Lincoln Park neighborhood dates back to the settlement of Auraria, the area north of Colfax Avenue where the Auraria Higher Education Center is now located. Today's Lincoln Park neighborhood was annexed by Auraria City, the area of the original congressional grant, under the Territorial Session Laws of 1874 and 1883. The boundaries are West Colfax Avenue, Speer Boulevard, West 6th Avenue, and the South Platte River. William N. Byers, co-founder of the *Rocky Mountain News*, was significant to the area's development, as were leading Denver philanthropists, the Mullens. The development and growth of Franklin/West High School, Denver General Hospital, St. Joseph's Parish, and the Buckhorn Exchange restaurant also had lasting impact.

Traditionally, the neighborhood was called La Alma, a Spanish word for "spirit" or "mind." In the 1970s, however, it was

Several men stand on Walnut Street near the crude office of the Rocky Mountain News *in Auraria in 1859.*

named for a park the city established in 1885. At that time, the city purchased 15 acres of land from a military post called Camp Wheeler near West 11th Avenue and Mariposa Street. The site became Lincoln Park, one of Denver's earliest planned parks, and a setting for the La Alma Recreation Center. La Alma is sometimes linked to the neighborhood's traditional name, making it La Alma/Lincoln Park. Due to its origins, neighborhood residents have hosted numerous Mexican-American festivities over the years.

William N. Byers

William N. Byers, a 28-year-old surveyor, came to Auraria with a printing press and plans to launch a newspaper. He claimed 160 acres along the South Platte River, built a cabin at the river's edge near West Virginia Avenue, and lived there with his wife, Elizabeth, and their children, Mollie and Frank. Byers and his partner, John L. Dailey, printed the first newspaper on April 23, 1859, from the attic over "Uncle Dick" Wootton's General Store on 11th Street. They called their publication the *Rocky Mountain News* and built an office on the dry bed of Cherry Creek. After the 1864 flood demolished the wooden office building, the newspaper moved to rented quarters. Dailey eventually opened his own printing and bookbinding business. Byers later sold his interest in the paper but continued to push for civic improvement through his visionary efforts for a united community.[1]

In 1877, Byers' subdivision had water from the Platte Water Canal, tree-lined streets, and no city taxes. Railroad workers and entrepreneurs built small brick homes on vacant lots and opened shops in the neighborhood. Nearly every building had some ornament that made it unique. More than 90 percent of the blocks were developed by 1900 and the remainder by 1915. The commercial block surrounding 1369 Kalamath Street housed various dry goods, grocers, barbers, tailors, and other small businesses.

William N. Byers, a young surveyor, traveled west with a printing press and was the founder of the Rocky Mountain News *in 1859.*

The Westside Historic District

Several blocks in the Lincoln Park neighborhood are listed on the National Register of Historic Places as an example of early Denver's working class community. The Westside Historic District is situated on Kalamath, Lipan, and

Mariposa Streets between West 13th Avenue and West Colfax Avenue. Although floods along Cherry Creek destroyed buildings in 1864, 1897, and 1912, many of the remaining original structures are listed in the *Denver Inventory* because of architectural or historical significance. Published in 1974, the *Denver Inventory* lists more than 2,200 historically significant buildings throughout the city.[2]

A typical one-story brick home on Lipan Street featured a rectangular floor plan with two bays, vernacular Doric detailing, a front gable with projecting eaves, and wood front porches. Other Victorian residences included row houses, such as the five units at 1102–1118 West 13th Street.

Franklin/West High School

Denver's education system advanced due to the efforts of O. J. Goldrick, an Irishman educated at New York's Columbia University. In a city swarming with miners and fur traders, the smartly dressed Goldrick created quite a stir in 1859 when he drove a team of oxen into Denver. He wore a broadcloth suit, stovepipe hat, and kid gloves. Goldrick also caught people's attention in front of the Lindell Hotel in 1860 with pleas for public education and with persistent oratory at Colorado's first legislative assembly in Denver in 1861.

Goldrick opened the first school, a private school, in a log cabin on the west side of 12th Street between Larimer and Market Streets. As the first superintendent of Arapahoe County Schools, he divided the area into five school districts. At that time, Arapahoe County encompassed all the land to the present-day Kansas border.[3]

Separated by Cherry Creek, District 1 (East Denver) and District 2 (West Denver) competed once again for prominence. East Denver was the first to organize its school board, but West Denver (Auraria) opened the first free public school in Colorado on December 1, 1862, near 10th Avenue and Larimer Street. In spite of floods in 1864 and scarce school funds, determined Westsiders raised $700 to purchase the Arsenal Building, which stored federal military supplies during the Civil War, and thus became the first school district to own a building. The two-story brick structure at 11th Street and Lawrence Street became the Eleventh Street School, housing about 200 students through eighth grade.[4]

Schools struggled for funding because of the unusually large population of transient men with no families and little interest in education. At the close of the 1869–1870 school year, persons of school age numbered fewer than 1,200 in a city of 4,000 to 5,000.

Lack of funds eased after 1870 when new railroads brought added commerce to Denver and a legislative act provided for more permanent funding. As the demand for public schools grew, the city opened the new Central High

School in 1880 near 10th Street and Kalamath Street for pupils in grades 7 through 11.

Central High School students transferred in January 1884 to a new building with gables and embellishments in the style of Denver's residential mansions. The grand school at West Colfax Avenue and Mariposa Street was called Franklin High School. It was often referred to as West Denver High School, however, so the names became interchangeable.

Charles R. McDonough, the first graduate of Franklin/West, was among the elite 10 percent of the school-age population able to attend high school. Not only at Franklin but across America most young people completed only up to sixth or eighth grade, then went out into the world to earn a living. McDonough, who was educated in the classics and the Bible, was said to love God and his country. He believed in a strong work ethic, and his oration at the graduation ceremony on June 13, 1884, focused on "A Nation's Wealth." He was one of six who graduated that day. His son Randolph graduated three decades later. As class orator also, Randolph talked about "The Effects of the American Revolution Upon Human Rights Throughout the World."[5]

The Franklin High School graduating classes of 1884 and 1885 met jointly in June 1885 and elected Ferdinand Jeffries as first president of the Alumni Association. Known from its beginning as Franklin/West, then Baker West, and finally West High School, the school rallied community pride. Residents of District 2 loved its one and only high school. Graduates became the "guardians" of West High, supporting the school through its growing years, a tradition that continued as alumni gave "their money, their time, their hearts" to the West High School Alumni Association.[6]

The Shwayder children were pupils at Franklin/West in the early 1900s. Their large Jewish family operated a neighborhood grocery, then opened a more profitable secondhand furniture store. Son Jesse, a promising vocalist, developed other talents as the inventor and founder of Samsonite, America's largest luggage company. As the story goes, when workers in his plant complained of extreme noise, Jesse came up with the idea of hiring deaf mutes and even organized a softball team called the Shwayder Silents.[7]

West Denver, an up-and-coming place to live, was proud of another new high school completed in 1893, on the corner of 5th Avenue and Fox Street. Designed by Frank E. Edbrooke, famed architect of the Brown Palace Hotel, the school featured an auditorium for daily assemblies and public debates that were so popular the students received prizes for oratory, essay, and Shakespeare reading contests. Known as Baker after 1926, the red sandstone building was demolished in 1959.

Several high schools, including East, South, and West, were built between 1922 and 1932 as part of Denver Public Schools' $12 million expansion program. Franklin/West High School helped fulfill the vision of Mayor Robert Speer in his campaign for a "City Beautiful." An element of Speer's master plan was to create parks to serve as settings for public buildings. With its mountain background and modern architecture, the new West High School at 951 Elati Street overlooked Sunken Gardens and Speer Boulevard, the parkway named after the mayor.

Principal Harry V. Kepner helped plan the new building and presided at the dedication on March 26, 1926. Designed by architect W. Harry Edwards, the building featured English Collegiate Gothic style, an adaptation of Neo-Gothic architecture, popular for early 20th-century skyscrapers in New York and Chicago. General contractor William Tamminga oversaw construction of the school, with its 110-foot central tower, 65 classrooms, and an auditorium that seated 1,500.[8]

Major changes on the West High campus occurred in the 1970s and again in the 1990s. A red brick structure was built in 1974–1975 west of the main building to house a modern gymnasium. The original gymnasium was remodeled in 1977–1978, and a new academic center opened with a first-floor science center and a second-floor music wing. A district-wide bond issue in 1990 provided funds for a swimming pool and an outdoor patio connected to the main building by a three-story bridge.

New West High School, overlooking Sunken Gardens, was built in 1926 as part of Mayor Speer's City Beautiful movement.

In cooperation with the State Landmark Commission, the school planned a library addition, which was dedicated April 19, 2002. The second-level library media center, one of the most modern in Colorado, features four large bay windows with both downtown and mountain views.

The Singing Christmas Tree

West High School's internationally known Singing Christmas Tree choir began as a musical assembly for students. Pearle Mayberry was a senior at West in 1937–1938 and sang in the Acapella Choir with 35 other music students under the direction of Warren Turner. "The Singing Christmas Tree wasn't a big deal then," she said. "The choir filed in to different rows on wood plank risers and sang several selections during assembly. I was amazed that it became so great."[9]

Planning and preparation for the Tree's official debut began in 1939, springing from the dream of English teacher Willa Girault. Introduced to the public in December 1941, the Tree represented the efforts not only of the music department but of other pupils as well. Home economics students made ornaments for the choir robes, the stage crew assembled the frame, and the shop class printed programs. Families attended evening performances each year as part of their Christmas celebration, and children aspired to follow in the footsteps of family members who sang on the Tree.

The school added improvements over the years, including a steel frame, glittery collars for singers, and colored spotlights. Choir students vied for the honor of star soloist for the traditional closing song of "Silent Night," which was sung as artificial snow fell gently on the Tree.

The Tree gained national fame in 1973 when it was invited to appear in the Christmas Pageant of Peace, an annual observance on the White House grounds in Washington, D.C. The Tree's 5-ton frame, its lights, and its student singers were sent to Washington with funds raised by the West High School community. Students and alumni also traveled to Vienna, Austria, as the only public high school choir in the world invited to sing in the 1993 International Advent Sing Festival. In addition, the 1994 Singing Christmas Tree participated in the International Three Kings' Night Festival of Brotherhood and Peace Through Music held in Paris, France, as the only choir from the United States invited to perform.[10]

In December 2004, the school presented an additional Alumni Tree, composed of former choir members. Previous directors James Fluckey, Richard Eichenberger, John Thorin, Stephen Nye, and current director Brian Eichenberger rehearsed with former music students for five months prior to the special performances.

Alumni of Franklin/West High School

Pearle Mayberry moved to west Denver in 1923 at age 3 and lived with her parents and three older brothers at West 9th Avenue and Acoma Street. "My uncle owned a grocery store in the neighborhood and let me pick out candy or a special

The 1954 West High Singing Christmas Tree.
Introduced in 1941, the Tree is a tradition that has grown to international fame.

treat each time I went there," she said. "When my family bought acreage at West 6th Avenue and Utica Street, we raised vegetables, chickens, and rabbits for show. Each spring we ordered 100 chickens. We kept some for eggs, raised roosters for meat, and sold the others. My job was to sit by the road with a stick to keep the chickens out of the road so they didn't get hit by a buggy. I made two cents an hour. We also raised worms and sold 100 worms in a can for a dollar.

"In those days, West 6th Avenue was a two-lane road. I walked one mile to catch the street car at West 6th Avenue and Knox Court to go to high school at West. I met my husband, Duncan, there. He gave me a kiss each day before going to his class across the hall and we danced in the gym at lunchtime. On Old Fashioned Day, which later became Color Day, we wore old-fashioned clothes. My girlfriend and I borrowed a horse and buggy and took friends for rides.

"Sunken Gardens, across the street from West, was a beautiful park with a pool where people cooled off in the summer and ice skated in the winter. The city paid people to pull dandelions in the gardens and each family got so much per bag."

A year after graduation, Pearle married Duncan John Cameron, who became a lawyer and municipal judge. He also served as president of the West High Alumni Association. Typical of most mothers of the 1940s and 1950s, Pearle stayed home with her three children: Diane, Duncan William, and Dawn. Diane and Duncan went to West High School as their parents had. Like his father, Duncan William was elected president of the West High Alumni Association; Diane later became treasurer of the association, which had grown through the years to a membership of more than 9,000.

The Student Body of Franklin/West High School

From its early days of serving white, upper-class, mostly Protestant students— since Catholic youth usually went to St. Joseph's Parish—West High School reflected significant changes in society and changes in the neighborhood at its 100th year. A broader ethnic enrollment composed the student body. Of the 1,833 students enrolled in 2000, 82.9 percent were Hispanic, 9.3 percent were white, 3.1 percent were Asian, 2.9 percent were black, and 1.7 percent were American Indian.

West High School was named a national 2000 School of Excellence by *Hispanic* magazine as one of two U.S. high schools that displayed a significant impact on education. Two unique programs helped the school win the honor— the Center for International Studies, aimed at developing intercultural communication, critical thinking, and articulation skills; and a VIP partnership with the University of Denver to encourage and help students attend college.[11]

Sunken Gardens

In 1910, one of the most significant city improvements in the neighborhood involved conversion of an ugly dump site at Elati Street and Cherry Creek to one of Denver's beauty spots, Sunken Gardens.

Landscape architect and city planner Saco Rienk DeBoer patterned the formal gardens after those laid out in St. Louis and Portland. Originally planned by George Kessler, the gardens faced Elati Street and could be seen easily from Speer Boulevard. They served as a park for the neighborhood as well as a front lawn for West High School and Denver General Hospital. Non-motorists reached the park from a nearby trolley line.

Extending from Elati Street to Speer Boulevard and from West 8th Avenue to West 11th Avenue, the park consisted of two triangles on the south side of Cherry Creek. In its glory, the informal image of the east triangle suggested a forest glen with scattered picnic tables and a rustic shelter. By diverting water from Cherry Creek, DeBoer created a waterfall and stream flowing through a cottonwood grove to an open meadow on the 12.6-acre site. He also designed a rock garden, the first to appear in a Denver park.[12]

The west triangle presented formal gardens with views of West High School, open lawns, and terraces—similar to the English landscape design of a manor house with gardens. Flower gardens probably graced the grand staircase up to

Children cool off in the pool at Sunken Gardens on a hot summer day in the 1930s.

the high school, and trees were planted to frame a view of the school building. Terraced lawns dropped 10 feet below ground level, a unique feature in Denver parks since most parks were set on hills to capture a good view.

A reflection pool with concrete walls featured the play of fountains in summer and ice skating in winter. When a wooden pergola given to the city by Westinghouse Electric Company was damaged during a windstorm, it was replaced by a concrete Florentine pavilion next to the pool. Both pool and pavilion were illuminated with multicolored lights at night, offering a serene beauty after dark. West High School students chose the pavilion as a favorite setting for yearbook pictures until its demolition in 1933. Due to a polio epidemic, the pool was closed to swimming in the 1940s and subsequently filled in.

Sunken Gardens was listed on the National Register of Historic Places in 1986. In 2000, the Colorado Historical Society awarded a $60,000 grant to study the park's historical significance as the first step toward renovation.

The Hospital

An institution with continued effect on the area is Denver Health Medical Center, formerly Denver General Hospital and County Hospital before that. Denver General Hospital started as the "Poor House" when Arapahoe County bought 3 acres of land for $1,250 from R. E. Whitsitt in 1873 and erected its first public building to house the unfortunate infirm. The building seemed far from town, at West 6th Avenue between Evans (Cherokee Street) and South 14th Street (Bannock Street). The city named the institution County Hospital in deference to the feelings of those who depended on public assistance but shrank from going to the "poor house." About that time, the county also acquired a "poor farm," a large infirmary on farmland north of Denver near Henderson.[13]

From the beginning, County Hospital served poor and destitute people and those who temporarily became public charges. A nurses' training school was added in 1887 with Miss Hattie Shepherd as superintendent of nurses. The nurses' home was erected in 1889 with hospital work on the first floor and quarters for student nurses on the second and third floors. The hospital's bed capacity increased to 150 with the addition of a new ward in 1891.

By 1925, the first-rate hospital offered 500 beds for "poor and stricken humanity" and was well equipped to meet any emergency, according to Louise Boyd's book, *The Colorado Training School for Nurses*. Renamed Denver General Hospital, the facility also contained a Police and Fire Ward for exclusive use of public servants who were injured on duty.[14]

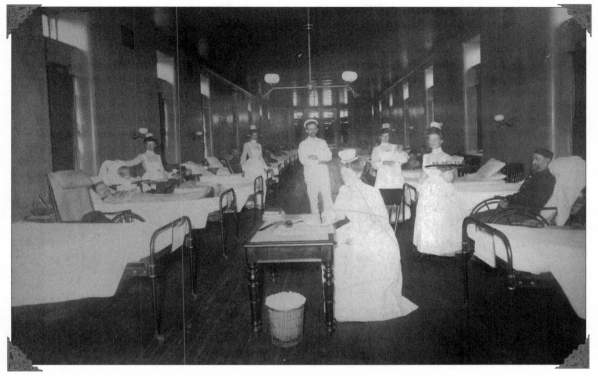

The Men's Chronic Ward in 1907 at Arapahoe County Hospital, West 6th Avenue and Bannock Street. The hospital was known later as Denver General Hospital and is now Denver Health Medical Center.

Excited young nurses moved from cramped quarters into a spacious new four-story residence in December 1927. The main floor featured a large lobby flanked by a library on one side and a spacious living room with two large fireplaces on the other. The three upper floors contained 56 sleeping rooms, 12 baths with showers, an infirmary, and three small apartments for school officials. The basement housed classrooms, a kitchenette, and a large gymnasium with a stage. With its location on 8th Avenue between Bannock and Cherokee Streets, the nurses enjoyed the advantages of Sunken Gardens as a front yard, plus a garden roof that overlooked the city. A tunnel linked the residence to other hospital buildings. Two other units opened that year—the Medical Building and the Chapel.[15]

Changes continued in the 1930s with plans for a two-story pavilion to increase operating room facilities. Denver's civic and welfare leaders approved a Children's Building at Denver General Hospital (DGH) as a memorial to the late Robert W. Speer, who was known as "Denver's Builder Mayor." In 1939, Denver received a grant from the federal government to match a gift from the estate of U.S. Senator Samuel D. Nicholson for a two-story addition to the existing structure and a new four-story building to be known as the Nicholson Wing. Twenty-one student nurses graduated in 1942 as the 54th graduating class.

Dr. Florence R. Sabin instigated major health-care reforms, which were enacted in 1947. After retiring from a distinguished career at the Rockefeller Institute in New York, Sabin moved to Denver and served on the governor's panel, heading the medical subcommittee. Appointed by Mayor Quigg Newton as manager of Health and Charity, she promoted active health outreach programs and significantly improved DGH, making it a model public health center. Sabin retired from her Denver health work in 1951 at age 80.

Dr. Sabin began her distinguished career as one of the first women accepted for a medical education at Johns Hopkins University. After earning her medical degree in 1901, she was asked to remain at the university as a faculty member and became known as the first woman in the country to serve as a full faculty member of a graduate school. An outstanding researcher, Sabin attained prestige as the first female member of the National Academy of Sciences and was recognized as one of the top scientists and female physicians in the world. She often visited her sister Mary, who taught mathematics at Denver's East High School for many years. Notable herself, Mary Sabin, the first woman in Denver to obtain a driver's license, co-founded the Colorado Mountain Club. Honoring the sisters' contributions to Denver, Sabin Elementary School, at 3050 South Vrain Street, was named after them when it opened in 1958. In fact, Dr. Sabin, along with astronaut Jack Swigert, was chosen to represent Colorado at the National Statuary Hall in the U.S. Capitol Building. The hall showcases statues donated by each state to honor great Americans.[16]

After a new tuberculosis (TB) ward was added to DGH in 1948, the former building was remodeled and redecorated to house a division of the Bureau of Health and Hospitals, Sanitation, TB Control, Health Education, Maternal and Child Health, Communicable Disease Control, and the Visiting Nurse Service. It was dedicated in memory of the late Dr. B. B. Jaffa, manager of Health and Charity from 1927 to 1931. Dr. Emma M. Kent became director of Mental Health Services when the psychiatric ward was established at DGH in 1950. The Police and Fire Ward was abolished in 1951, and the Denver Farm at Henderson closed, thus ending the old "country poor-farm idea" that many cities had already abandoned.

During the 1960s, DGH struggled with its image as many Denver residents interpreted its initials as "Don't Go Here." Phil Frieder, deputy manager of Health and Hospitals, initiated steps to reach out to people rather than only providing emergency care for those without other options. As a result, the Neighborhood

Health Program opened six clinics and two health stations in the mid-1960s. DGH was then one of the few facilities in the country to combine public health and hospital functions as one comprehensive unit.

After some talk of abandoning DGH completely, numerous improvements occurred, allowing demolition of most of the early 1900s red brick buildings along West 6th Avenue. In October 1970, Denver General dedicated a new $12.5 million main patient facility at West 8th Avenue and Cherokee Street. During the 1980s, DGH struggled with finances and operated at a deficit for several years. The 1990s saw additional major changes as the Rocky Mountain Poison Center was located at DGH. Operated by the Denver Department of Health and Hospitals, the center serviced eight counties.

As Denver's population swelled with new ethnic groups, the hospital and its network of clinics faced the challenge of communicating with patients who spoke no English. By hiring full-time interpreters, DGH became the city's leader in providing language services to non-English-speaking residents who were among the city's poor and often uninsured. In April 1996, the hospital had nine interpreters on staff and called for volunteers who spoke Spanish, Russian, and Southeast Asian languages such as Vietnamese, Lao, and Hmong.[17]

By May 1996, DGH was poised to enter a new era as a semi-independent authority. The name changed to Denver Health Medical Center, signaling a complicated transition to cut costs and remove constraints of the city's bureaucracy. The hospital transferred from the Department of Health and Hospitals into a separate city department. Although the name changed, the mission remained the same—to serve as a safety net hospital for those who could not afford to pay for medical care. Mayor Wellington Webb said in 1995 that 17 percent of all indigent medical care in Denver was provided by the hospital. "We will never turn our backs on the people who need help," Webb said, as he announced the hospital's new corporate identity. "The change will allow more freedom in economic and personnel decisions by freeing it from rigid budgetary cycles of city government."[18]

Part of the credit for the hospital's turnaround goes to Patricia A. Gabow, M.D., who joined the hospital staff in 1973 as chief of the Renal Division. She became director of Medical Service in 1982, deputy manager of Medical Affairs in 1989, and CEO in 1992, when she was also appointed to the mayor's cabinet. She helped move Denver Health from a department of city government to an independent public entity.

"We wanted to create an infrastructure that matched the quality of care of the community. We wanted to redesign hospital care to create a meaningful relationship with doctors, nurses, and patients in a whole new way," Gabow explained.[19]

In 2002, 160,000 people—one-fourth of the city's population—turned to Denver Health for treatment. *U.S. News and World Report* named Denver Health one of its Top 50 Best Hospitals, ranking it 13th in neurology and neurosurgery, 20th in rheumatology, and 38th in nephrology.[20]

To further the goals of this unique institution, city voters approved a $148 million expansion project in May 2003. The project proposed a 242,000-square-foot addition at West 8th Avenue and Delaware Street to increase the number of hospital beds from 311 to 450. Plans also called for new outpatient surgery suites and enlargement of the intensive care unit.

Denver Health evolved into a highly integrated public health-care system that contributes to the health of people in Denver and the whole Rocky Mountain region. The only hospital in the southwest Denver city limits, Denver Health combines acute hospital and emergency care with public and community health services. The health agency encompasses the Rocky Mountain Regional Trauma Center, Denver's 911 emergency medical response system, Denver Health Paramedic Division, a Community Health System with 8 family health centers and 12 school-based health centers, Rocky Mountain Poison and Drug Center, Denver Public Health, Denver Health Medical Plan, and the Rocky Mountain Center for Medical Response to Terrorism, Mass Casualties and Epidemics. A new addition is the Denver Health Pavilion for Women and Children, featuring private patient rooms and state-of-the-art birthing facilities, a 24-bed MICU, and the Wellington E. Webb Center of Primary Care.

St. Joseph's Parish

Prior to 1883, the only Catholic parish west of Cherry Creek was St. Elizabeth's (now surrounded by the Auraria campus). Traveling by horse and buggy, parishioners had to cross one of the two bridges spanning Cherry Creek to attend services there. Some working people found it extremely difficult.

Mr. and Mrs. Stephen Wirtz petitioned Bishop Joseph Machebeuf to form a new parish for Catholics living in the southwest part of the city and suggested the parish name of St. Joseph, patron saint of Bishop Machebeuf. With the purchase of property at West 4th Avenue and Clark Street (now Inca Street), a small frame building on the grounds was fitted as a temporary church.

The first pastor, the Reverend Percy A. Phillips, came to Denver because of ill health, which forced him to resign after three years. During his term, however, the growing parish moved to a store on West 4th Avenue and South Water Street (now Galapago Street). The Reverend Thomas Malone, known as an outstanding lecturer, was appointed pastor in 1886. Progressive and energetic, Father Malone built a frame church at West 6th Avenue and Galapago Street and lived with his mother and sister in an adjoining cottage.

As West Denver developed, the parish outgrew the frame church and erected a larger, more substantial structure. Dedicated in November 1889, the new Victorian-Gothic style, two-story brick building contained American-made stained-glass windows fashioned with clear prisms. The windows were unique for that time, since church windows were usually imported from Europe. Worshippers, mainly of German and Irish ancestry, gathered on the upper level, leaving the first floor for school purposes. Father Malone invited the Sisters of Mercy, who had just come to Denver, to take charge of the school.

The original frame church housed the first pupils in 1889, with a partition allowing two classes to be held at the same time. Sister Mary Evangelist, one of the first teachers, had 90 students in her room at one time. She taught the ninth grade when it was added in 1897. Other faculty members of the time included Sister Mary Regis, Sister Mary Philomena, and Sister Mary of Mercy, who was destined to continue at St. Joseph's for many years as teacher and principal. For years the Sisters lived at St. Catherine's Home or Mercy Hospital in East Denver, enduring the hardship of traveling back and forth to St. Joseph's School.

St. Joseph's Parish suffered greatly when the Silver Panic of 1893 suddenly paralyzed the country. Unemployment and bank failures swept away the life savings of many West Denver residents, undoubtedly contributing to the parish's financial difficulties. However, records also show charges of embezzlement and misappropriation of funds against the Reverend Malone.[21]

With foreclosure threatening, Bishop Matz appealed in desperation to the Redemptorist Fathers of St. Louis to rescue the church property from confiscation. They consented to his appeal, and Matz then appointed the Reverend Daniel Mullane as pastor. Faced with a shaky economy, unsympathetic parishioners, and debts of nearly $39,000, Father Mullane worked to gain the goodwill of the people. For six years Father Mullane and his associates received no salary from the church, which was renamed St. Joseph's Redemptorist Parish. As the associates received aid for the church by taking mission trips, the financial situation gradually improved.

A high school was established in 1908, with 10 students enrolled. Showing significant growth, the grade school had 278 pupils when the first high school students graduated in 1911.

Gene Fowler, author of *A Solo in Tom Toms*, told of growing up in the Westside neighborhood when St. Joseph's Church was the center of life for Catholics and non-Catholics alike, who met there for social as well as religious activities.

He remembered the bells of St. Joseph's summoning the faithful to Sunday mass and to devotions throughout the week.[22]

The church retained its significant interior and exterior architectural features in spite of many alterations during the years. St. Joseph's Church was designated as a historic landmark in 1982, on the eve of its 100th anniversary. Concerned about the church's survival a century after its founding, Sister Alicia Cuaron organized the FaithAction task force to fund repairs and renovation of St. Joseph's and other historic sites in Denver. FaithAction rallied support from various organizations, including the Clergy Committee, Historic Denver, Inc., Piton Foundation, Wartburg West Program of Wartburg College (Waverly, Iowa), and the Governor's Commission on Community Service.[23]

John and Catherine Mullen

Two of Denver's philanthropists, both charitable Catholics, identified with the working-class community in West Denver. John K. Mullen was born in Galway, Ireland, in the famine year of 1847. His father made barrels for oatmeal and flour mills before the famine forced them to leave Ireland. The family settled in Oriskany Falls, New York, and John quit school for a job sharpening granite millstones at a flour mill. As one of his family's primary wage earners, he earned $2 per week.

At age 19, John traveled west for better employment opportunities. After working awhile in Kansas, he arrived in the rough city of Denver in 1871. The town brimmed with miners, asthmatics, frontiersmen, bankers, and saloon keepers at the time. Mullen found a job at Merchant's Mills in West Denver where he advanced to manager in two years. Eight years later, he was president.

The stocky, 5-foot-8-inch Mullen signed a pledge of sobriety at a young age and practiced temperance and regular church attendance throughout his life. He volunteered to teach a boys' Sunday school class at St. Mary's Catholic Church. A "blue-eyed, pretty, bright-souled" Irish girl named Catherine "Kate" Smith was the girls' instructor. Kate had ministered to poor, sick, orphaned, and homeless people in Central City before moving to Denver. With investments from her brothers' freighting company, she bought property and various notes of debt. Attracted by their shared interests in church, charity, and business ventures, John and Kate married on October 12, 1874, at St. Mary's Catholic Church. They purchased a new, two-story house at 339 9th Street.

With a growing family and successful flour mills, the Mullens moved four years later to a larger, 12-room house at 1178 9th Street, where they lived for the next 20 years. In 1898, they joined the elite on Pennsylvania Street. Their first, smaller house in the working-class neighborhood of West Denver symbolized their struggling pioneer days, and the family always referred to the house on the corner of 9th Street as the Mullen homestead.

A shrewd and progressive businessman, John Mullen adopted a new process, developed in Hungary, that produced purer, whiter flour for his mills. He remodeled the existing Excelsior mill, and he built a new frame grain elevator between Blake and Wazee Streets on 7th Avenue, which he called the Hungarian Elevator. In 1885, J. K. Mullen and Company was the leading flour producer in Colorado. In fact, Mullen and the other local millers made Denver the leading mill city in the West at that time. With mills operating in five states, Mullen became a millionaire, real estate mogul, bank director, and prominent civic and religious benefactor. Acting upon his belief that he was charged to use his wealth for the public good, he donated more than $2.4 million—about one-third of his personal net worth—to public, private, and religious causes. In addition, he gave checks and cash gifts to charity, friends, and even strangers.[24]

Many of the Spanish-speaking people who came to west Denver in the early 1920s attended St. Leo's Catholic Church, which was built for Irish parishioners on land donated by Mullen. When conflict developed between the two ethnic groups, the Hispanic immigrants asked for their own church. Once again, Mullen donated land for a church, along with a small house to serve as a rectory and money to begin construction of St. Cajetan's Catholic Church at 9th Street and Lawrence Street. The basement was finished by January 1925, shortly after the Mullens celebrated their 50th wedding anniversary, and members held services there until the bills could be paid.[25]

When Catherine Mullen, a strong supporter of St. Cajetan's, died two months later, her devoted husband agreed to retire the church's outstanding construction debts as a memorial to her. Many parishioners donated carpentry, masonry, and woodcarving skills to help finish the church. St. Cajetan's was consecrated on March 21, 1926.

Magdalena Gallegos, who was born on 10th Street, said the lives of the Spanish-speaking people in Auraria revolved around their church since the Hispanic people had no other public institution where they could mix and feel important. "Every girl sang in the choir and men played in the band. The organist played rumbas, sambas, and boleros before 10:30 Sunday mass on a magnificent organ donated to the church from the old Tabor Grand Opera House."[26]

In 1967, the Denver Urban Renewal Authority declared the neighborhood as the site for the 127-acre Auraria Higher Education Center. Even though concerned residents campaigned against the bond issue to fund the project, Denver voters approved it. Longtime homeowners and renters received money for relocation.

Historic Denver, Inc., saved the old church building and other historic structures along 9th Street from demolition. The preservation group raised $900,000 to restore exteriors and refurbish interiors of the early homes and businesses that now serve as office space for faculty and staff of the three colleges. The old St. Cajetan's church was remodeled as a campus auditorium with classroom space in the basement. Ninth Street Historic Park was declared a Denver landmark and listed on the National Register of Historic Places.[27]

John Mullen outlived his wife by four years and established the John K. and Catherine S. Mullen Benevolent Foundation to make sure their fortune would continue to help people after their deaths. The millionaire philanthropist died in his Capitol Hill home from pneumonia and a weak heart on August 9, 1929. Mullen High School at South Lowell Boulevard and West Kenyon Avenue is named for John K. Mullen.

The Buckhorn Exchange

A colorful character arrived in Colorado in the person of Henry Zeitz, who worked as an Indian scout for William F. "Buffalo Bill" Cody. Because of Zeitz's short stature, he was nicknamed Shorty Scout by Sioux chief Sitting Bull. The chief later sent Zeitz a saber

Henry Zeitz opened the Buckhorn Exchange in 1893 at 1000 Osage Street and displayed his collection of hunting trophies.

taken from Gen. George Custer after the Battle of Little Bighorn. While traveling with Buffalo Bill, Zeitz learned hunting skills he used all his life.

In 1893, Zeitz opened a restaurant/saloon at 1000 Osage Street. The restaurant was originally started by his father, Theodore Zeitz, on Market Street in 1871. It featured a white oak bar crafted in Germany and shipped to Wisconsin with five wooden beer tables, which were then transported to Denver by a team of oxen.

Zeitz's Osage restaurant was first called the Rio Grande Exchange because of its location near the railroad, but it became known as the Buckhorn Exchange due to the stuffed Buckhorn ram heads mounted on the walls along with hundreds of other Colorado animal heads. In its early days, the establishment not only served food and beer but also cashed checks for the railroad workers who ate there.[28]

During Prohibition, the Buckhorn operated as a grocery store, and when Prohibition ended it gained Denver's first liquor license. A lounge on the upper level once served as living quarters. The tavern/museum added an impressive collection of antique firearms and Native American artifacts, drawing famous diners such as Buffalo Bill, Theodore Roosevelt, Princess Anne of England, and actor Ronald Reagan, who left autographed photographs for display. The Buckhorn Exchange, still open today, was designated as a historic landmark in 1983.

Santa Fe Drive Development

Santa Fe Drive developed between 1885 and 1890 as a thriving commercial corridor first called Jason Street. The community petitioned the city to change the name to the historic-sounding Santa Fe, since it was the original road that headed south from Denver in the direction of the old Santa Fe Trail and Santa Fe, New Mexico. A major thoroughfare for Westsiders, the corridor deteriorated when businesses moved to outlying districts. However, structures received a facelift in the 1990s as art galleries, theaters, and other businesses found low-rent headquarters along Santa Fe Drive. The area is also home to the Museo de las Americas, a museum dedicated to Latin American and U.S. Hispanic art.[29]

The Byers Branch Library

The Byers Branch Library at 675 Santa Fe Drive opened its doors to enthusiastic patrons following the outdoor dedication ceremony on June 22, 1918. Businesses closed early so their employees could attend the patriotic program, which featured schoolchildren singing under the direction of Wilberforce Whiteman, music supervisor for Denver Public Schools. Clark W. Bond, founder of the *West Denver Hustler* newspaper, donated a flag for the 35-foot flagpole given by the community in honor of the West Denver men serving in World War I.

Named for William N. Byers, pioneer newspaperman, the library was the sixth library building in Denver, and the first on the west side. Money from the Andrew Carnegie Foundation funded the Italian Renaissance structure, which cost $22,000. Helen Campbell, a graduate of Westminster College and the New York Public Library School, served as the first librarian.

Shelves for 7,000 volumes lined the walls of the single-room library. A large mantel of Indiana limestone crowned the fireplace. The basement contained an auditorium for community events and two rooms used by the Red Cross for garment workers and those making surgical dressings for the war effort.

The library continued as a center for the active neighborhood until the 1950s, when city library officials considered closing the branch because of

Excited patrons gathered June 22, 1918, for the dedication of Byers Branch Library, 675 Santa Fe Drive.

higher costs than at other branches. Alarmed citizens circulated petitions against closing the branch and argued that Byers Library was important to the community not only as a learning center, but also as an activity center for adults and children. Angry residents said they had been "long neglected and ignored" by the city, citing the loss of the West Side Auraria Community Center, which was cut from Community Chest (now Mile High United Way) appropriations.[30]

West Denver residents won their battle to keep the branch open when a large number of neighborhood representatives from labor unions, schools, PTA groups, churches, women's clubs, and businessmen's associations showed up at a public hearing in March 1952 and persuaded the Library Commission to reverse its recommendation.

By the mid-1960s, many of the original settlers had moved. The racial makeup in 1966 was 61 percent white, 37 percent Hispanic, and 2 percent black. As people of Hispanic descent increasingly moved into the neighborhood, the Library Commission allotted funds for magazines and materials in the Spanish language.[31]

The library experienced a change of status from a "branch" library to a "neighborhood" library in January 1963, due to declining circulation attributed to a more industrialized neighborhood divided by West 6th and West 8th Avenues. This meant a reduction in staff and a reduction in available publications.

An $11,575 facelift in late 1966 resulted in a new sidewalk and steps, new paint, renovation of the basement rooms, and other exterior and interior improvements. Innovative programs started in the 1970s with the Right-to-Read project (funded by the U.S. Office of Education) and English as a Second Language classes.

Friends of the Denver Public Library commissioned a Denver artist, Carlota Espinoza, to paint a mural for Byers Library in 1977. Painting on her own time, Espinoza depicted the story of Chicano people "from Aztec empires, through Spanish imperialism, from alienation, to the struggle to re-win a people's identity, pride and future." The epic 5-by-20-foot mural is called *Pasado, Presente, Futuro*. A focal point for the library, the painting was an official Colorado creation for the 1976 Centennial-Bicentennial celebration.

Housing Developments

North Lincoln Park Development, 1449 Navajo Street, was built after World War II to alleviate crowded conditions in the Curtis Park and Five Points areas. A 1940s barracks-style complex, it contained 685 units for low-income families.

Denver Housing Authority (DHA) erected the South Lincoln Park Homes at 1000 Navajo Street in 1952–1954. Rows of simple two-story brick apartments housed 800 low-income residents, who occupied one- to five-bedroom units.

By the 1970s, the residential atmosphere of the neighborhood had declined because of industrial expansion from the south and west, commercial expansion along Broadway and Santa Fe Drive, and development of the Auraria Higher Education Center on the north, which replaced many houses of the original German-speaking, working-class citizens. In 1972, the Denver Community Renewal Program designated Lincoln Park a "blighted" neighborhood and began revitalization efforts. Part of the plan envisioned housing that could accommodate members of the press if Denver became the site of the 1976 Winter Olympics. When voters rejected the proposal to host the Olympics, the city developed a new plan that included 350 units of housing for elderly and low-income families.[32]

In 1979, Lincoln Park received a $13.5 million federal Urban Development Action Grant from the Department of Housing and Urban Development to purchase land for middle-income housing. Other money from the grant was allocated to rehabilitate owner-occupied single-family and multifamily units.

Residents helped plan improvements on a block-to-block basis, using funds for exterior painting, mending fences, planting trees, repairing walks, and adjusting curbs for handicap access. In addition, funds covered a new senior citizens' housing complex called Court House Square at West 14th Avenue and Santa Fe Drive, and rent subsidies under HUD's Section 8 program for longtime, low-income residents displaced by revitalization. Brothers Redevelopment, Midland Federal Savings, and the Colorado Housing Authority committed money and assistance for a pioneer program to help middle-income renters buy their homes.

Revitalization

Revitalization of Lincoln Park started in the 1980s as young singles and couples moved to affordable homes in the neighborhood and began fixing up deteriorating and neglected houses. Auraria students sought nearby apartments, bringing new vitality to the community as well. Workers found jobs in manufacturing, transportation, communications, and utilities and were mainly employed by the Denver Water Board, Denver General Hospital, and Gates Rubber Company.[33]

Hispanics made up 75 percent of the neighborhood's population, whites made up 16 percent, and blacks made up 5 percent. Forty percent of the residents were under age 18. Del Pueblo School opened in 1973 at 750 Galapago Street, helping to accommodate the large number of children in the community. The facility, new in 1973, marked Denver Public Schools' first move away from neutral colors, with bright, bold graphics emblazoned on the interior and exterior walls reflecting Aztec, Toltec, and Mayan cultures.[34]

Bilingual classes at Del Pueblo Elementary School.

La Mariposa Health Station, at West 11th Avenue and Kalamath Street, also displayed the southwestern architecture preferred by the changing community. In addition, Zocalo Center, a commercial plaza at West Colfax Avenue and Kalamath Street, was developed under the Denver Urban Renewal Authority's Neighborhood Development Program.

In 1994, the Denver Housing Authority tore down the old North Lincoln Park homes and erected Victorian-style townhomes to blend with the original bungalows in the neighborhood. In addition to the 131 townhomes, the development included a 5-story senior citizen apartment building and a family learning center wired for high-speed Internet access with a computerized link to the Auraria campus across West Colfax Avenue. Called the North Lincoln Campus of Learners, this successful partnership between the Community College of Denver and the Denver Housing Authority promotes education and job skills so tenants can move up and out of public housing. Tenants agreed to participate in educational, job training, or community service programs during the five years they lived there.

"Public housing can never be the same again if this model can hold," said Henry Cisneros, secretary of the U.S. Department of Housing and Urban Development, who attended the ribbon-cutting ceremony in September 1996 to emphasize the national significance of the North Lincoln project.[35]

CHAPTER FOUR

Baker

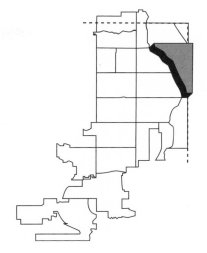

*A*round Broadway and Alameda Avenue, you will find an incongruous collection of Victorian homes in various states of gentrification. This is
the Baker neighborhood, eclectic since its 1870s beginnings. Featuring tightly
packed "shotgun" houses and elegant Queen Annes, the area was once home to
many prominent citizens, particularly in the Baker Historic District. As the
neighborhood aged, it deteriorated, only to be renewed in the 1980s as younger
residents and many neighborhood amenities moved in.

*St. Peter's Episcopal Church, 126 W. 2nd Avenue, was constructed in 1891
by Cornish miners to resemble an English country church.*

The Early Days

Englishman Frederick J. Greenway, a typical settler, bought the block between South Broadway, South Bannock Street, West Byers Place, and West Alameda Avenue in 1877 for $500. At the time, Greenway lived in a dugout with living quarters below ground level. As one of many early residents who raised fruit, vegetables, and poultry for market, Greenway used the roof above ground level and the remainder of his land for growing 18 varieties of strawberries.[1]

The Baker neighborhood consists of 21 additions and subdivisions of various sizes, from half a block to many blocks, which were platted between the early 1870s and the mid-1880s. It extends west of Broadway to the Platte River, from West 6th Avenue to Mississippi Avenue. Broadway Terrace, one of the largest additions to the neighborhood, was first platted in 1873 by John L. Dailey, a printer, who was impressed by the "broad and beautiful plateau with a magnificent view of the Rocky Mountains." Dailey Park at Ellsworth Avenue and Cherokee Street was named after him.

The Baker area derived its name from James Hutchins Baker, who actually never lived in the neighborhood. Baker was an educator who served as principal at East High School (1875–1892) and president of the University of Colorado (1892–1913). His name was given to the school building at 5th Avenue and Galapago Street, originally called West High School. The building became Baker Junior High School in 1926, when West High School moved to its new facility at 951 Elati Street. In the 1970s, when they organized Denver into specific neighborhoods, city planners chose the name Baker for the area.[2]

By 1874, small brick houses, 40 lots to a block, covered half the area. These early houses contained a simple "shotgun" floor plan of single rooms placed directly behind each other. The plan got its name because one could stand at the front door and fire a shotgun clear through the house and out the back door. A small shotgun house still exists at 111 West Archer Avenue, possibly built in the 1870s. A larger frame cottage with a picket fence at 151 West Archer Avenue dates back to the 1880s. Few of the early shotgun homes survive elsewhere in Denver neighborhoods.

In the 1880s, the area east of Broadway from Cherry Creek to Yale was known as the Southside and west of Broadway was the Westside, which included Auraria. However, the Baker neighborhood was identified more closely with the Southside because of its proximity to Broadway and the influence of Southside leaders.[3]

In 1887, Greenway sold his block of land and bought building sites. He built a large brick Queen Anne house on the corner at 98 West Byers Place. Home construction boomed in the area after Denver Tramway Company built a cable car line along Broadway in 1888. Early pioneers tore down their crude pine slab cabins and dugouts to build permanent brick houses.

To augment the building, the Fleming Brothers, the first to sell houses on the installment plan, and House Construction Company built a number of houses designed by architects William Lang and Marshall Pugh. Lang produced some of the most interesting houses in the city, including landmark homes such as the Zang House at 1532 Emerson Street and the Molly Brown House at 1340 Pennsylvania Street. In contrast, his Baker houses were modest and downscale, but they still had a flair of individuality.

The Baker Historic District

Today, extending from Broadway west to Fox Street and south from West 5th Avenue to Alameda Avenue, the small Baker Historic District is a residential neighborhood featuring Victorian homes situated in the northeast corner of the larger Baker area. Its development actually began in the 1870s as a sparsely scattered rural settlement of log and frame homes.

By the 1890s, the area had become an attractive middle-class neighborhood featuring many Queen Anne homes. The neighborhood attracted people of varying social and economic status, forming an eclectic mix of large and small houses. Well-to-do families usually built on corners or along Broadway, with smaller lots spaced between. Although not as exclusive or as expensive as the Capitol Hill area, the Baker District had 41 families in Denver's 1892 *Blue Book*, a registry of the city's elite.[4]

One of the elite was Dr. Isaac Perkins, a renowned physician and surgeon, who resided at 132 West 4th Avenue from about 1890 to 1929. Dr. Perkins was one of the founders of Presbyterian Hospital in 1921.

Prominent women in the neighborhood included Sadie Likens, Denver's first police matron and president of the Florence Crittenton Home; Alice Polk Hill, Colorado's first poet laureate; and Dr. Mary Elizabeth Bates, activist for the rights of women, children, and animals.

John H. Blood lived at 50 West 2nd Avenue. A hardware merchant, inventor, journalist, and

The musically talented family of Wilberforce Whiteman, his wife Elfrida (seated), and their children, Ferne (standing) and Paul, in front of their Queen Anne–style home in the 1890s.

realtor, Blood co-founded the *South Denver Eye* newspaper. His house served as the meeting place for South Broadway Christian Church members before the Romanesque Revival–style church was erected at 23 Lincoln Street in 1891.

Paul Whiteman, musician and band leader, lived at 135 West Ellsworth Avenue in the early 1900s. He attended Fairmont Elementary School and West High School. His well-known father, Wilberforce Whiteman, taught music for the Denver Public Schools.

Mary Coyle Chase, who authored the Pulitzer Prize–winning play *Harvey*, grew up in the two-story, seven-room Queen Anne–style house at 532 West 4th Avenue.

The sudden Silver Panic of 1893 hit hard, and the resulting economic depression affected all residents of the Baker Historic District. When home construction resumed, new 20th-century styles filled the few empty lots, including the following:

> Dutch Colonial Revival, 227 W. 5th Avenue
> Terrace Style Multifamily, 305–313 W. Irvington Street
> Classic Cottage, 523 W. 3rd Avenue
> Bungalow Twin House, 235 and 237 Delaware Street
> Edwardian, 147 W. Irvington Place

The oldest of the five churches in the Baker Historic District is St. Peter's Episcopal Church, built in 1891 by Cornish miners who garnered their wealth in Colorado mines. Constructed of volcanic rock from the Castle Rock area, the distinctive building at 126 West 2nd Avenue was patterned after an English country church.

The Four Winds Survival Project, which helps American Indian families in urban areas, now occupies the Gothic Revival–style building at 201 West 5th Avenue The structure was built in 1912 for the Danish Evangelical Bethany Lutheran Church, which held services in Danish until 1930.

In 1902, Byers School was built at 108 South Bannock Street to replace the "old tin school," an 1891 one-room schoolhouse on the same site. Prominent Denver architects Aaron Gove and Thomas Walsh designed the Mission Revival–style structure. The name changed to Alameda School in 1921, when Byers Junior High School was built. A site for the Denver food stamp office in the 1970s, the building was converted to condominiums in 1982 and later became known as The Lofts at Byers School, with a new entrance at 106 West Byers Place.

Fairmont Elementary School, 520 West 3rd Avenue, reflected the City Beautiful philosophy with its setting and 1924 Collegiate Gothic–style design by architect Harry James Manning. Unique because of its endowed library, the

Barrel maker Henry Roth salvaged metal barrel lids as well as stones for the homes he built on South Fox Street in the 1930s and 1940s.

new school replaced the old 1880s building on the corner of West 2nd Avenue and Elati Street.

Works Progress Administration (WPA) workers constructed Fire House #11, at 40 West 2nd Avenue, around 1936. The Art Deco–style structure with its three façade bays replaced the 1903 fire station at 301 Cherokee Street.[5]

The Henry Roth Residence

The Henry Roth Residence, listed on the National Register of Historic Places, showed a marked contrast to the neighboring Queen Anne homes of the Baker Historic District. Roth built three homes in the Craftsman-inspired bungalow style between 1927 and 1941 with cobblestones collected from the nearby South Platte River.

The homes, at 5, 7, and 9 South Fox Street, represented Roth's ingenuity in using recycled materials for several buildings constructed by hand during the Great Depression. Roth and his sons hauled river stones for the walls and chimneys. A barrel maker by trade, Roth salvaged metal barrel lids from a railroad-tie factory on South Santa Fe Drive. He cut the barrel lids into shingles for the roof and coated the roof with a waterproof asphalt mixture.

Roth also built several sheds with the same materials to provide rental income for his family and sleeping quarters for transients who needed a cheap, temporary place to stay. Each shed had a window and enough room for a small bed or cot. The structures were arranged around an open courtyard, typical of motor courts (collections of cabins similar to motels) gaining popularity in the 1930s.[6]

Gentrification

The aging neighborhood experienced a transition in the 1980s, showing gains in the young adult population (age 25 to 34), similar to a trend in the Washington Park area. Youthful residents moved into the deteriorating community, channeling energy and financial resources into renovation of the older houses. This increased property values, and the housing market changed. Business renovations along Broadway also added to the attractiveness of the Baker neighborhood. Two senior housing facilities, Hirschfeld Towers and Lutheran Apartments, afforded Baker residents an opportunity to move from their homes but stay in the same neighborhood.

Doretta Philpot, former director of Mother-to-Mother Ministry and retired home visit coordinator for the Denver Department of Human Services, bought a Queen Anne–style home with two friends in 1983. Impressed by the original stained-glass windows, they paid $72,500 for the house—20 years later it was valued at three-and-one-half times that much.

"Some people prefer to live in the suburbs and stay away from downtown," Philpot said, "but we like the excitement of the city. We can walk, take the bus

Byers School, built in 1902 in Mission Revival style, was renamed Alameda School in 1921. Converted to condominiums in 1982, the Lofts at Byers School are located at 106 W. Byers Place.

or light rail to theaters, concerts, and city events, so the location is very convenient. The Number 0 bus runs south on Broadway and north on Lincoln Street. We're also close to major streets if we want to drive."

Philpot served on a neighborhood committee to help save the 1930 Mayan Theater from demolition in the 1980s. "When our church mission group heard the historic building was to be torn down, the committee suggested that children's films be shown on Saturdays as a step to revive business. We printed flyers, took them door to door, and the theater gained new life as people attended the Saturday movies." Restoration took place in 1984 and the Aztec-style theater began to draw patrons of all ages from the entire Denver metropolitan area.

"We enjoy the diversity and friendliness of our neighborhood," Philpot said. "Professionals, blue-collar workers, young married couples, and elderly residents all get along—taking in mail, watering plants, or babysitting for one another."[7]

Numerous "pocket parks" provide picnic tables and playgrounds for leisure-time activities, while community plots give gardeners a place to plant a few rows of vegetables. Many of the larger homes have been converted into apartments for rental income, and real estate values remained stable in the face of an economic downturn early in 2003.

Residents are near law offices, insurance companies, a cat hospital, a violin maker, and other businesses that operate from Victorian houses. A variety of services are available through agencies such as La Familia Recreation Center, with its Olympic-size swimming pool; Mi Casa resource center for women; Sobriety House, featuring a 12-step alcohol recovery program; Atlantis Community, serving disabled persons; plus nearby grocery stores, a post office, a library, and restaurants.

CHAPTER FIVE

Sun Valley, West Colfax, and Villa Park

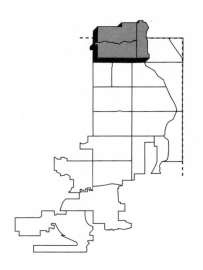

*A*fter the rush for gold died down, men and women continued to pour into Denver for its promise of better health and new business opportunities. Starting in the 1870s, the area developed as a working-class community, although you will hear famous names such as Barnum and Buchtel associated with it. Anchored by Rude Recreation Center, the industrial Sun Valley neighborhood once housed many Jewish families, who eventually migrated west along Colfax Avenue. Today, a primary feature of the area is Invesco Field at Mile High. Specifically, Sun Valley includes the strip containing the stadium, between West 20th Avenue and West 6th Avenue and between I-25 and Federal Boulevard. The West Colfax neighborhood's boundaries are West 18th Avenue, Dry Gulch, Federal Boulevard, and Sheridan Boulevard. Meanwhile, Villa Park, which includes the Stuart Street Historic District, is bounded by Lakewood/Dry Gulch, West 6th Avenue, Federal Boulevard, and Sheridan Boulevard.

Sun Valley

As Denver grew, poorer families tended to settle along the banks of the South Platte River, where farming and industry attracted workers. Jacobs Addition, the first development in the Sun Valley neighborhood, was in place by 1872, bounded by Golden Avenue (now West Colfax Avenue), Federal Boulevard,

Morrison Road, and Holden Place. By 1885, Sun Valley had been entirely platted. Jacobs Addition, Brinkhaus Addition, and the Denver Brick and Building Company were situated north of Lakewood Gulch. The residential additions of Fairview, West Fairview, and South Fairview claimed land south of the gulch. The whole area was part of the town of Colfax, incorporated in 1891. Children growing up in the poor but close-knit families attended Fairview School, built in 1902–1903 at 11th Avenue and Decatur Street.[1]

Nearby Bloomfield Park, at 13th Avenue and Decatur Street, was a favorite spot for social events in the early 1900s. The British owner decorated the park with Japanese lanterns and provided an orchestra for summer weddings. He also kept a trout pond and tanks of the fresh fish necessary for Jewish holidays.[2]

The Rude Park Community Center near West Colfax Avenue and Federal Boulevard offered stenography classes in 1934.

Private donors purchased the 10-acre Bloomfield Park for $22,525 in the 1920s, and they presented it to the city of Denver as a play area for the families of West Colfax, many of whom were Jewish. A Jewish tailor and philanthropist, I. Rude, gave half of the purchase price. L. Guldman, a wealthy merchant, helped endow the I. Rude Community Center and later developed the Guldman Community Center in West Colfax.[3]

On the east side of the Platte River, children grew up in Jerome Park and attended Garfield School at 11th Avenue and Yuma Street, where outdoor summer concerts and movies provided neighborhood entertainment. Old-timers remember roasting potatoes and frog legs by the stream that ran parallel to 12th Avenue—perhaps that is why the area was dubbed "Frog Hollow," a term that was offensive to some who lived there.[4]

Garfield School was supposed to be abandoned when nearby Fairview School got a new building in 1924. However, parents in the district did not want their young children crossing South Platte River. So, classes for kindergarten and youngsters through third grade continued at Garfield while the older children went to Fairview, west of the river at West 11th Avenue and Decatur Street Clara F. Gard served as principal for both schools from 1915 to 1934. Garfield added grades four and five in the 1940s to accommodate children from the Las Casitas federal housing project. After additions to Fairview in the 1950s, Garfield was discontinued in 1959 and torn down in 1962. The old Fairview structure, which has served as an annex to the newer building, was demolished in 1975.

Scattered industries included a dairy, a clay pottery factory, a bakery, and auto service and sales south of 9th Avenue; Standard Wrecking and Lumber at 10th Avenue and Federal Boulevard; and Centennial Brick Company at Mulberry and Decatur Streets. Public Service Company's Zuni Plant and warehouses along Old Colfax Avenue stood at the north end of the neighborhood. Las Casitas, Denver's first public housing project, was built at 11th Avenue and Federal Boulevard in May 1951. Two additional large public housing projects, Sun Valley Homes and Decatur Place, went up in 1954 and 1956.[5]

Jerry Garcia grew up in a family with 14 children. He lived in a house on West 13th Avenue near South Decatur Street, and his father worked for Burlington Northern Railroad. "I wore hand-me-downs, learned to share, and enjoyed large family gatherings at holidays," he said. "We had a tight-knit family, and our parents taught us good values and good work ethics. As a boy, I played baseball and football at the old Rude Recreation Center. The old center was small and didn't have a pool, but it offered lots of youth sports programs."

After attending Fairview Elementary, Lake Junior High, and West High School, Garcia started a career with the city of Denver as recreation program coordinator at Rude Recreation Center, 2855 West Holden Place. Using his carpentry skills, he now works as a construction maintenance supervisor for Denver Parks and Recreation. In the 1970s, the city bought the house he grew up in and demolished it along with other homes on West 13th Avenue to build a parking lot for Bears Stadium, which has since been replaced by Invesco Field at Mile High.[6]

Many children from the housing projects hung out at the Rude Recreation Center. A modern building, dedicated May 31, 2003, replaced the poorly constructed 1968 facility, which was torn down to make way for the new center. Youths from Fairview and Eagleton Elementary Schools; West, North, and Lincoln High Schools; and Mountain Peak Academy now participate in the swimming, sports, and recreation programs offered year-round. "We serve from 3,000 to 4,000 members yearly," said Edgar "Nick" Nichols Jr., recreation supervisor. "The 9,000-square-foot weight room brings in a lot of people.[7]

"A number of our programs are coordinated with other agencies such as Christian Charities, Denver Human Services, and public health staff. Food Bank of the Rockies serves a hot meal, funded by Denver Rustlers, at 4 p.m. on weekdays. We noted a big improvement in the children's behavior when we started the hot meal program," Nichols said. "Our community is the poorest in the city—and the youngest, with 82 percent of the households under 18 years of age, many headed by single parents. We also have quite a few homeless people, who mostly come in for showers."

The center has also offered a program for deaf children for more than 15 years. The program recently changed its focus to work only with deaf children from deaf families.

Nichols, a director at the center for 29 years, has worked with grand-children of the first youngsters he got to know. "My father was a pilot and we moved several times when I was young, so I envied the kids who grew up here in the neighborhood with the stability of adult supervision and friends they've known all their lives."

In 1999, a new Denver Human Services Center opened across the street at Federal Boulevard and West 12th Avenue (formerly Holden Place). The 300,000-square-foot facility contains offices for more than 1,000 employees representing several human resources providers, such as Denver Social Services, District 1 Police Community Office, Mayor's Office of Employment and Training, and child welfare, child support, and food stamp services. A day-care center, child evaluation center, community room, and small police substation are located there, as well as a cafeteria for employees. Phil Hernandez, manager of Denver Social Services, described the Human Services Center as a one-stop career center where people can file for unemployment and look for a job all at once.[8]

Primarily an industrial area, today's Sun Valley neighborhood encompasses Invesco Field at Mile High and the Zuni Power Plant along the South Platte River.[9]

West Colfax

Wishing to escape the crowded cities of the East Coast, early entrepreneurs eyed the hills west of the rowdy town of Denver for home sites offering pure air and excellent views of the mountains. Avondale, near present-day Federal Boulevard and West Colfax Avenue, started as one man's vision for an area reminiscent of his hometown in Stratford-upon-Avon, England. Built in the late 1800s, the settlement of small homes was demolished in the early 1960s to make way for new apartment buildings, businesses, and a shopping center—one of Denver's first urban renewal projects.[10]

Ralph Voorhees, a young athlete from New York, arrived in Denver in 1872 and worked as a ticket agent for the new Denver & Rio Grande Railroad. A record holder in New York for the 800-yard dash, he was a valued member of the volunteer fire department because of his speed and strength. Voorhees married in 1885 and had four children. He was successful in real estate and became a member of the Colorado legislature, where he introduced a bill to establish Colorado's Flag Day on June 14. He was one of the founders of Colorado Women's

College and helped finance the Larimer Street trestle that brought cable car service to Denver's western suburbs.[11]

In the early 1900s, Jewish immigrants fleeing the pogroms in Eastern Europe first settled near Colfax and the South Platte River alongside those coming from the east for Colorado's dry climate. Outside peddling proved ideal for immigrants, who salvaged what they could, bought a horse and wagon, and headed west on the "Golden Road" (Colfax) toward mining camps or agricultural areas to sell their wares. Many peddlers in the early 1880s were not listed in the Denver city directory because they had no need for an address.

Jews also started small businesses, such as iron dealer, tailor, watchmaker, and pawnbroker along Colfax Avenue. A grocery business founded by Jacob Miller grew into a national chain of supermarkets. Other Jews became farmers and ranchers or organized large salvage houses for rags, wastepaper, and bottles. As they prospered, they opened shops along Colfax Avenue, spreading west to Sheridan Boulevard, and built small brick homes and synagogues on both sides of West Colfax Avenue. This "ghetto" was described as unique because of the tidy one-story houses with clean unpaved streets, compared with the large, overcrowded Jewish quarters in New York and Chicago.[12]

Some of the wealthy families lived on higher ground west of the Platte. Isaac Goodstein left Russian Poland and came to Denver in about 1878 to join his brother-in-law, Philip Rosenthal, in the smelting business. Goodstein paid $400 for an acre of land and another $35 for the well in a section near West Colfax Avenue called "No Man's Land."

Voorhees plotted lots for the West Colfax subdivision in 1891. When Colfax became a town, the commercial section along Golden Avenue—9.5 blocks long and 2.5 blocks wide—seceded and called itself Brooklyn. The town of Brooklyn emerged as a link to Denver due to the roads that connected the city with the agricultural towns of Golden and Morrison to the west. Because of double taxes and other problems, Brooklyn soon gave in and rejoined the town of Colfax. After the town's annexation by Denver in 1897, Golden Avenue was renamed Colfax Avenue.[13]

Voorhees built a seven-home enclave in the area from Perry Street on the east to Tennyson Street on the west and from West Colfax Avenue south to West 13th Avenue. Four of the seven homes built by Voorhees were designated as historic landmarks. They became part of the West Colfax neighborhood in the 1970s when the city set the boundaries as West 18th Avenue on the north, Dry Gulch on the south, Federal Boulevard on the east, and Sheridan Boulevard on the west.

Stuart Street Historic District

The tiny Stuart Street Historic District includes only Stuart Street from Colfax Avenue to the southern corners of West 14th Avenue. It encompasses the luxurious stone palace designed in the 1890s by Lang and Pugh at 1471 Stuart Street for the Voorhees family. The family liked to gather on the third-floor balcony to watch fireworks at North Denver amusement parks.

Ralph Voorhees, successful real estate man and member of the Colorado legislature, erected a stone house in 1890 designed by the well-known Denver architects Lang and Pugh. The home still stands at 1471 Stuart St. in the Stuart Street Historic District.

The Frank I. Smith family, with six energetic children, occupied a three-story home just south of the Voorhees residence. In fact, the Voorhees and Smith homes had adjoining gardens. The Smith home, looking more like a church than a residence, featured a rusticated stone house with a square cupola on the north and five narrow stained-glass windows along the south stairway. Paul Smith, one of the sons, married Ferne Whiteman, prominent vocalist and sister of jazz musician Paul Whiteman.[14]

Elizabeth McNulty, a teacher at nearby Glen Park School, lived with her two aunts in a house at 1390 Stuart Street for many years. The three-story house has a steep roof, a bay window, and a balcony. Roady Kenehan, an Irishman who served as state treasurer and auditor, also lived in the home at one time.

The house at the southeast corner of West Colfax Avenue and Stuart Street was razed. It was the residence of F. W. White, longtime drama writer for the *Denver Post*, who signed his columns "F. W. W." Mike Spangler and his wife, who was a sister of Voorhees' wife, lived in a large stone and shingle house at 1444 Stuart Street. Dr. Gerald Bliss, a Civil War veteran and member of the honor guard over President Lincoln's casket, lived at 1389 Stuart Street. A similar house across the street is of brick and shingle construction with steep roofs, small dormers, and balconies.

Villa Park

Daniel Witter, an early real estate speculator, received the first federal patent for 160 acres of land southwest of Denver in 1865. Witter borrowed money

Organized in 1872, Villa Park School District 21 erected this building at West 8th Avenue and Hazel Court in 1891. Its name was changed to Eagleton in 1929 in honor of longtime principal William H. Eagleton. The four-story school was torn down in 1975, after a newer building was erected in 1973.

from his brother-in-law, Republican vice-presidential nominee Schuyler Colfax (for whom Colfax Avenue is named), to buy out three other developers, boosting his holdings to 760 acres of hilly terrain overlooking the Platte Valley. Witter transferred ownership of his land to the Denver Villa Park Association, which negotiated loans to develop the area for construction of "stately residential homes." The villas never materialized and creditors brought lawsuits against the association after the financial panic of 1873. The association filed for bankruptcy in 1878 and the land was sold by court order.[15]

Famous showman and circus owner Phineas T. Barnum purchased the 760 acres, through his agent Julian Gorham, for $11,000 in 1878. The area stretched roughly from Colfax Avenue south to Alameda Avenue and from the Platte River west to Sheridan Boulevard. Believing the unrestricted hilltop view of the mountains and valley would draw the city's elite, Barnum imitated earlier plans of the Denver Villa Park Association to create Denver's grandest neighborhood, with tree-lined streets, wide boulevards, and a dam to contain an artificial lake.

When his grandiose plans failed as well, Barnum turned over the property to his daughter, Helen Buchtel, who had moved west with her husband, William, because of his tuberculosis. (Colorado's dry, sunny climate was rumored to help the disease.) Dr. William Buchtel was the brother of Henry Buchtel, who became chancellor of the University of Denver in 1899. William and Helen Buchtel built a 21-room summer home known as Villa Park Hotel, where they hosted dances and other neighborhood gatherings before the building burned in 1910. Although Helen sold some of her holdings in the community, she continued to fight for major improvements and helped finance projects such as road paving and park irrigation.[16]

The school district expanded on the west side of the Platte River and established four schools in District 21: Glen Park School, built in 1887 at West Colfax Avenue and Stewart (Alcott) Street; Barnum School, built in 1889 in the town of Barnum; Cheltenham School, built in 1891 near West Colfax Avenue and Irving Street; and Villa Park School, erected in 1891 at West 8th Avenue and Hazel Court. In 1900, the new District 21 registered 1,534 students and 21 teachers. High school students attended classes in the Villa Park school building, which changed its name to Eagleton in 1929.[17]

Scattered development left many vacant lots, which filled with apartments as the demand for multiple-unit housing grew during the late 1950s, the 1960s, and the 1970s. Cowell Elementary School was erected in 1954 at West 10th Avenue and South Utica Street for the increasing number of children in the neighborhood. A new Eagleton School was built in 1973 at West 9th Avenue and South Hooker Street, and the old building was demolished in 1975. The Villa Park neighborhood today extends from Lakewood/Dry Gulch on the north to West 6th Avenue on the south and from Federal Boulevard on the east to Sheridan Boulevard on the west.[18]

In 2006, Denver Parks and Recreation opened the city's first 18-hole regulation disc golf course along the hilly ground of Lakewood/Dry Gulch, Knox Court, and West 13th Avenue. Councilwoman Rosemary Rodriguez represented District 3 at the opening celebration, which activated the passive park area for more community use.

A new Eagleton Elementary School went up at 880 Hooker Street in 1973
to replace the old 1891 building first known as Villa Park School.

CHAPTER SIX

Barnum and Barnum West

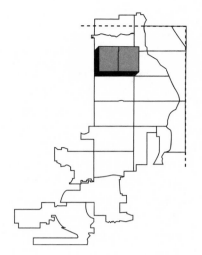

O riginally intended as an exclusive enclave, Barnum actually became a working-class neighborhood with a "live and let live" attitude. Infrastructure has always been a challenge here, although neighbors have banded together for improvements despite years of changing demographics. The area was influenced by founder P. T. Barnum, architect William Norman Bowman, and local publications such as the *Barnum News*, which became the *Denver Herald–Dispatch*.

Development started in the Barnum area around 1878, and the towns of Barnum and Villa Park were incorporated in 1887. Between West 8th Avenue and West Alameda Avenue from Federal Boulevard to Tennyson Street was Barnum. Villa Park included the area north of Barnum from West 8th Avenue to West Colfax Avenue, between Federal Boulevard and Sheridan Boulevard. Today, Barnum and West Barnum are bounded by West 6th Avenue, Federal Boulevard, West Alameda Avenue, and Sheridan Boulevard.

The P. T. Barnum Subdivision

When Phineas T. Barnum of circus fame bought land in West Denver in 1878, he envisioned an elite hilltop neighborhood with winding boulevards and comfortable homes around a man-made lake. The "P. T. Barnum Subdivision to Denver" was platted into 5,012 lots and advertised as a grand development for "homes, gardens, and manufacturing" on Denver's "New West Side." The lots were priced at $15 to $112 each. In spite of enticements such as furnished homes valued from $2,500 to $7,000, advertising failed to spark a boom of home construction. A sparse water supply and difficult access to the rest of the city foiled Barnum's ambitious plans.[1]

In 1884, Barnum transferred the property, which included Villa Park, parts of Sun Valley, and present-day Valverde, to his daughter Helen, wife of Dr. William Buchtel. The Buchtels had moved to Denver hoping to cure William's tuberculosis with the dry climate. William's brother, Henry, was a pastor and chancellor of the University of Denver; Buchtel Boulevard is named after Henry Buchtel.

P. T. Barnum died in Connecticut in 1891, but his name and descendants remained in the West Denver neighborhoods. Two adjacent houses on King Street are associated with the Barnum family. The larger 14-room house dates back to 1878 and features a conservatory, parlor, kitchen, third-floor bedrooms, and maid's quarters, along with a cistern in back and a hitching post for horses in front. The red brick guest cottage next door was supposedly fashioned after one Barnum had seen in Sudbury, England. A descendant, who calls himself Bart Barnum, has lived in the two houses for many years.[2]

Although he never really resided in Denver, P. T. Barnum did have an impact on the area. For example, Hazel Court was originally called Jumbo Avenue, after Barnum's best-known elephant. Barnum also named streets after some of his favorite people and places: 1st Avenue was called Emerson Avenue, after Ralph Waldo Emerson; 2nd Avenue was Beecher Avenue, after the famous preacher Henry Ward Beecher; and Ellsworth Avenue was dubbed Holmes Avenue, after Oliver Wendell Holmes. Newton Street was called Waldemere, after Barnum's mansion in Connecticut, and Raleigh Street was Connecticut Avenue. Stuart Street was known as Pequonnock Street, recalling the river running by Barnum's eastern estate. Barnum honored his daughter with Helen Avenue (Julian Street), her husband with Buchtel Avenue (Knox Court), and his granddaughter with Lelia Avenue (Hooker Street). He even named a street after himself (King Street was Barnum Avenue). The street names changed to an alphabetical system when the Barnum neighborhood became part of Denver in 1896.[3]

Even though many stories circulated about Barnum wintering his circus animals on land named for him, circus historian "Cappy" Fox said the circus owner never wintered his animals anywhere but his home base in Connecticut and later in Florida. "Colorado was too impractical for winter grounds. The season opened in New York every year, and the distance from Bridgeport, Connecticut, to Brooklyn, New York, was only a hop, skip, and a jump for his animals," Fox stated. Records show the circus traveling to Colorado most seasons in the early days, but Barnum himself visited Colorado only four times, according to local author Ida Uchill. She said Barnum visited Greeley in 1870 and returned in 1872 to lecture on temperance. He came to Colorado again in 1877 to check on properties he owned in Greeley, Douglas County, and Denver and made a final journey in 1890, the year before he died.[4]

After plans to attract well-to-do residents proved unsuccessful, Helen Buchtel sold lots in the area to people with meager incomes. Dreams of Barnum becoming Denver's most exclusive neighborhood faded as it turned into a community for the working class. Families of all types moved beyond the city limits to "be free from the contaminating influence of downtown city streets," said F. S. Kinder, a pioneer resident. "Many a man put up his home with the help of his good wife," Kinder noted.[5]

American-born families worked as professionals, tradesmen, and laborers, many in railroad jobs. Germans and Swedes came as skilled cabinetmakers, masons, teamsters, manufacturers, and manual laborers. Other foreign-born residents from England, Ireland, Scotland, Canada, and Russia sought employment as carpenters, paper hangers, and stonecutters. Residents overcame their ethnic differences as they cooperated with one another in tackling common concerns. As longtime resident Nell Thompson stated, "When you're poor, you work together."[6]

Numerous families kept barnyard and domestic animals in the rural area, and town officials were faced with issues of roaming dogs in addition to the major problems of water, public transportation, and unpaved roads. Seeking revenue for improvements, the town council passed a measure to tax the ownership of dogs. Responding in anger, residents threatened riots. The city fathers soon reversed the ordinance. To foster good feelings, they sponsored a picnic in Barnum Park with money collected from the dog tax.

To address water concerns, two existing artesian wells at the corners of 1st Avenue and Hazel Court and 7th Avenue and Knox Court were refurbished. By the mid-1890s, the town was able to pay for mains that supplied water from Denver Union Water Company.

But transportation was a headache for residents who worked downtown and could not afford a horse and buggy. Most depended on the streetcar for the nearly 2-mile trip from Barnum across the prairie to Denver. After proposals from three railroad companies failed to materialize, the first streetcar connection to Denver began on January 1, 1893. The Denver, Lakewood & Golden Railroad ran from the downtown loop on Larimer Street to a stop at West 8th Avenue and Grove Street. However, service still proved unsatisfactory. Streetcars ran one hour apart and passengers had to transfer to the Tramway Company line and pay another fare to reach the city. Free transfers were not issued, because the two lines operated independently.[7]

The town of Barnum united with Denver in 1896 and by 1900 was established as a homogenous working-class community. West Barnum was annexed in 1901 but remained largely undeveloped until after World War II. Its area pushed west from Tennyson Street to Sheridan Boulevard between West 6th Avenue and Alameda.[8]

Local residents and the city shared the cost of paving 1st and 2nd Avenues between Sheridan and Federal Boulevards in 1909. However, many streets remained unpaved until the 1940s. "If you stick with Barnum, Barnum will stick with you," became the community's unofficial, sarcastic slogan as pedestrians trudged through muddy streets on their way to work or school.[9]

The Bowman/Savio House

One of Barnum's wealthiest residents, architect William Norman Bowman, settled in Denver in 1910 with his wife, Alice May, and built a large red brick house for his family at 325 King Street Born in New York, Bowman first worked as a carpenter, then became a businessman who sold steel. He amassed a comfortable sum of money by the age of 40 and looked for a suitable place to start his architectural career. He selected Denver over Los Angeles, a city of the same size at the time, because of its climate and people.[10]

A pleasant, gray-eyed man who wore subdued suits, bat-wing collars, and tortoiseshell glasses, Bowman was a prolific architect. He designed the 1929

Prominent architect William Bowman designed his 1890 hilltop home overlooking the Platte River valley. Once owned by the Sisters of St. Francis as a tuberculosis sanitarium, the building is now known as Savio House and serves troubled youths.

Mountain States Telephone Building at 14th and Curtis Streets, the State Office Building at Colfax Avenue and Sherman Street, the Colburn and Cosmopolitan Hotels, Byers and Cole Junior High Schools, and scores of other Denver buildings, many of which still stand today. In addition, he designed Adams State Teachers' College at Alamosa and buildings for the Cañon City Penitentiary.

Bowman's home stood on a high hill in the Barnum neighborhood. The stately two-story house, called Yamecila—his wife's name spelled backward—afforded a majestic view of the mountain range to the west and the river valley to the south and east. Bowman designed the home with Colonial Revival elements, including a large porch, two prominent towers on the front, and an unusual floor plan with the living room open to the entry hall and the principal stairway to the second floor at the rear of the house.

The Bowmans lived in the house until 1924 when they moved to the newly constructed Norman Apartments, designed by Bowman, at 99 South Downing Street. Because of financial difficulties, Bowman sold his impressive mansion on King Street in July 1924 for $12,000 to the Sisters of St. Francis of the Congregation of Our Lady of Lourdes, Rochester, Minnesota, as a hospital for tubercular Sisters. Renamed Mt. Alverna Convent and St. Francis Sanitarium, the facility offered a dry climate and quiet haven for Catholic nuns suffering from tuberculosis and other lung ailments.[11]

The Sisters purchased additional land, eventually owning most of the block between King Street on the east and Lowell Boulevard on the west, from West 4th Avenue on the north to West 3rd Avenue on the south, an area of 3 acres.

At the Sisters' request, Bowman designed a building in the area—a U-shaped structure around a garden court so tuberculosis patients could enjoy fresh air and sunshine prescribed by doctors as part of the treatment and cure. He also designed a new Colonial-style chapel built at the northwest corner of his original house to replace the makeshift chapel room used previously. Bowman died in 1944.

In 1966, the sanitarium was sold to a group of Denver businessmen who wanted to meet the needs of delinquent boys. Renamed Savio House after Dominique Savio, the Patron Saint of Youth, the red brick building provided a home and school for homeless, abandoned, and abused adolescents in the Denver area.[12] Purchasers and founders were Gail Neiswanger, Alfred Wiesner, Charles Hughes, and Michael Reidy. Jerry Dennis, a local teacher, served as director.

Living their motto, "We Serve," the Lions Club of Denver enthusiastically participated in the growth of this new agency and took sole leadership of Savio House in 1974 at the request of the founders. As a community project of the Lions Club, Savio House evolved into an effective resource for distressed families.

Although interior remodeling occurred over the years, the Bowman/Savio House retained many of its original features, such as stained-glass windows, fireplaces, and the dining room buffet. The impressive exterior commanded attention of passersby, who assumed it to be Barnum's house, based on its stately appearance. The circus descendant's actual house was smaller than one might imagine considering the showman's reputation, but his home near West 3rd Avenue and King Street was considered grand at the time it was built.

Rosenberg's "Barnum News/Denver Herald-Dispatch"

J. Ivanhoe "Ivan" Rosenberg moved with his family to Barnum in 1925 at age 5. Ivan's father, Joseph, was the son of a Russian Jewish immigrant—a rabbi who settled as a printer in New York and typeset the Bible by hand, the first to do so in Yiddish. Joseph migrated to Wyoming and eventually ended up in Denver, where he bought out Kimberly Printery.

"We moved to 36 South Federal Bloulevard on Mother's Day in 1926," Ivan said. "I attended Barnum School at West 1st Avenue and Hooker Street and got beat up many times over as I walked to and from school because I was Jewish."

When Joseph opened his Barnum print shop, anti-Semitism had penetrated Denver government and the Ku Klux Klan, which dominated Denver's politics in the 1920s and terrorized Jewish citizens. "The Ku Klux Klan didn't want Jews and burned a cross in our front yard and gave tough messages to get out of the neighborhood," Ivan related. "My father wasn't intimidated by the Klan and decided to fight back. He started the *Barnum News* in October 1926. Friends and supporters wouldn't advertise in the paper but gave him money secretly. This money helped him survive in the early days. The more active the Klan, the more donations he got."

Ivan remembered going with his father to the potato cellar at Joe's Cave when the business started as a fruit and vegetable stand at West 1st Avenue and Federal Boulevard. "The cellar in back was a cool place to store food in the hot summer. It was the first business in the neighborhood to get a liquor permit," he said.[13]

Joseph and Judith Rosenberg raised their five children—Ivanhoe, Quentin, Amy June, Evalea, and Juanita Illene—in Barnum and all five attended West High School. Ivan's sisters, however, married and moved away.

Quentin Rosenberg belonged to Mensa, an organization for people with genius-level IQs. After serving in the Army Air Corps in World War II, he held responsible positions in many organizations, including American Legion state commander in 1967–1968 and colonel in the Colorado National Guard. Known by friends as Rosie, he moved easily in political and military circles in the nation's capital.

He remained active in politics, befriended scouts, and worked with young people until his death in 1997. He was 75.[14]

Ivan and his wife, Shirley (Hall), had six children: Joe, Margie, Eileen, Donna, Gary, and I.V. In the footsteps of their parents, they attended West High School and became successful businessmen and businesswomen. The three sons followed their father and grandfather into the printing business.

Ivan took over as publisher and editor of the *Barnum News* when his father, Joseph, died in 1955. He changed the newspaper's name to the *Denver Herald-Dispatch* in the early 1960s, using the slogan "The only newspaper in the world that gives a darn about Southwest Denver," and continued his father's tradition of campaigning for community improvements. The newspaper operated for 12 years at 47 South Federal Boulevard, then moved back to its original location at 314 Federal Boulevard. Barnum Publishing Company, also owned by Ivan Rosenberg, printed more than 60 publications, including high school and college newspapers and weekly magazines. His company also published *La Voz*, which is still Colorado's leading Hispanic newspaper.

Ivan Rosenberg with his sons, Joe, Gary and I.V.

Ivan owned another business, too, a snowplow manufacturing company called Sno-Skat. The company promoted Ivan's invention, a light-duty snowplow designed to fit on the front of an automobile, van, or pickup. After his 80th birthday, Ivan sold the Barnum Publishing Company to his youngest son, I.V. Rosenberg, who moved the presses to 6888 Grove Street. The senior Rosenberg continued to conduct his innovative Sno-Skat business from the South Federal Boulevard office.

On July 21, 2001, Ivan Rosenberg announced that the newspaper, which had published 3,952 consecutive editions since its founding in 1926, would fold because of declining circulation and decreased support from local advertisers.

Fortunately, the newspaper did not miss an issue and in the following week proclaimed, "We're Back!" after a business partnership formed between Rosenberg and publisher Robert Sweeney. Sweeney took over as the new publisher/owner in August 2001 and incorporated the *Sheridan Sun* to cover news for the town of Sheridan.[15]

In 2000, Ivan Rosenberg was inducted into the Denver Press Club Hall of Fame for his longtime newspaper career, which he had started as a floor sweeper (custodian) and delivery boy. Three years earlier, he received the Gold Medal award at the 40th annual Minnesota Inventor's Conference for his Sno-Skat snow-removal product. In previous years, Ivan drove race cars at the old Englewood Speedway and was active in the Colorado Automobile Racing Club at Lakeside Speedway. He celebrated his 81st birthday by riding in a sailplane. At 86 years old, he remains active and goes to his office daily.

Early Barnum Residents

With the demand for skilled and unskilled labor, a housing boom occurred in the 1920s. People added on to their houses as their families grew. The first school, which started in 1873 in a two-room house, moved to different locations in the neighborhood for more than 30 years. The newly constructed Barnum Elementary School opened its four classrooms in 1921 at the corner of West 1st Avenue and Hooker Street. Resourceful families included the Leopolds, Garlingtons, Broses and Jeffses, many of whose members stayed in the area, working and raising their own children.[16]

The Leopolds

Charles and Madge Leopold and other enterprising residents took advantage of Denver's healthy climate by renting rooms to tuberculosis sufferers who came to the city for a cure. After moving from New York City to find a new life in the West, the Leopolds responded to a Denver newspaper ad and bought a four-room house at 148 Osceola Street for $725. They paid $400 down and $10 in monthly installments including interest, then rented rooms for $6 a week to eastern TB patients.[17]

Charles worked as a painter at the Pullman shops, leaving home at 6 a.m. to walk a mile over the prairie to the Lawrence streetcar. In 1907, Madge helped establish Bethany Methodist Church at West 1st Avenue and King Street; pioneers recall it as the first church in the community.

The Garlingtons / Broses

An early Barnum resident, Waldon Garlington moved with his family to Barnum in 1923, at age 3. He recalled that his father, Jesse Garlington, built a house on Short Place out of whatever he could find. Raised on a farm, Jesse Garlington knew how to shoe horses and make his own tools. He worked at Midwest Steel as a layout man (a specialized welder) and taught welding at Emily Griffith Opportunity School. Jesse Garlington was also a baseball buff who organized teams, managed, and played. Semi-pro baseball, popular in the 1920s and 1930s, drew 1,500 to 1,800 people to watch teams such as the Barnum Boosters, Barnum Merchants, White Elephants from Five Points, and the House of David bearded players. The teams played at Merchants Park at South Broadway and West Center Avenue.

With no money for entertainment, young Waldon and his friends burned weeds off flat land to make a rough diamond for playing baseball. They created slingshots with long leather thongs and could throw rocks 200 feet to knock tin cans off a log. They used caves in the creek bank to build fires and roast potatoes. The boys swam in the Platte, skinny-dipping on hot summer days, and caught crayfish. Never bored, they raided watermelon patches and munched on Pascal celery grown along the river. In winter they cleared snow off the frozen creek and skated on the rough ice.

Waldon met his future wife, Dorothy Brose, in kindergarten. Dorothy was the only child of Mary and Arthur Brose, who bought a house on Hazel Court. "I walked to school every day with Waldon Garlington and we became good friends," Dorothy said. "Then he went on to Lake Junior High. I stayed at Barnum School through eighth grade, aspiring to become a writer like Lenora Mattingly Weber, who I interviewed as Head Girl at Barnum. Waldon and I both attended Seventh Avenue Congregational Church where my mother taught Sunday school and Dad helped stage plays," she said.

"Barnum had a great mix of houses and people," Dorothy recalled. "The neighborhood ranged from large brick houses of the well-to-do to tiny frame homes of very poor families. People there were most genuine. Many had little material wealth but displayed compassion, respect, and appreciation for others. They helped each other and shared what they had.

"Everyone planted gardens. We raised lettuce, carrots, beets, beans, peas, strawberries, corn, also chickens that gave us eggs.

When there was a water shortage, we saved wash water and dish water and threw it on the garden to keep it growing. As a girl I

enjoyed walking to the tiny park on the hill close to my house where I looked for flowers and sat listening to the train's lonely whistle, wondering if I would ever get out of Denver and go places. I liked to gather sand lilies and johnny-jump-ups for the driver of the horse-drawn bakery wagon. He gave me cookies in exchange," Dorothy said.

Mary Brose with daughter Dorothy near their garden, where they raised lettuce, carrots, and other vegetables in the 1920s.

"In ninth grade I went to West High, riding the '75' streetcar, which crossed Cherry Creek near 12th Avenue and passing truck gardens and a vinegar factory close to the river. Fascinated by hobos camped along the river bank, I imagined what it would be like to eat out of cans and not wash dishes."

Waldon and Dorothy both graduated from West High School, then he joined the Navy. She went on to college and eventually landed a job in the U.S. State Department in Washington, D.C., where they were married. They returned to Denver in 1958 to care for Dorothy's mother and to raise their daughter, Carol.[18]

The Jeffses

Waldon's contemporary, William "Bill" Jeffs, moved to a sparsely populated Barnum in 1923 and started kindergarten in the annex, the original Barnum School, where desks still had inkwells. His father worked for J.S. Brown Mercantile Company, noted for its roasted coffee, and his mother was governess to a lawyer's children. The Jeffs family lived at West 1st Avenue and South Hazel Court.

Young Bill worked for Joseph Rosenberg, earning 10 cents a week delivering newspapers. Each Friday he took the *Barnum News* to neighborhood houses and blew a whistle to let people know the paper was there. During his senior year at West High School, he earned 25 cents an hour as a sweeper boy (custodian) and later worked as a sweeper boy at the University of Denver for 30 cents an hour.

After graduating from the University of Denver, Bill Jeffs taught science at West High School, served as assistant principal at Kepner Junior High School, and returned to Barnum Elementary School as principal in the 1960s, completing the cycle begun as a Barnum kindergartner. After retirement, he remained active as a Barnum and West High School alumnus.[19]

A Push for Improvements

In the late 1920s, Barnum still had no sidewalks, curbs, or paved streets. Progressive Barnum citizens organized civic associations, held meetings, and took petitions to the city to push for improvements in their neighborhood. Even so, the town continued to grow as businesses appeared along West 1st, West 5th, and West 7th Avenues, as well as Knox Court, Federal Boulevard, and West Alameda Avenue. A market, a barbershop, a drugstore, and the Comet Theater were among the 54 businesses counted in 1933. The Comet, which became the Paris Theater in the late 1950s, was eventually destroyed by an explosion.

During the Great Depression, resourceful people used every opportunity to stave off hunger and unemployment. With a surplus of shotgun shells and no buyers, one merchant gave the ammunition to local hunters, who went to eastern Colorado to shoot jackrabbits that were destroying crops. The rabbits made tasty meals for hungry Barnum residents. Others survived by planting gardens, raising chickens, eating liver at 5 cents a pound, and going barefoot in summer to save shoes for winter.[20]

The *Barnum News* reported in 1933 that more than 2,000 Barnum residents had jobs with the Civil Works Administration (CWA) maintaining mountain parks, tearing down the old city courthouse, and designing and building water projects. The government also paid laborers to complete the 12-mile extension of Alameda Avenue, from Knox Court to Red Rocks Park.

Forty years after annexation, Barnum still lacked paved streets, streetlights, traffic signals, and additional improvements enjoyed in other parts of the city. Residents battled with municipal officials of Mayor Ben Stapleton's administration, and the *Barnum News* fought for a swimming pool, park improvements, and pavement on streets west of Knox Court and south of West 1st Avenue.

Finally, street improvements began as the city completed two main arteries between 1941 and 1944. The rough, rutty 8th Avenue highway was paved at a cost of $43,000. Construction of the four-lane West 6th Avenue freeway provided a high-speed route to the Denver Ordnance Plant, known later as the Denver Federal Center. A shared project of the city, state, and army, the freeway cost totaled $200,000. On the downside, the new thoroughfare separated a portion of Villa Park from the rest of the neighborhood, deflating the dream for a big lake with a beach and boating in the park.[21]

A Multicultural Mix

The homogenous nature of the area changed as new cultures moved into the neighborhood because of nearby employment and low-cost housing. By the mid-1940s, many of Denver's Westside Hispanics worked at Gates Rubber Company on South Broadway in skilled and unskilled labor positions, in railroad work, in meatpacking, and in smelter and refining jobs. Manuel L. "Sam" Sandos, former councilman, remembered working on the Gates fan belt assembly line after World War II for 67 cents an hour. Barnum homes attracted people because of the convenient location for workers. The average rent in 1945 ranged from $19.90 to $21.40 a month.[22]

From 1950 to 1970, the number of Hispanic residents rose while Anglo numbers declined. The vacant lots were annexed as Barnum West exploded with middle-class homes, reflecting the post-war construction boom. In contrast to the varied dwellings in Barnum, Barnum West was developed uniformly by construction companies such as Happy Homes. The population there swelled from 1,734 in 1950 to 5,887 in 1960, surpassing Barnum by 600. Barnum West residents earned an average salary of $11,500 a year in 1960, compared with Barnum's yearly average of $10,000.[23]

Additional long-awaited improvements occurred in the 1950s as Denver acquired and developed the neglected park at West 3rd Avenue and Hooker Street, expanding Barnum Park to 39 acres, including an artificial lake built in 1959. With increased money from property taxes, the city finally installed curbs and paved streets and alleys in 1954–1955.[24]

Some early residents chose to stay in the neighborhood. Nell Thompson resided in Barnum for over 50 years. Sometimes referred to as the "Mother of Barnum," Thompson knew how to get things done. She said "If the city doesn't get to it right away, we do it." Over the years, she developed Girl Scout troops, organized the effective Concerned Citizens of Barnum (CCB), and convinced the city to build a swimming pool at the Barnum Recreation Center and an addition to the Ross-Barnum Library. She and Nina Eason were instrumental in forming the Barnum Senior Center. Thompson received recognition from the Denver City Council on her 82nd birthday for "volunteerism for the good of the greater area of Barnum." She died in 2003 at the age of 95.[25]

Changing Demographics

A Denver District Court mandate in 1970 increased city council membership from 9 to 11 seats and rearranged district boundaries, allowing more minorities to serve in city government. Sam Sandos ran against J. Ivanhoe Rosenberg for the newly designated District 3 seat during the 1971 city election. Although Sandos grew up in "old Barnum" at West 7th Avenue and Lowell Boulevard and spoke Spanish, he was narrowly defeated by Rosenberg. The Jewish Rosenberg thought it ironic that the neighborhood where the KKK wanted to run his family out of town in the Klan-dominated 1920s elected him to represent them.[26]

Rosenberg and Sandos met again in the 1975 election, resulting in a runoff election won by Sandos, who said his greatest challenge in the campaign was convincing voters he would represent all people, regardless of race. As the first Hispanic council member, Sandos faced the task of building a bridge between white and Hispanic residents. Sandos, who died in 1987, is remembered for his efforts to improve the quality of life in his council district.[27]

Attendance patterns in Protestant and Catholic churches reflected changes in Barnum during the 1970s and 1980s. Archbishop James V. Casey of the Catholic Archdiocese of Denver approved relocation of St. Cajetan's Church from 1156 9th Street to a site that would better serve the city's Mexican-American population. During the 1970s, when Denver Urban Renewal Authority (DURA) razed many older homes to clear the way for the Auraria Higher Education Center, the original church building was preserved as a historic landmark. Since parishioners needed another worship location, a new facility was built in 1975 at the corner of South Raleigh Street and West Alameda Avenue, on Barnum's south boundary. This spurred many families to move close to the new St. Cajetan's Church and also increased attendance at the long-established Presentation of Our Lady Church at 665 Irving Street.[28]

Several businesses weathered changes in the community. The Krupa family opened The Little Store in 1940 at 1st Avenue and Knox Court and sold it to Lloyd King in 1950, when King started the King Soopers grocery chain. In 1970, King sold the store to Ted Zimmerman, who operated a thriving business for 17 years and was named "Grocer of the Year" for a five-state region in 1984.

Anthony Apergis opened the Columbine Steak House at 300 Federal Boulevard. in 1961. Originally from Greece, he worked at the famed Brown Derby Restaurant in Los Angeles and the Denver Country Club and the Brown Palace Hotel in Denver before starting his own business. Over the years he helped many Greeks come to America and go into business for themselves. After his death in 2000, his son, Socrates, said the family would continue to run the Columbine Steak House.[29]

A 10-foot replica of the Statue of Liberty marks the site of Federal Heating and Air Conditioning Supply, 175 South Federal Boulevard. Bo Ramsour, president of Federal Heating, said his grandmother purchased the building in 1911 and founded the business, which survived over three generations. The business stayed small enough to provide quality service to community residents.[30]

Ongoing Challenges and Improvements

With its deteriorating infrastructure, Barnum citizens continue to fight for neighborhood improvements in the tradition of community activism begun nearly 100 years earlier. In 1981, Concerned Citizens for Barnum, with support from Councilman Sam Sandos and the Heritage Conservation and Recreation Service, organized the Weir Gulch Action Group to coordinate a resident-based effort to improve the Weir Gulch corridor and make it a recreational asset to the neighborhood. With funds from the Community Development Agency's Neighborhood Small Projects program, volunteers planted trees, built a tot lot, upgraded ball fields, and installed basketball backboards, picnic tables, and park benches.

The 1940s building that served as Ethel's Beauty Salon and Gil's Barber Shop for 33 years was moved to the Lakewood Heritage Center when West Alameda Avenue was widened in the 1990s.

Funds approved in a 1989 bond election allowed for restoration of Barnum Lake to bring back wildlife and enjoyment of the lake. Work did not begin, however, until citizens pushed for the project through Concerned Citizens for Barnum. Finally, work was underway in 1998 to drain the lake and remove sediment to allow for excavation of new islands with lush grasses, wildflowers, shrubs, and trees, which provided habitat for birds and aquatic animals.[31]

Improvements to the major corridors began in 1997 and 1998. Plans called for widening roads, improving drainage and sidewalks, refurbishing the 6th Avenue viaduct, and adding a turn lane at the intersection of West 6th Avenue and Federal Boulevard.

The widening of Alameda Avenue over the years caused the popular Ethel's Beauty Salon and Gil's Barber Shop to move twice. Gil and Ethel Gomez married in 1955 and Gil started work in Herb Stuart's barbershop at West Alameda Avenue and South Federal Boulevard. Gil bought the business a year later with a $600 loan from his father.

In 1957, Gil moved the shop to 3126 West Alameda Avenue and Ethel opened a beauty salon next door in 1961. When the city widened Alameda a few years later, their parking was eliminated, so they moved across the street to a small building at 3043 West Alameda Avenue. Featuring rounded corners, exterior tile, and glass block construction, the unique building dated back to 1942. Topped with an eye-catching clock, it originally housed a dry cleaning business, then a struggling variety store, which closed in December 1962.[32]

With plenty of parking for customers, Ethel's Beauty Salon and Gil's Barber Shop shared the cozy space for 33 years until the city earmarked Alameda Avenue for expansion again in 1996. Gil, a master barber, won numerous awards and honors in his trade and taught razor cutting at Emily Griffith Opportunity School. He and Ethel lived near their shop and raised three children: Lisa, Les, and Timothy. After Gil died in 1996 at age 64, Ethel relocated her beauty shop to Harts Corner Center on West Mississippi Avenue.

The fate of the longtime landmark building wavered between demolition by a wrecking crew and rescue as a "typical neighborhood business" from the 1950s. A significant example of International-style architecture, Ethel's and Gil's caught the notice of history-conscious people in Lakewood. In 1998, the former beauty/barber shop building rolled to a new home at Lakewood's Heritage Center at South Wadsworth Boulevard and West Ohio Avenue. Denver sold the 1,000-square-foot building to Lakewood.

Barnum residents overcame many obstacles through the years to keep their neighborhood alive and well. As community activist Jan Belle concluded, "This will always be a working class community that built itself. It will never be southeast Denver or west Washington Park. The people who live in Barnum value it for what it is. There's a spirit of live and let live."[33]

CHAPTER SEVEN

Valverde and Athmar Park

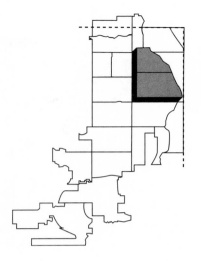

A former celery capital of the United States and birthplace of the Colorado state song, "Where the Columbines Grow," the Valverde and Athmar Park neighborhoods in the Platte River valley flourished around rich farmland. Development started in the late 1800s on Valverde, which includes the area between West 6th Avenue and West Alameda Avenue from the South Platte River west to Federal Boulevard. Today, the old town of Valverde is actually contained within the Athmar Park neighborhood, bordered by the South Platte River, South Federal Boulevard, West Alameda Avenue and West Mississippi Avenue. The fertile location, unfortunately, left residents vulnerable to severe flooding of the South Platte River. The flood in 1965 had a major impact on businesses and families in the area until the construction of Chatfield Reservoir mitigated the possibility of a repeat flood. The neighborhood attracted many Hispanic and Asian immigrants, producing today's rich multicultural offerings in shopping and restaurants.

The Fassett Farm

One of Valverde's first settlers, Joseph W. Fassett, traveled to Denver from Illinois by ox and wagon in 1859. The ambitious 23-year-old and his comrades gathered supplies and headed for Golden to make their fortune in mining. They secured claims to mine gold in Russell Gulch, and Fassett made a considerable amount of money working his claim. He invested in other enterprises and made a good living by freighting between Denver, the mountain towns, and the military post. Later, he worked as a farmer. In the spring of 1869, he applied for a homestead patent from President Ulysses S. Grant and received 160 acres of land overlooking the South Platte River.[1]

Fassett married Nancy Caroline Janes in 1886. He sold 80 acres of land to Donald Fletcher for $1,000 in 1889 and then hired an architect to design a large home and carriage house on the remaining property. The distinctive three-story brick house, finished in 1890, sat on a bluff looking down on flourishing willow and cottonwood trees along the river, in an area early developers called Valverde (Spanish for "green valley").

From its hilltop location at what is now 50 South Alcott Street, the extraordinary home could be seen for miles. A winding driveway from West Bayaud Avenue (originally called Fassett Avenue) ended at the gabled-roof carriage house. Fassett's farmhouse featured Colonial Revival–style architecture with characteristics of Victorian styling and embellishments of the Arts and Crafts period. Facing east, the three-story, 5,000-square-foot home had two sunrooms on the main floor and one on the third floor. Wide woodwork of solid oak followed the mode of the day. A carved coat of arms on the newel post of the elaborate oak stairway greeted visitors, who no doubt were impressed by the two striking, stained-glass windows above the stairs and a stained-glass transom over the front door.[2]

Joseph, Nancy, and their children often gathered on the front porch, enjoying the view of Denver City and the valley below. They lived comfortably, relying on the help of a female servant who occupied basement quarters. The family's food was prepared in the basement kitchen and then traveled on a dumbwaiter to the elegant first-floor dining room furnished with a built-in mirrored buffet. On winter days, fireplaces warmed both the front and back parlors and the front bedroom upstairs. The house featured six bedrooms along with five bathrooms on the upper two stories, and the five children put their dirty clothes in the laundry chute, which shot them down to the main-floor laundry room.

A prominent Denver citizen, Joseph Fassett was a charter member of Union Lodge No. 7 of the Masons and served 15 years on the Villa Park School Board. He died in 1907, a year after his wife.

Over the years, Fassett family members sold off parcels of property to Globe Fuel and Feed Company, Park Hill Investment Company, Denver Clay Products Company, and Morningside Homes Inc. In 1946, the Tuckaway Home for Homeless Children purchased the family home to care for orphans. Five years later, Victoria Hatfield bought the historic property and converted the two-story carriage house into four two-bedroom units called Victoria Apartments.[3]

Lawrence and Ada Haley bought the house in 1961. After Lawrence died, Ada managed the place by herself. She hired Clyde Miranda, who was looking for work. They became friends and ended up marrying—when she was 90 and he was 70. Ada sold the property to Jim and Jeanne Amen in 1994.[4]

The enthusiastic Amens began remodeling the run-down property even though they both had jobs. "At first we planned to open a bed-and-breakfast to be known as The Fassett Farm Guest House," Jeanne explained. "We did some preliminary research and learned that it would be very costly to bring the house up to Denver's requirements for food service and handicap access. So we decided to keep it as apartments."

The Amens lived on the first floor and rented out five apartments on the upper floors and four in the carriage house. They both participated in community activities and served different terms as president of the neighborhood organization. After failing to gain historic landmark designation for the old mansion, the Amens sold the property in 2000 and moved to a retirement community.

The Town of Valverde

Edward A. Reser platted Valverde in 1882 along the line of the Denver and South Park Railroad. The town was incorporated in 1888 while still in Arapahoe County. Industrious pioneers published their own newspaper, the *Valverde Vedette*, which later operated as the *Valverde Progress*. Baron Walter von Richthofen sold lots for $25 to $75 north of Alameda Avenue, between Bayaud and Irvington Avenues from Tejon to Pecos Streets, promising easy payments on the installment plan and easy access to railroad transportation. Citizens voted to annex Richtofen's Addition in 1892, casting 22 votes, 13 in favor and 9 opposed.[5]

The old town of Valverde ran along both sides of Alameda Avenue (Spanish for "avenue lined with trees") from West Tejon Street to South Lipan Street, extending south to West Virginia Avenue on the west boundary and south to West Exposition Avenue on the east boundary. The town had 750 residents by 1900.[6]

The town functioned with a municipal government that included a town hall, marshal, jail, saloon, hotel, and school. Sam Hamilton, the first real estate agent, held the job of postmaster, and Dr. Edmond Dillard provided health care. Florist, jeweler, dressmaker, shoemaker, and bicycle repair businesses sprang up along Alameda Avenue east of Tejon Street, forming the nucleus of the old Valverde community along with the adjacent industrial areas of the present-day Athmar Park and Sun Valley neighborhoods.[7]

The Denver Fire Clay Company produced pottery and brick at its large factory. The Kuner Pickle Company prepared a variety of condiments, pickles, and canned goods for Denver consumers. The Western Glass Manufacturing Company made flint-glass merchandise until 1905, then became Western

Feldspar Melting Company, with its rock-crushing plant next door. The Western Chemical Company, established in 1898, became a landmark for the town. After changing owners in 1920, the company was known as General Chemical Company until 1928, when it consolidated with five other divisions into the Allied Chemical Company.[8]

In 1897, fearful residents filled sandbags to protect their homes and businesses from floodwaters. The water rose as far as the glass factory at the corner of what is now South Pecos Street and West Bayaud Avenue, and when it subsided people collected many stranded fish in washtubs.

A residential area mostly made up of single-family homes blossomed on the bluffs while industry spread to the east in the lower Platte River valley. Early builders developed Weir Addition and Allen's Heights neighborhoods in the northwestern section, which was close to the old Barnum community on the west. In the early 1900s, South Federal Boulevard was narrow and carried little traffic, so the street did not present the barrier that separated the two communities when businesses sprang up along Federal.

Children from the area attended Valverde School, which was built purposely on high ground at West Exposition Avenue and South Navajo Street. Girls in dainty white dresses and boys in dress slacks walked miles to school. They trudged along the sandy path up the hill to the 1890 schoolhouse and when it stormed, they dodged several gullies along the way, including one between Dakota Avenue and Alaska Avenue, where sand lilies and johnny-jump-ups often bloomed. If they veered from the path, they risked losing their shoes in the mud.[9]

The view from Inspiration Hill, south and west of the Valverde schoolhouse, impressed E. J. Clark, M.D. "From the top of the hill one looks down at the green valley lying close at your feet and you can realize why it should be called Valverde. . . . 30 acres belonging to the Tramway and the Water companies need only a few dollars of expenditure to give this section of the city a park that will out-rival any of the artificial parks of our city. The trees there are magnificent specimens, growing in a rich soil that needs only grading, seeding and caring to make it one of Denver's most beautiful natural resorts. The Valverde ball nine [baseball players] have cleared a portion of this ground and have there fought and won some hotly contested games," Clark wrote in a 1913 article.[10]

The town of Valverde was dissolved in 1902 and annexed to the city of Denver. The Valverde Improvement Association formed in 1909 and helped bring about the West Alameda subway under the railroad tracks near Santa Fe Drive, a new steel bridge across the river, a tramway extension into Valverde, culverts at street crossings, electric arc lights where needed, improvement of the town hall, a branch public library, street signs, and widening of West Bayaud Avenue at the glass works.[11]

The Celery Industry

During the late 1800s and early 1900s, Valverde earned a reputation for the best celery in the country. Farmers utilized the rich soil along the South Platte River to grow 2,880,000 bunches of celery each year. A large celery plot filled the corner of West Nevada Avenue and South Raritan Street, a portion of the 60 acres planted by 25 to 30 local growers.

"Thirty years has made 'Valverde celery' a name for all that is excellent in celery. It means the topnotch in crispness, in color and in flavor. It is a synonym for super-excellence," E. J. Clark, M.D., wrote in 1913. Besides supplying

Valverde earned a reputation for the best celery in the country in the early 1900s. Each year, growers shipped 65 railroad cars loaded with celery to cities as far away as St. Louis and Chicago.

quality celery for Denver dinner tables, the hardworking gardeners shipped 65 railroad cars of Valverde celery each year to cities as far away as St. Louis and Chicago.[12]

Many families made a good living while the celery industry flourished—and they also put money aside for a rainy day, since Valverde celery growers were not only industrious but frugal. The growers received an average of 20 cents per dozen. Each year more than $50,000 was divided among the growers and their employees. Not satisfied with raising one crop, these enterprising citizens followed the early celery with a second crop of lettuce. One farmer expected to clear about $300 per acre from his celery and about $125 from his lettuce crop.

Carpenters, contractors, and mechanics grew celery as a sideline business. S. P. Merman on West Center Avenue managed a successful gasoline and oil route while raising more than an acre of celery and other crops. Those with greenhouses raised four or five vegetable crops each year. Specializing in celery and lettuce, Frank Hollberg also grew cucumbers and tomatoes in a greenhouse with an up-to-date heating plant. An observer described the Hollberg greenhouse as "one of the most beautiful sights in the valley in springtime with tomato plants growing straight toward the heavens until stopped by the glass roof at a height of 8, 10, or more feet."[13]

Early Development

The Valverde Neighborhood House, built in 1921 at 1415 West Alameda Avenue, served in a dual capacity for many years as community center and place of worship. The Wright Memorial Methodist Church on South Navajo Street disbanded in 1921 and joined the Valverde Presbyterian Church. Both congregations traced their beginnings to 1891. The expanded congregation held services in the Valverde Neighborhood House from 1923 to 1957, then members moved to a higher location at 430 South Tejon Street. They installed the bell from the old Wright Memorial Methodist Church on the new church building.[14]

A historical tree, dubbed the "Hangman's Tree," met its demise during the area's development in the 1920s. The towering cottonwood, estimated to be 150 years old, stood at the northeast corner of West Alameda Avenue and South Tejon Street, across the street from the site for a new school. After Alameda Avenue was covered with gravel in about 1918, the 70-foot tree, 7 feet in diameter, lost its water supply and began to die. The landmark tree was demolished in 1923 to make way for increased traffic through the growing neighborhood. Early settlers told stories of criminals hanged from the tree, including a man named Youngblood, who supposedly robbed a tavern on West Mississippi Avenue.

After Valverde's annexation by Denver, city workers constructed the 1,300-foot Alameda subway in 1909 to avoid collisions at the railroad tracks near West Alameda Avenue and South Santa Fe Drive.

Local historians, however, deny that the huge tree was actually used for hangings.[15]

The new Valverde School was built in 1923–1924 on the south side of West Alameda Avenue at South Tejon Street, which became part of the Athmar Park neighborhood. The cost of the building and the 6-acre site totaled $121,492.64. Designed in Italian architectural style, it contained 10 classrooms, an office, a clinic, restrooms, and an auditorium. A total of 349 pupils, kindergarten through eighth grade, attended the school, which employed eight teachers. Mr. A. J. Fynn was principal at Valverde School from 1919 to 1928.[16]

Valverde School added a new wing in 1951 to keep pace with the increasing population. Kitchen, lunchroom, gymnasium, library, and additional classrooms expanded the school's capacity and usability. Enrollment rose to 500 pupils, kindergarten through sixth grade, and teachers numbered 24. Classes extended from 9 a.m. to 3 p.m. If the weather was nice, children went home for lunch. If it was too cold or snowy, pupils brought their lunch pails and ate homemade grape jam sandwiches at their desks. The original school building was sold to the Adventists, who continued to use it for education until its demolition sometime after 1951.[17]

After World War II, the vast alfalfa, wheat, and celery fields in the area gave way to home construction, mostly single-family dwellings, starting in 1949 and continuing into the 1950s. Industrialization increased in the river basin as farmers began selling their land for redevelopment.

The Colorado State Song

Valverde has ties to Colorado's state song, which was written by A. J. Fynn, the principal of Valverde School from 1919 to 1928. The chorus of the song references the Colorado state flower, the columbine: "Tis the land where the columbines grow / Overlooking the plains far below / While the cool summer breeze in the evergreen trees / Softly sings where the columbines grow." An act of the General Assembly on May 8, 1915, adopted "Where the Columbines Grow" as the official state song.[18]

The song remained relatively unknown, and after several unsuccessful attempts to change it lawmakers voted in March 2007 to make John Denver's balled "Rocky Mountain High" the state song as well.

Valverde Memories

Karen Gowans, who moved to Valverde at the age of 3, has fond memories of the area. "I played with children at the orphanage called The Tuckaway Home for Homeless Children, which was just two doors from my house," she recalled.

The oldest of three children, Karen started school at Valverde Elementary School and went to Byers Junior High until Rishel Junior High was built in 1959. She attended Rishel in the ninth grade and then advanced to West High School. Her grandparents lived close by on Lipan Street and she often hopped irrigation ditches and crossed the road to visit them. The road eventually became the Valley Highway, later designated as I-25.

"My grandmother warned me to stay away from the gypsies who camped along the Platte River. They went door-to-door telling fortunes and trying to sell things," Karen explained. "The circus set up tents each year on the grounds at West 3rd Avenue and Lipan Street where Xcel Energy is located now. I remember being absolutely amazed by the Hilton Sisters who appeared in the side show. They were Siamese twins joined at the side and waist.

"I was raised in a large, Catholic, Spanish-speaking family that gathered often at my grandparents' house. The adults played guitars, sang, told stories, and drank homemade chokecherry wine. My grandfather, 'Daddy Joe' Trujillo, told us children about tending sheep as a child.

"In those days houses were scattered, built one at a time, until developers started constructing tract homes. There were hills to slide down, summer and winter, before builders cut away the hills to put in low-income housing units. Two irrigation ditches from the Platte River provided water for fields of bell peppers, celery, cabbage, and onions," she continued. "Clay mines and obsidian mines on the bluff in front of the big Fassett house had collapsed and were closed so kids couldn't go in, but the beams were still there. We liked to walk on them, balancing like gymnasts."[19]

Later Growth

The low-income complex north of Alameda Avenue and east of Tejon Street was built by the Denver Housing Authority in 1956. Approximately 400 people moved to the complex, called Columbine Homes.[20]

Today, Valverde includes the area between West 6th Avenue and West Alameda Avenue, from the South Platte River west to Federal Boulevard. Valverde's children go to schools in adjacent neighborhoods because no schools are located within the neighborhood's current boundaries. Students attend Valverde Elementary School in Athmar Park, Barnum Elementary School in Barnum, Munroe Elementary School in Westwood, Rishel Junior High School in Athmar Park, West High School in Lincoln Park, or Abraham Lincoln High School in Harvey Park.[21]

Construction of two major thoroughfares contributed to the industrialization of Valverde—Interstate 25 in the mid-1950s and the West 6th Avenue freeway in the 1960s. Many interchanges, including on and off ramps at West 6th Avenue and Federal Boulevard, Bryant Street, and West Alameda Avenue, provided excellent access for warehouses, offices, and light industrial uses.[22]

The Flood of 1965

The severe flood of the South Platte River on June 16, 1965, caused major suffering for Valverde residents. Many lived in modest, well-maintained, single-story frame houses, some with basements. A few families occupied brick homes. Most of the residents were homeowners. One of the worst-hit neighborhoods, Valverde sustained approximately $500,000 in property damage—the equivalent of $3 million today. Flooding affected the area from the South Platte River to Tejon Street and farther north and west. About 324 homes were condemned, including 75 that were completely lost.[23]

The community pulled together during this crisis with the help of the Reverend Kent O. Mills, minister of Valverde Community Church (formerly

Valverde/Athmar Park residents and businesses faced a tremendous cleanup task after the South Platte River flooded in 1965.

Valverde Presbyterian Church). The Reverend Mills organized his congregation and opened the church building as a base for centralized flood relief and emergency assistance operations. Because of its location on higher ground, the church building escaped damage from the raging water.[24]

Members of the St. Rose of Lima Parish and friends from the community worked many hours cleaning and restoring the church and school, saving the parish approximately $40,000. People from other churches in southwest Denver also assisted in the overwhelming cleanup process. Some took home clothing and bedding to wash.[25]

Valverde had been a close neighborhood during the 1940s and 1950s and into the 1960s. The flood, however, damaged relationships as well as property. Many people moved to new areas—especially those who lived east of Tejon Street—and a few even left Denver. Others stayed. "In 1965 we lost everything," said Bea Silva, who remained on the same block as before the flood. "We lost two homes. There was nothing we could do—we had to rebuild."

Besides rebuilding their home, the Silva family began restoring relationships by organizing a yearly gathering of those who grew up together, attended the same schools and churches, and shopped at the same businesses. Encouraged by her daughter Clita, Bea contacted about 30 families for the first reunion in 1986. By 2001, the reunion had doubled in size, drawing about 60 families to a picnic at Huston Park. The last picnic was held in 2003, when Bea was 89 years old and most of the other neighbors had passed away. Bea died on March 21, 2006.

The flood damaged homes and property.

Bea's son, Norm, said, "The neighborhood had everything you could ever want." His memories included Geringer's Grocery Store, Valverde School, Ruth and Pinkies Grocery Store, Johnnie's Barber Shop, Coral Beauty Salon, O'Connor's Creamery, the American Liquor Store (now called the Great American Beer Store), K&Ko's (now known as Valverde Country Club), Graviette's Texaco, Bowman's Conoco, and the experience of watching TV for the first time at either the firehouse or the furniture store. Construction of Chatfield Reservoir by the Army Corps of Engineers in 1976 reduced chances of another major flood along the South Platte River, much to the relief of Valverde residents.[26]

Business and Industry

Trends between 1960 and 1990 show an overall loss of population and housing units due to smaller households, housing converted to industrial use, and the continuing aftereffects of the 1965 flood. The percentages of elderly and minority residents increased, however. Valverde's Hispanic population expanded from 11 percent in 1960 to 62 percent in 1990, part of a trend of Hispanics moving to west and southwest Denver.[27]

Valverde was known as a major area of employment, with an increase in manufacturing, wholesaling, and retailing from 1983 to 1988. King Soopers, one of Denver's most successful companies, operated from Tejon Street in Valverde. Around 2,000 employees worked in the company's corporate offices, bakery, meat-processing plant, and general merchandise warehouses. Office warehouses and showrooms of Denver Community Development Corporation's Park One employed about 100 people at the West Bayaud Avenue location. Overall, Valverde claimed many large and small businesses, which employed approximately 5,500 people.[28]

Catholic Charities of the Archdiocese of Denver moved to 2525 West Alameda Avenue in 1997. The 23,000-square-foot building housed administrative offices, family services, an Employment Resource Center, and community organizing services, offering about 70 jobs to the community. Built in 1970, the structure formerly served the Denver Department of Social Services food stamp office and other tenants.

Recreation

Residents and employees enjoy picnics and ball games at five mini-parks in the neighborhood. The heavily used West-Bar-Val-Wood Park derived its name from Valverde, the nearby Barnum neighborhood to the west, and the old Denver

Wood Products buildings that were demolished to make way for a City of Denver Public Works facility. High school baseball teams played league games at the lighted Crow Field in Barnum Park East at West 5th Avenue and Federal Boulevard. Crow Field also provides a popular spot for summer softball games.

In addition to the parks, the West 5th Avenue greenbelt offers recreational opportunities and serves as a buffer zone between residential and commercial properties. Bike routes link several of the parks, and the South Platte River Greenway hiking/biking trail follows the eastern edge of South Platte River Drive near West Cedar Avenue.[29]

Community Activism

Neighborhood residents rallied in 1997 to oppose two detention facilities proposed for sites in their community. Construction of a new Denver juvenile detention facility was planned for an open field at West Irvington Avenue and South Tejon Street, directly across the street from the King Soopers warehouse. After fierce community opposition, the city withdrew its proposal and looked elsewhere for a site.

On the heels of this concern came the city's plan to build a new Denver jail at 7th Avenue and Osage Street. During a meeting at the Denver Water Board, residents vigorously opposed this proposal for the same reasons they opposed a youth detention facility in their neighborhood: they feared negative effects on their children, on businesses in the area, and on property values. Because of community outrage, the city withdrew the proposal and assured residents that a new site selection process would involve city council, businesspeople, law enforcement, and the public at large.[30]

Athmar Park

The old town of Valverde is enclosed within the present-day boundaries of the Athmar Park community, bordered by Federal Boulevard on the west, Platte River Drive on the east, West Alameda Avenue on the north, and West Mississippi Avenue on the south. At the time of annexation in 1902, Federal Boulevard was a local street and some western areas of the neighborhood were identified as part of Westwood, then known as Garden Home. In 1904, the area south and west of the newly annexed Valverde was owned by three entities: the C. M. Stebbins Estate, N. K. Huston, and the State of Colorado "School Property."[31]

By 1932, the Mountain View Park subdivision had been established west of Zuni Street. In 1935, West Alameda Avenue was extended beyond Morrison Road into Jefferson County as a connection to Red Rocks. Denver annexed Mountain View Park in 1943. Street numbers in the new subdivision did not fit with existing numbers along West Alameda Avenue, but the numbering was never changed, so to this day street numbers between South Tejon Street and South Federal Boulevard do not follow sequence.[32]

Brothers Thomas and John R. McCusker bought the large section of school land at a 1946 auction. They planned to build a four-phase subdivision on the parcel stretching from Alameda Avenue to Mississippi Avenue. According to old-timers, the developers combined their wives' names, Athena and Mary, and called the area Athmar.[33]

The Owen J. Goldrick Elementary School, named for Denver's first teacher, was built in 1951 at 1050 South Zuni Street. Also during the 1950s, two shopping centers bordering the residential area broke ground. Alameda Square opened at the corner of West Alameda Avenue and South Zuni Street. The Athmar Park Shopping Center, developed by Perlmutter Construction Company, featured 23 businesses with Miller's Supermarket as its anchor store on West Mississippi Avenue.[34]

During this time, Americans were worried the Russians would drop nuclear bombs on U.S. cities. Government officials urged citizens to stock a month's supply of food and water in their homes for use in the event of a nuclear attack, and schoolchildren were instructed to practice dropping to the floor under their desks during safety drills. With all the paranoia, many contractors scrambled to build fallout shelters in homes during the 1950s, especially in the Athmar Park neighborhood. "A lot of unscrupulous developers offered to build so-called 'fallout' shelters in the new houses, but they were nothing more than basements without windows," said Randy Rice, Denver abstract clerk.[35]

Parks and open space occupied more than 40 acres of the neighborhood, including Huston Lake Park, created from swampland. The lake, known by old- timers as Frenchie's Lake, provided a place for ice skating in winter and swimming in summer. The Clifford Aspgren Park, with its great slope for sledding, was created on West Exposition Avenue near the industrial edge of the community. The park was named after a hilltop resident who served in the Colorado House of Representatives. Zoned as open space and part of the South Platte River Greenway, Vanderbilt Lake Park contained Habitat Park and Boy Scout Park.[36]

Don and Carol E. Campbell, comparatively new residents, found a moderately priced home that suited them in 1988. Carol forged a strong sense of community through participation in the Athmar Park Neighborhood Association (APNA), an organization she helped form in 1991. An artist who liked to make things happen, Carol and other APNA members organized a community cultural arts celebration in 1993. The project featured oral history presentations by longtime residents and a large mural painted by schoolchildren.[37]

Diversity

Rishel Junior High School, named after Principal John B. Rishel, was built in 1959 at 451 Tejon Street, next to Valverde Elementary School. As the neighborhood changed, the school recognized the increasing need for foreign-language tutors. Henry Tuoc V. Pham, a noted Vietnamese educator and author, was hired to join Denver Public Schools in 1978 as a tutor at Rishel. Pham had held a respected position as principal and French teacher at a private secondary school in Saigon but left the city with his three youngest children the day before Saigon fell to the North Vietnamese in April 1975.

On the staff at Rishel, Pham helped Hmong students introduce their native food, dances, and crafts during the Hmong New Year celebration. He also organized a Vietnamese New Year observance in which students dressed in traditional costumes and presented the principal with best wishes and flowers for good luck, in keeping with the Vietnamese custom of showing respect for educators.

Rishel Principal Glendon Schultz sponsored a citizenship class, and Pham became a U.S. citizen in 1981 at age 61. In addition to his work at the school, Pham served as president of the Vietnamese American Cultural Alliance of Colorado, an organization that promoted positive relationships between Vietnamese and other U.S. citizens through the exchange of history, literature, music, and other cultural teachings.[38]

As a community learning center, Rishel Junior High School offered evening classes for adults and children during the 1970s. Funded by the Colorado Department of Education, the classes were open to any resident of the metro area and included English as a Second Language, Beginning Spanish, and Platte River Valley History.

Colorado's Asian population as a whole increased significantly during the 1980s and 1990s, and many Asian families settled in southwest Denver and opened businesses. Khanh Vu, Hamid Simantab, and Daniel Yim bought the Alameda Square Shopping Center at 2200 West Alameda Avenue. Once thriving with many successful businesses, the center lost shoppers as people moved from the area or sought larger, newer shopping malls. The popular Organ Grinder Restaurant, which drew patrons from all over town with its pizza menu and pipe organ music in the early 1980s, sat vacant for over a decade and was eventually demolished.

In 1999, the Asian Supermarket moved from its cramped space on South Federal Boulevard to the 27,000-square-foot retail space vacated by REI. Owner Dung Vu citied growth in Denver's Asian community, a boom in the economy, and expanded interest in ethnic cuisine for its success. The store, which offered sauces, noodles, fish, exotic fruit, Asian cooking lessons, and seminars, also contained a 5,000-gallon tank with live fish for household menus.[39]

The Asian Supermarket was replaced by the Viet Hoa Supermarket, which served the community along with several other Asian businesses, including the Pacific Ocean International Supermarket. Even with the markets, the Alameda Square Shopping Center struggled for survival. The site was designated as "blighted" by the Denver Urban Renewal Authority in 1991. After years of pursuing different possibilities for the site—including a Wal-Mart store—the Athmar Park Neighborhood Association held a public meeting in March 2004 for community input. An overwhelming majority of residents and business owners who attended the meeting expressed a strong desire for redevelopment. Supporters mobilized to send letters, postcards, and petitions to the city for action, but no major developers stepped forward. One of the owners built a 22,000-square-foot, L-shaped brick structure along West Alameda Avenue and South Zuni Street at the end of 2005 and offered 16 units for rent. The center's future, however, is still uncertain.[40]

CHAPTER EIGHT

Westwood

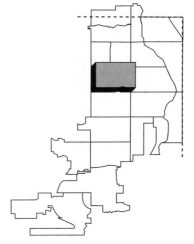

O riginally called Garden Home, the area between South Federal Boulevard, West Alameda Avenue, South Sheridan Boulevard, and West Mississippi Avenue was annexed by Denver in 1947 after a contentious annexation vote. Garden Home itself started as a small, 16-block community within the present-day boundaries of Westwood. The neighborhood of Westwood is thought to be named for the Westwood Telephone Exchange building on West Kentucky Avenue because residents of Garden Home were eager to be associated with a "modern" company rather than gardens or farming. The neighborhood has always been a working-class community marked by change and progress, including businesses springing up along Morrison Road, South Federal Boulevard changing to reflect the incoming Asian population, and the vanishing of old landmarks. For the past 20 years, a grassroots group called the Southwest Improvement Council has promoted improvements to the neighborhood.

Garden Home School

Rolling prairie stretched west from Valverde to Garden Home in 1889 when the two communities created a school district for their children. Garden Home, a small area with dairy cows and large gardens, extended north and west from the intersection of South Federal Boulevard and West Kentucky Avenue. Pupils traveled from scattered homes to learn their ABCs and arithmetic at Valverde's first school, a red brick building on West Exposition Avenue and South Navajo Street.[1]

After Valverde was annexed by Denver in 1902, the school district split. Still part of Arapahoe County, Garden Home made plans for its District 18 school. Denver contributed funds toward the purchase of 10 lots, which cost $150, and construction started on a two-room stucco building at West Kentucky Avenue and South Lowell Boulevard. Pupils met for a short time in the living room of Mrs. Alfred Anderson, on South Lowell Boulevard, then moved in 1904 to the new bungalow-type structure at 3615 West Kentucky Avenue.[2]

In 1917, the country school district consisted of 30 families. One teacher taught 12 pupils, grades first through eighth. Boys and girls carried their own water jugs to school along with their lunches, because they could not drink the school well-water. Fathers hauled sand to improve the mud-caked playground. All meetings were scheduled during daytime hours as the school did not have electric lights.

Flu hit hard in 1918, and the school closed five times because of sick pupils. The PTA organized in 1919 and received its charter in 1920, under the leadership of Mrs. Lillian Fotts, president; Mrs. T. J. Bellisle, secretary; and Mrs. Elizabeth Jackson, treasurer.

Garden Home School added a grade each year, and by 1934 the school had 12 teachers and an enrollment of 485 students, grades first through twelfth. Marie Baker was the first graduate, in 1934. The PTA numbered 167 members at the time. As a rural consolidated school, Garden Home received federal funds and served hot lunches, feeding an average of 200 children each day for 5 cents per child.[3]

Several additions were made to the school in the 1920s and 1930s, eventually attaching a three-story brick building to the smaller stucco bungalow. The school district received federal money for improvements in 1940, the start of an eventful decade for the small community. The PTA, one of the largest and most active in Arapahoe County, sponsored safety and vaccination programs, raised money for charity, and gave out 1,100 boxes of food and candy at Christmas. The parent group also provided clothing, books, and milk for children needing an extra boost.

By 1945, Garden Home School employed three principals—one for the senior high, one for the junior high, and one for the elementary school—plus a 62-member faculty. Student enrollment reached 1,699, and 544 parents belonged to the PTA.

Annexation by Denver

During the 1940s, Denver gobbled up portions of Arapahoe County with several annexations. Mountain View Park, the area west of Valverde from South Zuni Street to South Federal Boulevard between West Alameda Avenue and West Kentucky Avenue, was annexed on December 31, 1943. "We can't stop Denver from making outright purchases, and their annexation methods were upheld by the Colorado Supreme Court in the case of Mountain View Park," stated C. L. Harrison, Arapahoe County attorney.[4]

Garden Home School was built in the early 1900s at West Kentucky Avenue and South Lowell Boulevard for the Garden Home farm community in Arapahoe County. Known later as Westwood School, the building was demolished in 1994 and replaced by Castro Elementary School.

Denver city attorney Malcolm Lindsey said many city departments had received calls from homeowners outside Denver wanting to be annexed so they could receive the benefits of city services. However, some residents opposed annexation, fearing higher taxes because of additional services.

Garden Home citizens struggled economically through the Depression and into the war years. Then, when the Remington Arms Company offered employment at the Denver Ordnance Plant (today's Federal Center) just 4 miles west, the Arapahoe County community saw a number of newcomers. Because many students were from families employed at the government's Remington plant, the rural town qualified for federal assistance. Belmont Elementary School at 4407 Morrison Road and Irving Elementary School at South Irving Street and West Kentucky Avenue were built with the aid of government funds and the Federal Works Administration. Straining to provide necessary services, including public education, Garden Home incorporated as Westwood in 1943 and 1944, presumably taking its name from the Westwood Telephone Exchange building on West Kentucky Avenue and South Federal Boulevard.

Denver, however, was already eyeing it for annexation. "Apparently maddened by the independence of the people of Westwood, who recently voted incorporation to forestall a blitzkrieg upon themselves, Denver is striking at them through their children," stated the *Englewood Enterprise* in a strongly worded article on December 14, 1944. "The pillaging of land from the Westwood school district, in an apparent effort to make operation of the educational institution impossible, is calculated to break these stalwart souls. It is apparently planned to force them to cower before the might of the monstrous regime which is bleeding the tax-payers of Denver and which casts greedy glances at all of western Arapahoe county. The machine hopes to surround the little city which dares defiance and force it to supplicate for the annexation it rejected.

"The 700-acre grab by which Denver seeks to isolate the little city is based primarily upon land recently purchased in that district by the machine as an 'airport site.'" According to City Attorney Malcolm Lindsey, the airport site was a 1.25-mile strip of land, 2 blocks wide, along West Jewell Avenue, which could provide a suitable runway for a small-plane airfield.[5]

Faced with the loss of federal money for the school's financial support, Westwood voted on November 2, 1946, to be annexed by Denver as a way out of a mounting problem. At about the same time, the Westwood community became aware of the scandal involving William C. Gehrke, superintendent of schools, who was eventually charged with criminal activities involving misuse of funds.

Later in the year, a group called Westwood Citizens Association succeeded in having the election voided on grounds that it had not been well publicized and had been held on a blizzardy, bitter winter day and therefore voting was too light to be representative. When a second, "valid" election was held March 11, 1947, Westwood residents still voted for annexation by a ratio of three to one. Westwood included the area between South Federal Boulevard, West Alameda Avenue, South Sheridan Boulevard, and West Mississippi Avenue.[6]

Life changed dramatically for families when Westwood was finally annexed by Denver. The following September, senior high students started at West High School, 8 miles away at 951 Elati Street. Many faced ridicule as "country bumpkins" and some students quit school or transferred elsewhere. Junior high pupils remained in the larger school building, renamed Westwood Junior High School, while elementary students stayed in the small building called Westwood Elementary School. Denver Mayor Quigg Newton's administration announced plans for paved streets, sewers, streetlighting, better police and fire protection, and low-income housing for its new acquisition.[7] One hundred and ninety-two public housing units, called Westwood Homes, were constructed at 3401 West Kentucky Avenue in 1954.

Many old-timers still identify with the area as Garden Home, and their memories of living in the community include family gardens, low-cost entertainment, and hard work.

The Allens
Charles Allen moved to Garden Home from Globeville in 1926. His father worked for the city dog pound, and the Allen family

lived in one of the few houses on West Exposition Avenue. Charles thought the house was big. "It had a bathroom and full basement, but no furnace. We used a kerosene heater to warm the bathroom. We were lucky—some of our friends had outhouses. Farmland extended between Alameda and Kentucky Avenues, with fields of wheat, oats, and mainly alfalfa. Dad had rabbits, and my job was to cut alfalfa to feed them.

"We didn't have a lot of money, so we found cheap entertainment. We swam in summer and ice skated in winter at Frenchie's Lake [Huston Lake] and at Anderson Lake [Garfield Lake]. We caught little sunfish and bass from the lakes. On Thanksgiving Day, kids gathered at Anderson Lake for a big skating party. The weather seemed to be colder then, and we skated from November through March. Sometimes we had a bonfire at the lake. It was a great life with good pals, no gangs. We went to a 5-cent matinee occasionally at the Comet Theater in Barnum. As a teenager, I hunted pheasants on the shale cliff near Yale Avenue, which was a one-lane dirt road, and did odd jobs at Progress Plunge Swimming Pool so I could swim there free."

Charles joined the Coast Artillery in 1939 and mustered out in December 1945. He returned to Garden Home with his wife, Raye, and built a cinder-block garage house on South Hazel Court and worked at a service station on Morrison Road. "When we traded land for a house on South Utica Street, the postman said to take whatever address we wanted since there were only two houses on the block. I ended up working for Mountain Bell and we moved to a new house in Harvey Park after our son was born in 1957."[8]

The Bradleys

Wanda Bradley, one of nine children born to Artie and Mary Cathryn ("Mamie") Bradley, grew up on South Lowell Boulevard and West Kentucky Avenue, directly east of the school. "Dad was a brick mason and built houses, mostly in the Bonnie Brae area. Mom raised strawberries on an acre of land near West Tennessee and South Knox Court, leased from the Andersons. She sold strawberries to the Evalona Dairy on Alameda for income," said Wanda. "Dad dug a basement where we lived until World War II, when we could afford to build on top. Both parents worked at the Denver Ordnance Plant during the war. Each payday, they bought building materials for the house. Mom and I laid flooring, tiled the bathroom, sanded and finished floors, and painted walls. We moved in just before the war ended.

"Since I was across the street from the school, I went home for lunch every day. The kids teased about going home with me because they could smell bread baking in our kitchen. Garden Home was like a big family. We knew everyone in our class, also their brothers and sisters. We were friendly with the teachers, too.

"Our school had girls' and boys' basketball teams that traveled to other schools where the girls played first, then the boys. My sister, Wilma, played on the girls' team. After 1939, we had boys' basketball only, besides football and track. Our teams wore blue and white uniforms and were known as the Garden Home Blue Jays," said Wanda, who served as a cheerleader.

Besides sports and dramatics, students could participate in band, orchestra, Glee Club, mixed chorus, Pep Club, and Girl Reserves (a division of the YWCA). Boys who lettered in sports belonged to the "G" Club. The school offered shop and sewing classes at night for adults.

Wanda remembered walking in the ruts cars made on the gravel streets and on a pipe crossing a swamp at South Lowell Boulevard and West Center Avenue. She and her friends often went to a movie at the Comet Theater in Barnum. After graduating from Garden Home High School in 1941, Wanda worked as an operator at the Westwood Telephone Exchange. When a fire was reported, the operators called the firehouse located at Kentucky and Knox Court and volunteer firemen responded.

She met Lorin Chase at a dance. After dating for two years, they married in Idaho while he was in the navy. They lived in Westwood following World War II, then moved in 1956 to a new home in Harvey Park where they raised three children: Sheryl, Terry, and Robyn.[9]

The Franks
Clayton and Gertie Frank lived on West Virginia Avenue in the 1940s. Their youngest son, Wayne, played football and graduated from Garden Home High School in 1942, then served in the navy. Clayton Frank worked as a carpenter, building houses and doing handyman work for Sebern & Sons Grocery Store, ABZ Lumber Company, and other neighborhood businesses.

Wayne Frank with his parents, Gertie and Clyaton Frank.

Many neighborhood children learned to roller skate at the Westwood Skating Rink, 4201 W. Kentucky Ave. Arthur and Marvis Merrifield owned the building from 1947 to 1957 and lived on the second floor with their children, Dean and Janet, who attended Westwood School.

The Mahanas

William (Bill) Mahana and Lue Setta Priddy met at Westwood School. Bill lived on South Perry Street. His father made a living as a car dealer, and his mother worked at the Remington Arms plant. Bill delivered papers for the *Denver Post* and *Rocky Mountain News* and helped at the Ice House, owned by Earl Maddox Jr. In school, he was elected class president and served on student council. He also played football and basketball and ran track. "It was surprising for a little man to make the all-star team, but I played on the championship football team as a freshman," he said. The Westwood Blue Jays were state co-champions in 1946. When the high school was phased out, Bill attended classes at the YMCA, then went to Alameda High School his senior year.[10]

Before moving to West Exposition Avenue, Lue Setta lived in Barnum, going to the Comet Theater for Saturday matinees. "On Saturday nights, they had a drawing for money, groceries, or a six-pack of Duffy's soda. My cousin and I saved balls of tin foil for the war effort. We also used coupons for meat, butter, and sugar when those items were rationed during World War II." Both parents worked at Remington Arms. When the war was over, her father took a job at Armour's packing plant and her mother went to work at Colorado Builders' Supply Company (COBUSCO) at West Evans Avenue and South Santa Fe Drive.[11]

Lue Setta finished high school at West and married Bill a year later. Their first home was at Shady Nook Mobile Home Park at 4325 Morrison Road. Lue Setta worked at the telephone company. Bill was employed at Miller's Supermarket until he was drafted. After his military service, he worked at Coors Brewery and studied in Greeley on the GI Bill, graduating with a degree in education. He taught mostly in Jefferson County high schools, specializing in drafting, architectural drawing, and driver's education until he retired in 1988. The Mahanas raised three children and kept in touch with their high school friends. They played bridge together and the women met for lunch once a month.

Westwood Teacher Uncovers Scandal

In 1945, following college graduation in Jacksonville, Illinois, La Rue White rode the train from Chicago to her Denver home. "People celebrated all night on the Denver Zephyr and people in Denver were still celebrating when I arrived on VJ Day [Victory over Japan Day]," said White. "I looked in the want ads for a job. There were two ads for a business teacher, one in Westwood and one in Bear Creek. I had no idea where Westwood was, but I thought it would be closer to my home than Bear Creek, so I began my teaching career at Westwood School, which had grades 1 through 12. I taught typing, bookkeeping, business, and sponsored the school newspaper and yearbook. Some of the boys had returned to high school after serving in the war and they were older than I was.

"For several months late in 1946 and early in 1947, the school district was struggling financially and Westwood teachers were paid in warrants [vouchers for later payment]. I was living at home, not going hungry like some of the teachers who had children and no money for milk or bread." Frank Merelli, owner of the Aeroplane Club, felt sorry for teachers who were not paid in cash and bought the warrants from them at face value. When student body president Mark McClanahan, 16, found out that teachers had not been paid for three months he called a student strike. This sparked an investigation.

One night White was at the school working late on the yearbook and happened to see Superintendent William C. Gehrke load a piano into his truck in the dark. Another night she and her students witnessed people loading tools and heavy equipment from the wood shop into the same truck. Everyone was up in arms about the stolen goods, and Gehrke was charged with embezzlement. McClanahan and several teachers testified at the two-week grand jury investigation. Ultimately, the Arapahoe County grand jury indicted Gehrke for misuse of public funds. The student, McClanahan, was expelled and finished classes at East High School because of the fervor in the community.

"The Garden Home kids didn't have many material things but were appreciative of what they had and were respectful of the faculty," White said. "The kids in my classes came from really poor households; some had a dirt basement as their home. Ninety percent of them became professional people and made real contributions in their communities. They've done well, have marriages intact, and don't have dysfunctional families. I keep in touch with some of my first students at a monthly luncheon and correspond with others who've moved away."[12]

La Rue White became Mrs. Richard Belcher in 1952, and many of her students attended her wedding. She was part of the faculty that opened Kepner Junior High in 1953 with John B. Rishel as principal. The new school at South Irving Street and West Kentucky Avenue utilized the old Irving Elementary School as an annex until its demolition in 1982. When Kepner, the first junior high school in southwest Denver, went on double sessions in 1955, Belcher switched to dean of girls for the afternoon session. One of her fondest memories was loading children on the buses at 6 p.m. "At that time we had real winters, so it was cold and dark," she recalled. "The faculty was very close and remained so for over 50 years, with reunions every five years."

Woody Takes Charge

After Westwood's annexation in March 1947, the Denver School Board assigned Wilford H. Woody, former West High School coach, to mesh the Westwood schools with the Denver system. Woody found a disorganized community with low economic standards, children without proper food and clothing, houses in poor condition, and unlighted, unpaved streets. First, he went to work and made sure the teachers got paid in cash on time.[13]

In the fall, Woody took over as principal of Westwood Elementary and Junior High School. He then organized the Westwood Service Association to work with the Westwood Lions Club to rid the area of trash and litter and push for parks and playgrounds. He helped start the Christmas food basket program, which became an annual event, and supported a clothing drive that spread throughout the city and eventually became part of the services offered by Goodwill Industries.

Woody said that when he went to Westwood as principal, there were no houses between Mississippi Avenue and Loretto Heights College, near Hampden Avenue. It was all farmland.

To promote a community feeling between Westwood and the adjacent Barnum neighborhood, Woody expanded the service organization in 1948 to become the Westwood–Barnum Service Association, which put on an annual hobby show. "The people had lots of hobbies," he said, "and we had marvelous exhibits."

Woody became principal at West High School in 1950 but remained active in the service association. By 1963, the association he started encompassed more than 70 organizations, extending south from West 12th Avenue to West Hampden Avenue.

DPS Careers

Houses were hard to find in 1951, when Juan and Lena Archuleta moved to Denver from Raton, New Mexico. A graduate of the University of Denver with a major in Spanish and minor in Latin, Lena chose Westwood Elementary School over East High School for her first Denver position as a full-time librarian. "We liked the neighborhood, which was very diverse, somewhat rural with modest cottages, a small community atmosphere, and people of the same socio-economic level working hard to make a living."

Lena continued her career as librarian at Kepner Junior High, which opened in 1953. "We were excited about the large new school with only three grades. The faculty was great and we got along well. We felt very 'uptown.' We had a new collection of books and a large library staff, including a pupil from every

Kepner librarian Lena Archuleta (standing at right) and her library assistants during the 1955–1956 school year. In 2002, Denver Public Schools named a school for Archuleta— the Lena Lovato Archuleta Elementary School in Montbello.

class. I involved students as much as possible and even organized an all-city convention with Boulder author Lenora Mattingly Weber as speaker.

"Juan and I shopped on Alameda and found people friendly, mostly inclusive, with no overt discrimination although there weren't many Latinos in the neighborhood. We were active in PTA, went roller skating, and enjoyed the community. I took dancing lessons and joined a women's group called 'Las Estrellitas Alegres,' which means 'The Happy Little Stars.' It was great exercise and we had fun performing Mexican folk dances and Spanish dances with castanets. Juan and I had saved money for a house but ran into difficulty when we tried to buy in Harvey Park. School principals Rishel and Carr helped us find a new brick house at 1840 South Federal Boulevard, which later became a music store."[14]

From Kepner, Lena went to the Denver Public Schools (DPS) Administration Building as coordinator of the Department of Library Services. Then she served in the School–Community Relations office and later in Federal Projects concerning bilingual education. She earned an administrative certificate from the University of Denver's Graduate School of Education and became the first DPS Latina woman principal when she went to Fairview Elementary School in 1976.

Juan Archuleta retired in 1979 as DPS Maintenance Department supervisor. Lena retired the same year. One of Denver's new schools is named after her —Lena Lovato Archuleta Elementary School. The school opened in Montbello in 2002 and is the only Denver school named after a living Hispanic person.

The Southwest Improvement Council (SWIC)

The Westwood neighborhood has made many improvements due to a grassroots group known as the Southwest Improvement Council (SWIC). Before SWIC came into being, Grace Methodist Church started an outreach ministry called Grace Community Center at 210 West 13th Avenue for people residing near Denver's business district. Organized in the 1930s, Grace Community Center looked for another site after industry spread into the area and people moved away. According to Marjorie Forrestal, secretary of the center's board of directors, the small town of Westwood had recently been annexed by Denver and was out in the country with potential for growth. The church bought a 5-acre parcel of vacant land next to the Forrestal family and constructed a building at 1000 South Lowell Boulevard with help from the Westwood Lions Club.[15]

In 1957, the center relocated to Westwood and changed its name from Grace Community Center to Southwest Community Center. The center offered family-oriented programs, including a day school, crafts, teen activities, and square dances for people of all religious, racial, and economic backgrounds.

A few years later, the center acquired adjoining property at 1001 South King Street, which included a three-bedroom house owned previously by Elizabeth R. Foley. This move allowed for construction of additional indoor facilities such as classrooms, a senior citizen center, and a larger all-purpose room, plus outdoor picnic, playground, and athletic areas. Services expanded with family and individual counseling, self-leadership development, a day-care nursery with a capacity for 57 children of working mothers, plus a variety of clubs, classes, and interest groups for all ages. The center also sent boys and girls to summer camp at Beaver Ranch near Conifer.

The Southwest Improvement Council (SWIC) received a $20,000 award from the Gloria Estefan Foundation for its Oye, Stop the Violence parade and daylong fair in the 1990s. Most of the money went to fund a variety of youth programs.

During the 1970s, the community wanted to add health-care services and expand child day care. To make this happen, the board of directors voted to donate their land and property to the city in order to qualify for a Model Cities grant. In 1972, the Southwest Community Center contributed $70,000 worth of equity in land and buildings to the city of Denver. The city then received a $239,000 Model Cities grant and a $300,000 HUD Neighborhood Facility Grant for construction of a new complex.

A new $2 million facility opened in 1976. The new community center encompassed the "Westwood Complex" and offered food stamp services, legal aid, a police storefront, and a branch of the Denver Public Library with books in Spanish as well as English. Praised as one of the finest designs in Colorado, the center included two adjacent buildings housing the Day Care Center and Health Station plus an outdoor play area. The United Way agency provided operating funds. Impressed with the entire center, Bob Hernandez, executive director, predicted that the Westwood Complex would become the focal point for all community activities.[16]

"The city did good things but took authority away from the community," commented Jan Marie Belle, a Westwood resident destined to link with the center. During the 1980s, the Southwest Community Center experienced internal problems and financial concerns. Meanwhile, a grassroots group began to sprout. Active at St. Anthony of Padua Catholic Church as coordinator for the Social Concerns Committee, Belle was angry about the unkempt neighborhood and frustrated with outside studies that failed to bring improvements. "I thought we should do something ourselves," she said.[17]

In 1985, Belle and her committee set up the Southwest Denver Dropout Prevention Program and St. Anthony Family Education program (SAFE), led by Barbara and Juan Sierra and Father Joe Sullivan. They wanted to provide after-school tutoring and periodic certificate awards to students to improve educational attainment in the Westwood community.

About the same time, Belle had gone as far as possible in her job as president of the Service Employees International Union Local 105 (AFL-CIO). Looking for new challenges, she left the union with $38,000 in severance pay, which she donated to help fund a new organization called the Southwest Improvement Council (SWIC). Father Joe Sullivan obtained a grant from the Bal Swan Foundation and together they set up SWIC as an incorporated nonprofit organization. Belle became executive director and Sullivan served as board president. Mayabella Abbott was vice president and Leo Urioste was treasurer. "It was a new idea to be incorporated rather than depend on government programs," Belle said.[18]

At first, SWIC operated from rent-free space at St. Anthony of Padua Center, 775 South Newton Street, with only two paid staff members, Belle and Dora Martinez, the volunteer coordinator. Belle began recruiting volunteers by knocking on doors and making telephone calls. Volunteers included men, women, boys, and girls from the various ethnic and religious backgrounds that made up the neighborhood (58 percent Hispanic and 36 percent white). With skills gained as a union organizer, Belle helped organize the 300 volunteers into teams for specific jobs and appointed 50 block captains to keep residents informed of community needs.

One team, the Urban Gleaners, gathered discarded building materials for volunteer craftsmen to use in improving homes. Gleaners also picked up old household items such as pottery, housewares, books, and toys for door prizes at SWIC meetings. Another team, the Youthful Yardbirds, cleaned yards and alleys and made sure trash was hauled away. The Snow Patrol shoveled sidewalks for those who were unable to. The Friendly Visitors team offered companionship to homebound residents. People trained as Respite Sitters stayed with ill or disabled elderly to give regular caregivers a break. The Prayer Warriors prayed for those who requested it. The SWIC Walkers distributed 5,000 monthly newsletters door-to-door while walking for good health, the Earth Movers did gardening, and the Graffiti-Busters painted over acts of vandalism.

From the beginning, SWIC leaders decided the organization should be forever independent and grassroots—not dependent on government agencies. No dues were charged, so that everyone could participate and have a voice in the decisions. Funds came from grants, fundraisers, and contributions by individuals and businesses.

"When looking at our neighborhood, we saw the problems and solutions simultaneously," Belle said. "In 1988, we presented our priorities for the Westwood neighborhood to the Denver Housing Trust Council. Our solutions were (1) fixing up vacant and abandoned housing for homeownership, (2) developing the Neighborhood Caretakers' fix-up program in collaboration with Brothers Redevelopment, (3) weatherizing homes through a collaboration with Bob Ridgeway and Westwood Energy Co-op, (4) upgrading Westwood alleys at no cost to residents with recycled crushed asphalt, (5) adding mid-block alley and street lights to prevent crime and danger, (6) fixing up rental property with low interest loans and grants, and (7) helping homeowners upgrade their property with repairs and landscaping.

Community residents improve their neighborhood by painting over graffiti during workdays sponsored by the Southwest Improvement Council (SWIC).

"Our goals continued: Creating a free tree-trimming program, organizing neighborhood small projects, developing a 'Neighborhood Plan,' starting a bike-hike path connecting Westwood, Garfield, and Huston Lake parks with the Platte River Greenway, starting a Food Share program, educating our youth and involving them in leadership for neighborhood improvement, organizing the community to get a new Westwood school, and, finally, showing everyone that neighborhoods can organize themselves into independent nonprofit corporations to accomplish community goals.

"We look back now and see how successful we have been, how many programs have had spectacular results—and we see how hard so many people have worked. Our unique success comes from our vision of answers found within the burdensome problems of our own experience and leaders found among those who are suffering from the problems."[19]

When SWIC took over the Westwood Community Center in 1993, they added a daily hot lunch program for seniors, in partnership with Volunteers of America. Local residents Simone Sedillo and Jane Hann coordinated the daily activities.

In 1995, SWIC continued efforts to develop affordable housing by forming a development group called the Southwest Neighborhood Housing Corporation (SWNHC). SWIC and its development corporation worked together to acquire houses to fix up for homeownership. They bought houses, remodeled them, and

Jan Marie Belle, executive director of SWIC, has helped the grassroots nonprofit organization secure important grants to finance first-time home ownership programs for low- to moderate-income families and individuals.

sold them at below-market prices to first-time homeowners—even giving financial assistance for the down payment and closing costs. SWIC bought and remodeled an apartment house at 3045 West Center Avenue. Next, they constructed 10 units of affordable housing at 1401–1402 West Louisiana Avenue with low-income housing tax credits from the National Development Council Corporate Equity Fund. Additional housing was built at 3316 West Walsh Place (a house) and 920 South Utica Street (four units). SWIC also started a housing counseling and homeownership program with support from the National Council of La Raza.[20]

Wilma Thin Elk coordinated the SWIC after-school program, which provided children with free snacks and daily homework help. Thin Elk raised her grandchildren and great-grandchildren and helped them learn traditions of their Lakota heritage. In addition, Thin Elk was active in a weekly Native American crafts class, which featured quilting, beading, doll-making, jewelry fabrication, crocheting, and canvas weaving. She sold her handmade quilts to support the four children who lived with her. Other Native American instructors and classes included A. J. No Braid and Richard Good Face teaching

dancing, Lionel Steele teaching drumming, and A. C. No Braid leading singing. Additional classes were added under the leadership of Steve Hann.

The 1998 Denver Bond Issue provided money for SWIC to hire architects to design a remodeled facility to be completed as money became available. Plans called for a new kitchen and classroom wing, remodeled administrative space, and improvements to the gymnasium.

The Vietnamese community met to talk about funding from the Southwest Improvement Council (SWIC) for English-language and citizenship classes.

SWIC hosted a free dinner in July 2003 to share results from the Survey on Community Needs in Westwood, coordinated by Debra Moulton, Ph.D., and Nick Cutforth, Ph.D., University of Denver. According to Belle, 5,500 surveys were mailed in three languages—English, Spanish, and Vietnamese—to ask people what they wanted in their neighborhood. She was pleased that more than

500 surveys were returned. Respondents were concerned about cars speeding in the neighborhood, college education and job training, and affordable housing. Forty-six percent said they had two or more families living together due to a shortage of affordable housing, and 26 percent had three or more families living in their home. These data revealed a "hidden homelessness" in the community.

To address housing problems, SWIC plans to develop homes between West Tennessee Avenue and West Mississippi Avenue with a Wells Fargo Housing Foundation challenge grant and matching funds raised throguh additional donations. SWIC will also use grant money from Xcel Energy Foundation to assist with a comprehensive counseling program in Spanish and English, focusing on financial issues and budgeting for people of low to moderate income.

After several delays, renovation of SWIC's building finally began in the fall of 2006 as the last project to receive funds from the 1998 Denver Bond Issue. "We are excited about the larger dining room and kitchen as well as a new Denver Public Library branch, with books for youths and seniors," Belle said.

Community Facilities

As the community continued to grow, Denver Health's new Westwood Family Health Center opened near Knapp Elementary School in July 2003. Located at 4320 West Alaska Avenue, just 7 blocks south of the old clinic, the new center offered well-child care, health screenings and preventive care, women's care, senior services, and prenatal care, as well as psychological and substance abuse counseling. An increasing number of people seeking health care in a limited space at the old center prompted construction of the new facility, which was funded by the 1998 bond issue. Colorful artwork by Knapp students brightened hallway walls and decorated restroom tiles.[21]

A new elementary school, replacing the nearly 100-year-old Westwood School, was built on the former Garden Home football field in 1993. Parents, teachers, and former students watched the old smokestack crumble as the original stucco bungalow and attached three-story brick extension came down in February 1994. Denver's Parks and Recreation Department then installed grass for soccer and softball fields where the old school had stood.

The new building erected at 845 South Lowell Boulevard was named for the late Richard Castro, former school board member, state legislator, and director of Denver's Human Rights and Community Relations office. Some residents wanted to keep the name of Westwood, but a community vote decided on Richard T. Castro Elementary School. Two terra-cotta reliefs from the old building were hung over the front doors. Castro School is representative of the Westwood neighborhood, a racially eclectic, multi-ethnic community, which includes Hispanics, Anglos, Native Americans, Asians, blacks, and those of mixed or multiracial heritage.

Schoolchildren once skipped through the doors of Belmont Elementary School at 4407 Morrison Road, a structure that was remodeled to house the Denver Indian Center. For 20 years beginning in the 1980s, the center offered adult education classes to help students receive a Graduate Equivalency Degree (GED) and work training. Unique in Colorado, the program concentrated on meeting the needs of Native Americans as they transitioned from the reservation to the urban community. A prestigious nationwide award was given to the program in 1994 when it received the Showcase of Effective Indian Education Projects grant. At that time, the program was the second largest in the western region.[22]

When funding from the U.S. Department of Education ceased in 1996, the Denver Indian Center had to close its adult education program. Classes resumed again with a new name and new location a month later when the Reverend Joseph Herrera and his son, the Reverend Israel Herrera, offered three classrooms at Eternal Life Temple, 745 South Lowell Boulevard The program's name changed to the Native American Multi-Cultural Education School (NAMES).[23]

Daryl Gray, of Blackfeet-Cree descent, was appointed executive director of the Denver Indian Center in January 2000. He said that needs of the American Indian people are complex because of their diversity. Although Denver's American Indians come from many different tribes all over the country, they are welcome to gather at the center to celebrate their culture and teach children their heritage. Services include youth programs, senior programs, employment assistance, social services, Head Start, and the Native American Cancer Institute. One problem, however, is that lack of bus service through the area makes it difficult to reach the center.[24]

The Morrison Road Business District

In 1899, County Road 8 cut diagonally southwest from West Alameda Avenue to the small town of Morrison; it became known as Morrison Road. As the automobile gained popularity, auto-related shops and services for motorists opened along the two-lane road. Emmett Cawood started a service station in 1937 at 3725 Morrison Road and sold gas at 6 gallons for $1. Most people bought only 25 or 50 cents' worth, and $2 was a big sale.

Mattocks Brothers Auto Body started when William "Bill" Mattocks built his shop at 4171 Morrison Road in 1944. He paid $1,800 for two lots, dug the footings and poured cement for the foundation, and purchased 100 cinder blocks at 25 cents each for the structure. Mattocks was raised by his grandparents on their farm at West 5th Avenue and South Utica Street. He began sanding cars at age 12 and later worked for Weber Auto Body, where he learned to weld. After he married Stella Brown, they lived on the farm until they built a home on South Raleigh Street, near the shop. Mattocks and his wife raised four children: Lester, Henrietta (Cookie), William (Billy), and Dennis. Their neighbors included the Bob Kerstyn family, who had a farm at West Kentucky Avenue and Morrison Road, and nearby businesses such as the John Abney Tire Shop, Lloyd Russell Garage, Suzy Q Bar, Edwards Hardware, Levitt's Cut-Rate Market, Hartley's Bicycle Shop, Kahn's Junk Yard, and Stones Garage.

Sixty years later, Mattocks' sons run the family business from a renovated and expanded facility at the original location. Billy Mattocks served as president of Morrison Road Business Association of Denver (MRBAD) in 2004.[25]

Over the years, Morrison Road buildings were abandoned by merchants, business façades deteriorated, trash accumulated, and the thoroughfare generally grew to appear run-down. Longtime, successful, and well-maintained businesses such as Mattocks Brothers Auto Body were in the minority. The situation changed when Cathy Kuykendall took the position of economic development specialist for the Morrison Road merchants in 1990. Envisioning a little Main Street U.S.A., Kuykendall scheduled cleanup days and other beautification projects funded through grants, loans, and private donations. Merchants and residents pitched in. During a six-year period, more than 100 tons of trash were hauled away—more than 70 tons in one day alone in 1991, as part of a Glad Bag-a-Thon. MRBAD organized and expanded under Kuykendall's direction as part of a Neighborhood Business Revitalization Zone grant to improve blighted areas.[26]

Merchants spruced up their storefronts, power lines went underground, metal street lamps draped with colorful banners replaced unsightly poles, and wider sidewalks with handicap access were installed. Trees and bushes added natural beauty through the efforts of Keep Denver Beautiful, Denver Digs Trees, and other organizations. MRBAD also started crime prevention programs and set up an educational scholarship program for Westwood youth.

Two mixed-use developments opened in April 2004. These developments were constructed on each side of the corridor. Paloma Villa I, 4200 Morrison Road, featured 44 two- and three-bedroom living units plus retail space for lease. Paloma Villa II, 3901 Morrison Road, offered 36 one-, two-, and three-bedroom rentals.

A Landmark Disappears

A popular landmark gave way to progress when the Aeroplane Ballroom, at West Alameda Avenue and South Irving Street, met its demise for the improvement of the intersection in 1998. Locals had gathered at the ballroom, restaurant, and bar for more than 70 years. The original owners, "Uncle" Frank Notary and his nephew Frank "Nookie" Merelli, named the Aeroplane in honor of Charles Lindbergh's famous 1927 flight across the Atlantic Ocean in the *Spirit of St. Louis*. Merelli managed the club with brothers Mike and Frank Vendegnia.[27]

The club's windows resembled those in an airplane, and a propeller hung over the bar. Since the club had a large dance floor, visiting bandleaders such as Dick Jergens practiced there and picked up local musicians for shows at the Lakeside and Elitch Gardens ballrooms during the 1930s, 1940s, and 1950s.

The Notarys and Merellis, who were well-known in the community, owned the club for most of its history. The two families had a lot of influence in Arapahoe County and helped finance the Mother Cabrini Shrine on Lookout Mountain. Tony Merelli and his wife, Lavera, still visit regularly to help maintain the grounds.

Merelli said the families have always believed in giving back to the community. They distributed boxes of food at Thanksgiving and gave out toys on Christmas up through the 1960s. Many times they helped with burial costs for those who did not have the necessary funds.

Howard Carroll and nephew Mike Carroll purchased the club in 1974.

The popular Aeroplane Ballroom opened in 1926 at 3310 W. Alameda Ave. near Morrison Road.

When Mike left the business in 1988, his brother and his sister-in-law, Terry and Jill Carroll, took ownership. After the Colorado Department of Transportation condemned the building, the owners staged a sale of the club's contents, including the original menus, vintage light fixtures, booths, restaurant supplies, and other reminders of bygone days.

Asian Influence

As old landmarks disappeared or relocated, new businesses reflected a growing diversity in the Westwood neighborhood. The face of Federal Boulevard changed dramatically during the 1980s and 1990s as Asian merchants offered goods and services to the expanding Asian population in southwest Denver.

T-WA Inn, at 555 South Federal Boulevard, was the first restaurant to introduce Vietnamese cuisine to Denver, opening January 1, 1984. Dining in a traditional setting, patrons learned about shrimp spring rolls, cheese wontons, chicken roti, Thai's salmon fillets, Vietnamese-style deep-fried bananas, and other tasty dishes.[28]

During the 1980s, the southwest corner of West Alameda Avenue and South Federal Boulevard was transformed into the Far East Center, featuring numerous Asian businesses. In the 1990s, Asian restaurants and retail stores also appeared along both sides of South Federal Boulevard southward to West Mississippi Avenue as many Vietnamese, Laotian, and Hmong people moved to the area.

In 2000, John Tong developed the southeast corner of South Federal Boulevard and West Kentucky Avenue, where Brooks Dairy Farm once stood. Tong's project included four houses 1,400 to 1,500 square feet each and a mini-mall with 14 units.[29]

CHAPTER NINE

Mar Lee

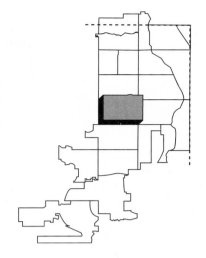

Similar to the Garden Home and Westwood areas, the area between South
Federal Boulevard, South Sheridan Boulevard, West Mississippi Avenue
and West Jewell Avenue was originally dotted with farms in the 1930s. As
the Depression hit, many farms failed and residents found other work. After
World War II, farms were often divided for development, and a fair number of
small frame houses went up in Mar Lee. But the area is also marked by houses
with character, including a round concrete house, a half barracks moved from
Buckley Air Force Base and converted into a house, a half house moved from
the Ken Caryl area, and the Davis mansion, which is now surrounded by
smaller homes. Two historical organizations that continue to have significant
impact on Mar Lee are the Garden Home Grange and the Greater Mar Lee
Community Organization.

The Jackson Family and Progress Plunge Swimming Pool

Fred S. Jackson and his wife, Elizabeth, came to the unincorporated area of
Arapahoe County around 1912. A blacksmith and farmer, Jackson moved his
family into an abandoned log cabin on McBroom's Ranch, where his second
son, Fred Harris, was born on June 1, 1913. Close to Bear Creek near South
Federal Boulevard, the cabin proved handy for Elizabeth, who washed clothes
in the creek. Later that year, during a blizzard, the oldest son, 4-year-old Emmett,
took on the chore of digging out the front door with a coal shovel so the family
could get out—snow had piled up to the second story and he was the only
one who could crawl through the small opening. This pioneer cabin was relocated to the Littleton Historical Museum in 1987.

Fred and Elizabeth homesteaded 80 acres bounded by South Federal Boulevard, South Lowell Boulevard, West Florida Avenue, and West Mexico Avenue and grew wheat on the tract they dubbed Progress Heights. Besides farming, Fred worked as a contractor, operated heavy machinery to move houses, plowed ground for lawns with his team of horses, and helped with the construction of Gates Rubber Company. The couple built a house at 1509 South Federal Boulevard. Elizabeth, a feisty activist, contacted Governor Johnson (who served a nine-month term in 1950) to get a postal route in the area.[1]

In the 1930s, the Jacksons built an indoor swimming pool at South Irving Street and West Florida Avenue and called it Progress Plunge. A popular recreation spot for the community, the pool attracted many neighborhood children, including Ruth Isom, who came to Denver with her mother in 1932.

"We lived with my grandparents, who owned Hill's Greenhouses at South Irving Street and West Arkansas Avenue. My grandfather, E. D. Hill, and uncles Ralph and Ernest, and Homer Hill, all worked in the floral business, and Homer was eventually inducted into the Floriculture Hall of Fame," Ruth said. "I was a cheerleader at Garden Home High School as a sophomore. Since I lived close to the pool and didn't know how to swim, I went there to watch. That's where I met young Fred [Harris Jackson], who was a lifeguard. We married in 1935 and lived in the basement of his folks' house. Then we moved to another house owned by the Jacksons at Iowa and Hazel Court. It didn't have a bathroom, so we bathed in a washtub in the kitchen.

"In 1939, we moved to our permanent home, a wooden building Fred bought and moved to South Hazel Court. He plastered the walls, put in a chimney and two wood stoves, and in time built on four additions. He also moved a garage from Valverde, put in a floor, and added on to it. We raised six children in that house—David, Marjorie, Sharon, Cyndi, Mary, and Rick—and never paid rent or made a mortgage payment."

During World War II, Fred worked at the Remington Arms plant (now the Denver Federal Center) making steel shells for .30-06 rifles. After the war, Fred and Ruth managed the pool. As senior lifesaving examiner, Fred took care of instruction, pool maintenance, service, and consulting; Ruth handled the bills, office help, and cleaning. "We provided swimming,

Jim Jackson on his pony, Skeezix, in front of the Jackson home on South Federal Boulevard, 1929.

scuba diving, and kayaking instruction. In later years, Martin Marietta used the facility for underwater training and water sled testing," Ruth added.

Elizabeth Jackson died in 1970. Each of her three sons, Emmett, Fred, and Jim, inherited 1 acre of the homestead site. Her house and property were sold for business enterprises, one of which is the Walgreens store at South Federal Boulevard and West Florida Avenue. Emmett worked as an electrician and managed the Jackson Electric store at the corner of South Federal Boulevard and West Arkansas Avenue. He lived in a house on West Florida Avenue that had been cut in half and hauled from the Ken Caryl area. Jim, 10 years younger, operated large machinery.

A snowstorm in 1972 damaged the roof of Progress Plunge Swimming Pool. By that time, city pools had been built at Abraham Lincoln High School and Harvey Park Recreation Center. Private pools, such as the Terrace Club and Pinehurst Country Club, also competed for swimmers. The family decided not to renovate, so the pool was demolished and the 10-acre site sold to developers, who then erected Prospect Park Townhouses at 3800 West Florida Avenue.

Fred and Ruth Jackson celebrated 61 years of marriage before Fred died of cancer in 1996. Ruth continues to live in the home they moved to 57 years earlier.[2]

The Davis Farm

Not far from the Jacksons, Harry Clayton Davis built a mansion on his farm, which extended from South Lowell Boulevard west to South Sheridan Boulevard between West Mississippi Avenue and West Jewell Avenue. Born on a farm near Medina, New York, Davis taught school for $5 a week at a country school near his birthplace before coming to Denver in 1890 at age 22. With a law degree from Cornell University, he was admitted to the Colorado Bar Association. He started his long career with Denver's pioneer law firm of Benedict and Phelps and became a charter member of the Denver Bar Association upon its founding in 1898, serving as its president in 1917.

After his first wife died, Davis married Jane Travello Humphreys in 1912. From 1922 to 1950, they owned a 3,802-square-foot, six-bedroom house commonly called the Clarefield Mansion. The large home at 1700 South Sheridan Boulevard was named for Davis' daughter, Clare, who preceded him in death. Frederics Brothers purchased the estate in the mid-1950s and platted the Parkview subdivision around the palatial home. With the addition of new streets, the home's address changed to 1674 South Zenobia Way. John C. and Elinor J. Campbell owned the home from 1958 to 1972; then Steven J. Burton and his wife, Leslie Merrill Burton, purchased the property.

Davis practiced law until the advanced age of 99. He was honored by the Colorado Bar Association in 1959 Law Day ceremonies and was recognized by the American Bar Association in 1966 for having the longest continuous law practice in the United States. He worked every day, even as he recovered from a broken hip at Spaulding Rehabilitation Center. When he came down with pneumonia, his secretary took calls and conferred with him by phone. His office was open on the day of his death, September 5, 1968.[3]

Early Residents

Scattered farms spanned the area in the 1930s, and early residents were separated by alfalfa fields, orchards, and greenhouses.

The Andersons

Alfred and Sigrid Anderson lived in a two-story farmhouse on South Lowell Boulevard and maintained an apple orchard with irrigation water from the lake near West Mississippi Avenue, commonly known as Anderson's Lake. The Andersons sold off parcels of land to early residents and deeded irrigation rights to the city after annexation in 1947. An irrigation ditch maintained by the Garfield Heights Water District ran south from Anderson Lake and the larger Garfield Heights Lake to all homes in the area. A concrete spillway emptied into a large gully with a small stream, which was lined with large cottonwood trees, ambling from northwest of Florida Avenue southeast to Federal Boulevard and beyond. The gully was eventually filled with dirt, and houses were built there. The city ultimately combined the two lakes and developed Garfield Lake Park.

The Kolacnys

William (Bill) and Geraldine Kolacny moved to South Knox Court about 1935. Like many residents, they kept cows, chickens, and a few pigs on their 1-acre site, once part of the Alfred Anderson farm adjacent to the Fred Jackson farm. Son Richard, who grew up close to Progress Plunge with his sisters, Eloise and Marian, said his parents met at a church in Englewood where his mother was the pianist. With experience as a teacher and director of a company band in Wyoming, his father worked as shop foreman for the Knight Campbell music store in Denver.

Richard Kolacny began his musical career in the Garden Home Grange Junior Orchestra and the Westwood High School band. He now owns Kolacny Music on South Broadway.

"After my father lost his job in the economic crash of 1929, he opened a repair shop downtown in the Barth Building. He repaired musical instruments for dozens of bands popular in the 1940s, 1950s, and 1960s—bands such as Ray Anthony and Les Brown, who appeared at Elitch's Trocadero Ballroom and Lakeside's El Patio dance hall."

Richard played trumpet in the Garden Home Grange junior orchestra and the Westwood High School band. He even formed his own band, called Rhythm 8, which performed at many events sponsored by the Westwood Lions Club. Richard now owns Kolacny Music, a business started years ago by his father. Located at 1900 South Broadway, the business rents, repairs, and sells musical instruments for private bands, school bands, orchestras, and individuals. The family business employs Richard's son, David, and daughter-in-law, Debbie, as well as daughter, Donna.[4]

Theda Marshall
While Richard Kolacny excelled in music, one of his Garden Home classmates who played coronet in the Grange orchestra and high school band made her mark as an athlete. Following graduation in 1946, Theda Marshall left a bank teller job that paid $25 a week to start a baseball career offering $100 per week. She played first base in the All-American Girls' Baseball League, which started during World War II and was featured in the movie *A League*

of Their Own. After playing baseball in Indiana and Illinois, she went to a professional softball team in Arizona for $250 a week. Theda retired in 1951, returned to Denver, and worked at the Lowry Air Force Base Accounting and Finance Center until 1981. She died in 2005 at age 80.

John Adams, Glenn and Jackie with first upholstered chair delivery to Daniels & Fisher, 1930s. They made and sold upholstered pieces to fashionable Denver stores.

The Adamses

John and Stella Adams opened a furniture shop in a former chicken coop behind their frame home at 1335 South Federal Boulevard. They made upholstered living room and bedroom furniture for Davis & Shaw, Daniels & Fisher (which merged with the May Company to become May D&F and then later became Foley's and then Macy's), and other well-known stores. Their five children—Glenn, Jackie, Joe, Elroy, and Bob—helped with the business, called Adams Upholstery, which also did re-upholstery work. "My job was to strip down the pieces for re-upholstery, and I got to keep any watches or rings I found," Elroy said.

"When lumber was scarce during World War II, we picked up bomb crates from the Federal Center to build furniture. In 1948, we built a big brick house at 1345 South Federal Boulevard and rented the older home. I was so proud to tell classmates at Westwood School that we moved to a new house—even if it was just next door," Elroy added. The growing business stayed in its original chicken-coop shop until the Adamses sold the property to Albertsons in 1969 and moved to a new shop in Lakewood. Albertsons eventually sold that supermarket to Grocery Warehouse.[5]

The Dallmann/Smith Home

Otto and Louise Dallmann, immigrants from east Germany, purchased land from Alfred and Sigrid Anderson in 1932 and erected a small frame house at the corner of West Louisiana Avenue and South Julian Street. Four years later, Otto dug the basement for a large two-story brick house, unique in the area. He also put up a chicken coop, a utility shed, a three-car brick garage, and a decorative wrought-iron fence. The enterprising couple raised chickens and operated a truck farm for a living. (A "truck farm" is a small farm that brings its goods to market via a small truck.)

Otto created a basement apartment, complete with wood cook stove and coal furnace, and rented it to a former German soldier. The renter, who worked as a landscaper at Pinehurst Country Club, eventually bought land from Otto and built a house next door. Otto also sold land to his brother-in-law, who operated a nearby greenhouse on West Louisiana Avenue and South Irving Street.

Jerry and Debbie Smith bought the Dallmanns' two-story brick house on West Louisiana Avenue in March 1996. Both grew up in southwest Denver: Debbie went to Abraham Lincoln High School, and Jerry graduated from Mullen High School. They married in 1984 and moved to the comfortable home 12 years later. Jerry worked as a criminal investigator for the Colorado Department of Revenue, and Debbie was a hairdresser.

Interested in history, the Smiths learned about the builders of their house from the previous owners, who had once rented from the Dallmanns. Striving to maintain the integrity of the property, the Smiths refurbished the home's interior and improved the grounds. They hung framed documents pertaining to the house on the walls, and Jerry added his own collection of Colorado license plates dating back to 1920. They gained a city variance to keep the chickens, extended the wrought-iron fence, and installed corner landscaping. "We enjoy gathering fresh brown eggs every day and relaxing in our spacious yard," Debbie said.[6]

The Garden Home Grange

Farmers started the National Grange in 1867, after the Civil War, at a time when growers could not move their products because of high railroad rates and banks charged prohibitive rates to borrow money. By banding together, farmers had a voice in government, bought supplies cooperatively, and secured favorable fire insurance rates.

The Garden Home Grange organized in March 1930 to bring both farm and non-farm people together to discuss rural concerns and to enjoy social and cultural events. Fourteen charter members elected officers headed by Master A. T. Monson. Another 15 members joined a week later, on March 12, 1930, and the group adopted its name from the surrounding community.[7]

Aided by state Grange officials, the new Grange initially flourished, adding 26 more members within a few weeks. Meetings took place at Garden Home School at 3615 West Kentucky Avenue. When the Depression hit, the Grange set up an employment agency to help members. However, economic conditions and lack of a regular meeting site led to a temporary halt of meetings during the summer of 1931. Determined to continue, the fledgling Grange struggled through the fall and elected Jack Cassias as master in 1932. The following year, Booster Night drew a crowd of 250. The rural Grange added a Ladies Auxiliary and Juvenile Grange, and by 1935 individual members owned $127,000 worth of Grange fire insurance.

At their 100th meeting in August 1936, Grangers agreed to purchase a building at West Alameda Avenue and South Federal Boulevard, with terms of nothing down and payments of $1 per month. The hall proved unsatisfactory, so members decided to buy land to build a new meeting place. In 1943, Garden Home Grange finally incorporated and purchased ground at West Mississippi Avenue and South Irving Street. "The women built the nucleus of the basement-level structure in 1944 and 1945, since most of the men were serving in the armed forces during the war," said Dorothy Ridgely, a charter member of the Grange. During World War II women also formed the Garden Home Ladies Square Dance team.

The new hall opened on August 1, 1945. By staging Saturday night dances for the community, the 276 Grangers paid off their entire debt at the end of 1946.

What started as a rural organization became an urban group as Denver grew around it. In 1959, the thriving Grange was recognized as the first and only Grange within the Denver city limits—Colorado's first rural-turned-urban Grange. The Grange has continued to offer its basement hall for square dances, church services, and other community events, even though the upper level was never added.

Members garnered trophies over the years in needlecraft, quilting, bowling, and other activities, filling eight trophy cases. They also helped at the local day-care center and Lutheran High School, plus supported national charities such as March of Dimes and Help for the Blind. During the 1960s, Hazelle Plambeck, Dorothy Ridgely, Diane Brown, and Ruth Graber competed nationally as the Garden Home Quartet, accompanied by Jackie Wennberg. Plambeck and Ridgely also sang in the 1974 Colorado State Grange Chorus along with Rose Barcelona and Dorothy Beeson from the Garden Home Grange. Ridgely said the Grange still meets twice a month, with programs of local interest and business meetings on alternate nights.[8]

The Cuhel and Intrery Homes

When Louis Cuhel mustered out of the army in Tacoma, Washington, in 1945, he and his wife, Waneta, headed for Denver and rented a "garage home" near Children's Hospital. Louis, who learned the baking trade in the army, went to work downtown at Merchant's Biscuit Company at 9th and Larimer Streets, which later became the Bowman Biscuit Company, and subsequently the Keebler Company. The Cuhels looked for a place to settle and decided to buy land and build a home themselves. They bought two lots in Sheridan Park close to Morrison Road and South Sheridan Boulevard for $800.

Young and energetic, the Cuhels purchased a half-barracks building from Buckley Air Field in east Denver, had it moved to their land, and began transforming it into a home. Working every evening, weekend, and holiday for a year, they put up walls and cabinets, hired out the plumbing and electrical wiring, and then did the plastering and painting themselves.

In the meantime, they made do without hot water. For five years, Louis took showers at work while Waneta and their two young daughters took "basin baths" with hot water hauled from their landlord's house. On laundry day, Waneta carried hot water to her wringer washing machine.

Louis and Waneta Cuhel converted a former Buckley Air Field barracks into a comfortable two-bedroom home and moved there in August 1950.

Finally, in August 1950, they moved into the two-bedroom frame house on South Yates Street. When daughter Jeanette was 8 and Barbara was 3, they enjoyed tub baths at last.[9]

The Cuhel's neighbors, Peter and Leona Intrery, moved from Honolulu, Hawaii, a few months later and purchased a frame house on the lot next to the Cuhels. Peter, a mason who at one time owned his own construction company, put brick veneer on their frame house and built brick planters several years later. "When we moved from Hawaii, I was one-and-a-half years old," said their daughter, Linda. "My brother, Robert [also known as Bosco], was born six months later in Denver."[10]

Growing up together, the Cuhel and Intrery children played games on the vacant land between their houses—games such as Swing the Statue and Billy Goat Gruff. "We also played on a sturdy swing set our dads built from four-by-fours. On snowy days, our street was closed off so we could sled down the hill safely," Jeanette said. The neighborhood girls had a favorite hiding place in a large weeping willow tree near Garfield Lake. The boys liked to look for crayfish and shoot their BB guns. "We all swam in the lake, rode our bikes on gravel roads, and borrowed books from the Barnum Library. When we got older, we rode the Bussard Bus to a movie at the Westwood Theater on West Alameda Avenue or went roller skating at Westwood Skating Rink on West Kentucky Avenue."

"The neighborhood women got together once a week for Tupperware or Stanley Home Products parties," said Waneta, who also belonged to the Mountain Do's, a group of women who met monthly for lunch, crafts, and tours of various places of interest. Waneta also created all the draperies for the house and regularly sewed clothes for her daughters.

"All of us girls learned to sew and make our own clothes," Jeanette said. "This skill came in handy years later when I made dresses alike for my five daughters, who sang together at church events." Waneta walked to the grocery store at Hart's Corner or bought food at Miller's when the Alameda Square Shopping Center opened in 1955 at South Sheridan Boulevard and West Alameda Avenue. But even closer was Miller's Supermarket in the Mar Lee–Garfield Shopping Center, which opened in 1956 at 4301 West Florida Avenue. Besides Miller's, the new center offered 18 other businesses, including Rexall Drugs, Hested's, Eakers, Dolly Madison, Vogt Shoe Service, and Mar Lee Restaurant and Lounge. Presumably using the family names of the developers and that of President James Garfield, the neighborhood center reportedly provided the largest parking area for its size.

Jeanette attended Belmont Elementary School on Morrison Road from third through fifth grades, then went to Westwood for sixth grade. She transferred to

Jeanette and Barbara Cuhel, 1952.

the new Kepner Junior High when it opened in 1953, then attended West High School, where she joined the Lariattes Pep Club. "Our 1960 graduating class numbered 609 and many of us celebrated afterwards at Elitch's amusement park in north Denver," she said. (Elitch Gardens, originally located on the southwest corner of West 38th Avenue and Tennyson Street, moved to the Central Platte Valley between the 1994 and 1995 seasons. Later, the park became Six Flags Elitch Gardens.)

Meanwhile, Louis Cuhel continued to improve their home by adding a 20-by-25-foot extension on the front of his house in 1965. After he retired in 1980, Louis built a shed on the patio to house a clothes dryer, a freezer, and a wood shop, where he made windmill clocks, wooden chains, and yard decorations as a hobby.

Cuhel's next-door neighbor, Peter Intrery, bought half of one of Cuhel's two lots and added an attached garage and second-story family room to his original house. Over the years, Intrery also built on an arched porch entry, a carport, and a large kitchen.

"My dad worked on every school I've attended," said Peter's daughter Linda, "with the exception of Westwood Elementary where I went to kindergarten. Because of crowded conditions, I was on split sessions all during my school years except for fifth and sixth grade at Force Elementary. I attended staggered sessions at Kepner Junior High and again at Abraham Lincoln High School. My 10th grade class at Lincoln started with a little over fifteen hundred kids. When we graduated at the Denver Coliseum in 1967, we were the largest graduating class in the history of Denver Public Schools."

Following graduation, Linda enrolled in college in Greeley to become a teacher. "There weren't many choices for women back then. Most became teachers, secretaries, or nurses." Linda received a bachelor's degree from the University of Northern Colorado and a master's from the University of Colorado. She taught math at Red Rocks Community College and retired after serving as department chair and associate dean of instruction.

The Concrete House

After World War II, Denver's population and associated housing needs continued to expand. At the east side of the Mar Lee neighborhood, Walter Bails built 15 houses on South Hazel Court near West Jewell Avenue. Constructed at an estimated cost of $4,000 each, most of the homes were frame and included a full

Constructed in 1948, this round house features concrete walls and floors, concrete fireplaces, and even a concrete foundation for the bed.

basement but no garage. Three of the homes had a one-car attached garage and cost about $5,000 to build.

Jack and Luella Terry, Clarence and Gracie Tollard, and Ed and Verba Moore erected post-war homes on West Bails Place, a short street apparently named for Bails, the original builder in the small community.

Unusual in its design and material is a 35-foot, round concrete house erected in 1948 by Edward Carpentier. A foreman at Robinson Brick and Tile Company, Carpentier and his wife, Esther, an employee at Gates Rubber Company, lived in a house built by Bails during the construction of their unique home. Carpentier reportedly planned a round structure similar to one he had seen in Italy during World War II. His 1,079-square-foot house was situated at the corner of West Bails Place and South Hazel Court. He added a detached 384-square-foot, six-sided garage in 1956.

The house featured concrete walls and floors, concrete fireplaces, and even a concrete foundation for the bed. A small enclosed room inside the living room held numerous electrical and communication wires. The basement contained a windowless storage room with an air pipe to the outside. Following Carpentier's retirement from Robinson Brick, he tutored students at Johnson Elementary School. He eventually moved to California to be near his daughter after living in his round house for 30 years, from 1949 to 1979. Several owners and renters occupied the house during the next 10 years.[11]

Eventually, the concrete home found a new owner. Candis Holmes moved from Valverde to the Mar Lee area when she was 7. "As a kid, I was always intrigued by the round house close to my school. I thought I would like to live there someday," she said. "Years later, when my son Joey and I were riding our bicycles in the area, I saw it was for sale." Candis and her husband bought the house in 1989 but divorced shortly after. She stayed in the house with her son and eventually married Greg Pilosi.

The Pilosis decorated the house with bold Egyptian-style furnishings that gave it a striking appearance. "We tore out the neon lighting along the living room wall and also the walls of the small room inside the living room, leaving beams that make a unique architectural statement," Candis stated. "Neither the upstairs nor downstairs fireplace was functional, so we hired people to rebuild the outside chimney that had deteriorated. We also put a wood floor in the kitchen and carpet on the rest of the floors. The designer, Carpentier's uncle, used a lot of brick in the kitchen and throughout the house. He certainly believed in storage as there are cabinets everywhere. A built-in lazy Susan in the corner cabinet is believed to the first lazy Susan installed in a kitchen, a feature popular in many kitchens today. Unfortunately, he didn't get a patent on it.

"There are no 90-degree angles in our home. When we first moved in, we became disoriented by walking into a wall instead of another room. Apparently Carpentier took note of the seasons, because the round window in the living room is host to the moon's positions during the year."[12]

Lutheran High School

As the neighborhood grew in the 1950s, the Lutheran Church Missouri Synod decided it needed a school in the area. After purchasing a 10-acre farm in 1955, the church started classes for 65 9th and 10th graders, using former farm buildings as temporary quarters. Lutheran High School, 320 West Arizona Avenue, opened the first wing of classrooms in 1956 and added the junior class that year. The second classroom wing was added to the campus during 1957–1958, and seniors completed the student enrollment of 220. Athletics were a vital part of the school program from the beginning, although 9th and 10th graders competed against teams from full four-year schools the first year. Known as the Lutheran Lights, teams played football, basketball, track, and baseball.[13]

The Chalmers Hadley Branch Library

Denver's suburbs continued to spread south and west as housing developments replaced farmlands. When the city failed to offer services for the new communities, spirited residents waged campaigns for such amenities. After a five-year fight for a new library, the city finally funded the Chalmers Hadley Branch Library at South Grove Street and West Jewell Avenue.

Denver Mayor Thomas G. Currigan came to the dedication ceremony on June 4, 1964. Named in memory of Chalmers Hadley, who headed the Denver Public Library from 1910 to 1924, it was the first DPL branch library built with city capital improvement funds. The building featured a contemporary expression of southwest regional architecture. The new facility contained adult reading areas for 40, children's seating areas for 20, a meeting room for 100, basement storage for 30,000 books, and a mechanical book lift from the basement to the ground floor. Stocked initially with 21,000 books for adults and 10,000 books for children, the library eventually reached a capacity of 50,000 books.[14]

Later Mar Lee Residents

In 1955, Bud and Dorothy Ridgely moved from Westwood to South Knox Court, across the street from the Kolacnys. The Ridgelys' brick house was built by Gil Venrick sometime during World War II. Bud worked for the railroad, and Dorothy was secretary at Munroe Elementary School until her retirement. They were active in the Garden Home Grange and the Boy Scouts while raising two sons, Ken and Smoke.

Other Scout Knox Court residents Steve and Peggy Hildmann were married at All Saints Catholic Church in 1979 and moved next door to the Kolacnys. The property still had a chicken coop and horse shed. The previous owners had secured a business license around 1935 and operated a furniture upholstery business called Tom's Upholstery. Steve was employed in the bakery business, and Peggy worked for the city. Their son, Zachary, attended Lutheran High School. Handy with home repairs, the Hildmanns began restoration work on their house. When they had to replace water pipes damaged by tree roots, they found an old grease trap from back when septic tanks served the neighborhood before the city installed sewer lines in the 1950s. They enjoyed the diversity of an older neighborhood and joined the Greater Mar Lee Community Organization to work for community improvements. They were concerned about decreasing property values because of low-income mortgage scams where realtors sold houses with no money down and no credit check.[15]

The Greater Mar Lee Community Organization

The Greater Mar Lee Community Organization formed in 1979 to discuss zoning issues. Citizens mobilized when the Colorado Corrections Office moved into the Mar Lee Shopping Center on August 16, 2000. Although more than 300 people showed up at a public meeting, the Corrections Center was allowed to stay. The State Department of Corrections had researched 74 other sites for more than two years before deciding on the Mar Lee location. The center oversees prisoners released before their full sentence has been served.[16]

Residents voiced security and community environment concerns—as well as alarm over the parole facility's proximity to Force Elementary School at 1550 South Wolff Street. Force's principal, Les Rank, said the school had a security officer on site to prevent problems.[17]

The Mar Lee neighborhood is split into two council districts, Districts 2 and 3. The active Greater Mar Lee Community Organization succeeded in its efforts to pass a state bill requiring the Colorado Corrections Office to notify a community before prisoner relocations take place.

CHAPTER TEN

Ruby Hill and Overland

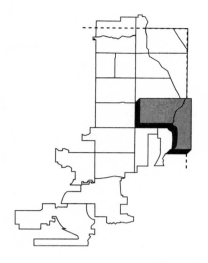

Known for the popular sledding hill in Ruby Hill and the golf course in Overland, this area's history is more industrial than agricultural. Marked by paper and cotton mills, the neighborhood also featured car, motorcycle, and horse racing in its early years. The Ruby Hill neighborhood is bounded by West Mississippi Avenue on the north, the South Platte River on the east, West Jewell Avenue on the south, and West Federal Boulevard on the west. The Overland neighborhood, meanwhile, comprises a narrow area between Broadway on the east and the South Platte River on the west, stretching from the old Gates Rubber plant at West Mississippi Avenue south to Englewood limits at West Yale Avenue. Today, with light rail and trains zipping through on one side of Santa Fe Drive and the Platte River Greenway offering an escape to nature on the other, Ruby Hill and Overland offer an interesting mix of urban and outdoor lifestyles.

Denver Paper Mills

More than 1,200 people turned out for the grand opening of Col. James Platt's paper mill on August 23, 1891. Excited to see the innovative factory, they traveled to Manchester, an unincorporated hamlet along the South Platte River, near what is now 1000 West Louisiana Avenue. Many took trains, filling 13 Union Pacific railroad cars, which left from Union Station. During the ceremony, city and state dignitaries praised the progress of Denver and talked about new opportunities for employment. "Next to Denver's great smelters, the successful establishment of cotton, iron, woolen, and paper mills are of the greatest importance to the rapid and permanent growth of our city. We have one of the largest and finest modern paper mills ever constructed in this or any other country," Platt told citizens, inviting them to tour the mill.[1]

After serving in the Civil War and in Congress as a representative from Virginia, Platt came to Denver in 1887 as president of Equitable Accident Insurance Company. He resigned from the insurance business to research the possibility of paper manufacture in Denver. Convinced that Denver was a favorable site for a paper mill, he furnished a large part of the capital and hired leading architects from Massachusetts to design the facility, which was 616 feet in length and 60 to 100 feet in width. Completed August 12, 1891, the plant cost $357,000.

Platt thought the location was ideal, with a running brook on the west and the South Platte River on the east to provide sufficient water. An artesian well supplied water for the boiler. The South Park Railroad ran by the mill and included switches so cars could be loaded or unloaded directly from the mill platform. In the spring of 1892, the mill expanded its operations. The *Rocky Mountain News* reported that $200,000 in improvements to the original plant were nearly completed, including a rag mill to produce a better quality of paper.[2]

A second paper mill at the Manchester site began operations in the fall of 1893 to manufacture book and writing paper. Containing 400,000 square feet of floor space, including the basement, the building was said to be the largest in the state. More than 300 carloads of stone and more than 7 million bricks were used in the structure, which extended 600 feet long, was 180 feet wide, and varied from two to five stories above the basement. The cost of the building with machinery totaled $500,000.

Soon after completing the grand paper mills, Platt took his family on a fishing trip to Green Lake near Georgetown, Colorado. On June 13, 1894, alone in a boat, he fell into the water and drowned.

Evidently Platt's death, and possibly the economic crisis around that time, affected the company. In 1900, eastern bondholders foreclosed on the property and sold the wagons, lumber, equipment, and supplies at a public auction. The two mills, known as the Denver Paper Mills and the Platte River Mills, along with the Denver Sulphite Fibre Company, were consolidated into the Rocky Mountain Paper Company, which took over properties costing more than $2 million, including pulp mills, paper mills, sulphite mills, and kindred industries.[3]

The new company owned the only mills between Wisconsin and California that manufactured newsprint, manila, book, and fiber papers along with roofing and wrapping papers. In addition to the plants, the Rocky Mountain Paper Company controlled all the waterpower, timberlands, sawmills, stores, sulfur rights, and other interests previously controlled by the individual companies. New management

In 1891, Col. James Platt opened a paper mill in Manchester, near what is now 1000 W. Louisiana Ave. The large smokestack was demolished around 1928; the mill and remaining smokestack were torn down in 1964.

from Pusey and Jones Company of Wilmington, Delaware, planned to increase plant capacity, double output, and increase payroll 50 percent by employing "many idle men."

The plans for expansion didn't work out, however, and the plant went out of business. A chemical company occupied the building through World War I (1918) and then the Denver Factories Company tried to revitalize the plant. In about 1923, Continental Paper Products Company occupied the buildings, and the large smokestack was demolished around 1928. Continental Paper Products moved to a new plant 100 yards south of the former location in 1958 but continued to use the old paper mill for miscellaneous storage.[4]

The Denver Carton Plant division of Packaging Corporation of America owned the old building in 1963, when the city condemned the remaining smokestack, which had served the original plant. Residents watched the demolition of the old mill and its 190-foot smokestack on a Saturday in March 1964. Another building west of the smokestack housed the Sells-Floto Circus at one time, according to E. W. Peiker, general manager of the Denver Carton Plant.[5]

Ruby Hill

Ruby Hill, near West Florida Avenue and South Platte River Drive, derived its name from the hill where early settlers found small red stones. Thought to be rubies, the stones were actually garnets. Over the years, the historical site that once saw

Arapaho Indians camped at its base also provided a lofty lookout for Sunday hot-air balloon ascents, horse and car racing, and early airplane flights across the river at Overland Park. A popular picnic spot and lovers' lane, Ruby Hill served as proving grounds for automobile and motorcycle enthusiasts around 1913.

White-robed Ku Klux Klan members burned crosses on the hillside during the 1920s and even as late as the 1940s. Klansmen gathered in the building at West Evans Avenue and South Mariposa Street, the former location of the Overland Cotton Mill, for meetings in the 1920s.[6]

For years, Denver citizens dumped and incinerated trash at Ruby Hill, located south of the old paper mill, drawing complaints about air pollution. Henry M. Duff, a 1946 south Denver councilman, requested an ordinance to abate the smoke nuisance. "An investigation disclosed that a rubber company was dumping truckloads of scrap rubber into incinerators on the hill to be burned. The smoke from the fire was black and dirty and hid the sun in some sections of my district," Duff said.[7]

Today in Ruby Hill, you will find children sledding in the winter and flying kites in the summer. The area is also popular with picnickers and families with disabled children, who enjoy a playground designed especially for them.

Radio Stations

This area of southwest Denver plays a part in the history of Denver radio. William D. "Doc" Reynolds, a dentist who had come to Denver for health reasons, placed a transmitter on Ruby Hill in the late 1920s and founded Colorado's first radio station. KLZ, dubbed the "Radio Pioneer of the West," reported news of the Moffat Tunnel and women's suffrage.[8]

In 1956, Gene Amole, born and educated in Denver, founded radio station KDEN with Ed Koepke. Amole met Koepke at radio station KMYR, where Amole started his broadcasting career as night announcer and Koepke was the night engineer. A year later, their FM station, KVOD, was licensed to broadcast from the transmission tower on Ruby Hill. Known as "The Voice of Denver," KVOD 99.5 FM played classical music for listeners as far away as Billings, Montana. Amole and partner Koepke started KMET in 1958 as a sister station to KDEN, which they sold in 1970.[9]

Amole said, "When competitors in broadcasting talked about our success, they would often say, 'Koepke had the brains and Amole had the mouth.'" Their radio station at 1601 West Jewell Avenue had a record library, recording room, and broadcasting room. Donations of art from listeners decorated the walls.[10]

Amole and Koepke sold KVOD in 1983 because Amole felt it was taking too much time away from home, according to his wife, Trish. Amole worked as a columnist for the *Rocky Mountain News* from December 1977 until his death in May 2002.

Ruby Hill Park

Denver acquired Ruby Hill Park in 1954. The 83-acre park was bounded by West Florida Avenue to the north, South Quivas Street and South Raritan Street to the west, West Jewell Avenue to the south, and the Burlington Northern Railroad to the east. In winter, sledders flocked to the large hill, rising 150 feet, for long rides in powdery snow. In summer, people of all ages marveled at the abundant wildflowers growing there and the splendid 360-degree hilltop view ranging from downtown Denver to Pikes Peak. Birds liked the Ruby Hill site, too, attracted by chokecherry bushes in the area. Members of the Audubon Society traveled to Ruby Hill as one of their stops for the annual bird census each New Year's Day.[11]

Early plans for Ruby Hill Park development showed a natural amphitheater with stage area and the layout for the Overland Golf Course. Authored by S. R. DeBoer & Company Landscape Architects, the plan proposed a scenic outlook point and contours that resembled the park's current topography. DeBoer started as city landscape architect for Mayor Robert W. Speer's administration in 1910 and opened his own business next to his south Denver home in 1924.[12]

Building on DeBoer's vision, the 1955 plan prepared by the Denver Parks and Recreation Department initially called for a large amphitheater to seat 25,000 people and a smaller amphitheater north of the scenic overlook to seat 4,000. The plan also included play fields, open space, picnic areas, and smaller parking lots. Another plan created by Denver Parks and Recreation in 1971 showed a large amphitheater in the central bowl that would host events such as the *Denver Post* Opera, a show wagon featuring local talent, and the Denver Symphony. A small amphitheater and a sledding area were proposed for the central bowl to the south. From this plan, the road configuration, two ball fields, and several parking lots were built.[13]

During the 1990s, area residents complained about gangs and rowdy people taking over the park and intimidating other park users. The Ruby Hill Neighborhood Organization (RHiNO) and sister neighborhood organizations in the Mar Lee, Godsman, Athmar Park, and College View areas worked with Denver police to make the park more family friendly. The neighborhood organizations also connected with city officials to protect views from the park by preventing high-rise development in the Platte valley east and south of Ruby Hill Park.[14]

Area residents gave input for the Ruby Hill Master Plan, which was approved in 2004. As money becomes available, plans may eventually be carried out to complete the oft-proposed amphitheater. This time, the amphitheater concept was retained as an informal flexible space for sledding in winter and summer events such as band or orchestra concerts and drama performances. Residents are working with the city to determine the best traffic route through the park for safety and to develop the master plan as funds become available.[15] In 2007, Denver and Winter Park Ski Resort developed a Rail Yard, the first snowboarding hill in a major city--and free to the public--at Ruby Hill Park.

Overland Cotton Mill

Not to be confused with the Denver paper mills, Overland Cotton Mill, another industry that sprang up near the South Platte River, started construction in 1890 at West Evans Avenue and South Mariposa Street. Denver parties invested $100,000 in stock, and eastern capitalists subscribed for the $350,000 balance. "For the mountain country of the West this opens up a new field of industry," stated the *Denver Republican* on June 4, 1890. "The manufacture of cotton and woolen goods has heretofore been confined to the East, especially the New England states. Henceforth the industry will be distributed and the West will get its goods as cheap as does the East."[16]

Grateful for work, many men found employment at the plant, headed by John L. Jerome, a prominent businessman, who served on the board of the Denver Stock Exchange and the University Club. The company erected a number of small cottages near the mill for families of workers in 1899, and the bell of the Overland Park Mission Church called people to worship and to social activities in the growing community.

The Overland Cotton Mill produced 12 million yards of cloth at the height of production in the 1890s but closed in 1903. Used in the 1920s by the Klu Klux Klan, the historic structure still stands at West Evans Avenue and South Mariposa Street, now within the boundaries of the South Platte neighborhood.

Concerned about children working at the mill, Judge Ben Lindsey prosecuted officers of the Overland Cotton Mill for abuse of child labor laws. Among his allies pressing for reforms affecting children were *Titanic* survivor Margaret "Molly" Brown and Denver journalist Polly Pry.[17]

At its peak, the mill's annual production reached 12 million yards of cloth in a variety of types and patterns. Even though the cotton mill ran successfully for several years, its days were numbered. The observation of an eastern labor agent helped explain the eventual demise of the textile business in Denver. Andrew Richardson, who served for 25 years as labor agent of a large woolen mill in Westerly, Rhode Island, looked into the trade on a pleasure trip to Colorado in 1901. Richardson said the average competency of Colorado's population was too high to allow the textile industry to flourish. He explained that textile industries employed uneducated men, women, and children who did not have the physical strength or manual dexterity for ordinary skilled work. "The higher a man rises in labor, the less willing he is either to have his wife work, except to make their home comfortable, or to have his children miss one day of school," he stated. "It is the girls who can't cook, the men who can't do skilled work, and the children of those who can't earn good wages at other things that we get to tend our looms and spinners. Now these Western states are settled by the peculiarly competent and enterprising. Except the women, who are widowed, neither they nor their children want employment in a mill," he said. "You couldn't find 50 men in Denver who would accept the wages that cotton mills pay, unless they are imported from other parts of the country. The Western climate does not produce them."[18]

No doubt Richardson's comments haunted mill owners as employees struggled to eke out a living. The winter of 1903–1904 proved disastrous for the poverty-stricken community. The mill closed in November 1903 when a coal strike cut off the supply of fuel. Since the mill paid low wages, even the most frugal families soon exhausted their savings.

Word of the terrible conditions reached O. E. Tuft, assistant secretary of the State Humane Society, who hastened to investigate the situation. According to a *Denver Republican* newspaper account, Tuft found unfortunates "who were without food or fuel at a time when the holiday season, with its attendant pleasures, is being welcomed in so many homes where gaunt hunger has never shown his hideous face. One family of 10 persons did not have a particle of food of any kind or description, and had spent the day wondering what could be done to avoid death by starvation."[19]

Mill superintendents John Gilligan and John Robinson had already taken action and food was delivered that day: 1,250 pounds of flour, 500 pounds of meat, 100 bushels of corn, 300 pounds of potatoes, 70 pounds of breakfast food, 100 pounds of coffee, a bushel of rolled oats, 100 pounds of salt, and other necessities. However, since nearly every family was entirely out of food, the supply lasted only four days. Attorney Robert Collier secured a carload of coal to heat the homes, and city leaders sought public contributions of food, fuel, and clothing.

More than 400 people, including Mary Duke and her three small children, suffered from the closure. Duke, washerwoman of the mill settlement, could not find work. People were now doing their own washing because they could not afford to hire her. Denver businessmen and citizens delivered substantial aid to the poverty-stricken families when they heard of the mill workers' plight. David Moffat contributed 40 tons of coal, the Atlas Coal Company donated 6 tons, and members of First Avenue Presbyterian Church sent 21 tons of coal along with 2,700 pounds of rations. Other church groups responded with aid, and many individuals left groceries anonymously.[20]

Mill owners responded also. "For the past five weeks we have not been charging rent for the houses occupied by the mill people," Assistant Superintendent Robinson said in December 1903.[21]

The death of mill operator Jerome complicated attempts to reopen the mill, and city leaders struggled with decisions regarding the welfare of unemployed workers. One plan involved chartering a train to transport the families to cotton mills in the South to find employment and make their homes in a climate less severe than winter in Colorado.

On January 21, 1904, the cotton mills went into bankruptcy. In March, John McGowan, an heir of the J. L. Jerome estate, which controlled the Overland Cotton Mill, expressed hope for reopening the mills. "There is an investment there representing $800,000, and of course that will not long remain idle. We are now working some men at the mills and finishing up the product that was left unfinished when the mills shut down." Twenty carloads of manufactured cotton goods were bought at auction by a St. Louis firm and shipped from Denver with hopes of finding more eastern buyers.[22] But the eastern market failed to materialize, and the optimism expressed by McGowan dissolved when Judge Hallett ordered the sale of the Overland Cotton Mill in April to satisfy creditors' demands.

The building's function from 1904 to 1920 is uncertain, but the 61,400-square-foot, Neo-Romanesque building may have been used for some type of manufacturing. In 1920, the Pittsburgh Radium Company bought the plant for radium processing. During the 1920s, the Ku Klux Klan met in the office wing of the old cotton mill. The Klan probably chose the site for its proximity to Ruby Hill, where Klansmen were known to gather and burn crosses on the hillside.

In 1930, James Maitland, a Denver businessman, purchased the building to manufacture ammunition that would be used against German tanks during World

War II. Named Mariposa Works, the munitions factory was so crucial to war production efforts that it was immediately repaired and restored to operational status after a half-million-dollar fire occurred in 1942. More damage resulted from the South Platte River flood in 1965. The plant was later designated as an Environmental Protection Agency Superfund project, and cleanup started in 1979.[23]

During the mid-1990s, Norsaire Systems Inc., a maker of swamp coolers, sold the building to Hercules Industries Inc. for $650,000. Norsaire remained as tenant of the building at 1314 West Evans Avenue, which was located next to the main building of Hercules, a sheet-metal manufacturing plant. Hercules owners Paul, Bill Jr., and Jim Newland applied for designation as a historic site and received approval in 2001 for listing on the National Register of Historic Places.[24] Although related to the Overland neighborhood, the building actually sits within the current boundaries of the South Platte neighborhood.

The Overland Golf Course

While some residents struggled to eke out a living in the early 1900s, wealthier citizens pursued interests such as horseracing and golfing and, later, flying and motorcycling at Overland Park near South Santa Fe Drive and West Jewell Avenue. Adjacent to the 1858 Montana City mining camp, the land was settled the next year by potato farmer Rufus Clark, who built a small cabin near the river and claimed 160 acres for his farm. In 1882, Clark deeded 70 acres to real estate promoters, who built a horseracing track and grandstands. The track was named Jewell Park after Charles A. Jewell, one of the investors and a former governor of Connecticut. Because of financial struggles, the park changed ownership in 1887. The new owner, Overland Racing Association, renamed it Overland due to its distance from Denver (a distance considered significant at the time).

In 1896, businessman Henry Wolcott plotted a nine-hole golf course around the 1-mile horseracing track. With its track, grandstand, and numerous arbors, Overland Park attracted fun-lovers who traveled on the Circle Railroad from Larimer Street, a half-hour journey to the "picturesque oasis," or by horse-drawn carriage along the old county road (Santa Fe Drive) that ran beside the South Platte River. Shaded by tall cottonwood trees, an elegant clubhouse provided dining and dancing for Denver socialites. The city's first country club attracted 300 members and had a long waiting list. The well-equipped club offered tennis and bowling as well as horseracing and golf. A sturdy new grandstand featuring 20 private boxes replaced the old one in 1901.[25]

In 1902, Wolcott moved his golf club to 1st Avenue and University Boulevard, the beginning of Denver Country Club, and left the luxurious Overland clubhouse as a residence for jockeys. The building served as a boardinghouse for cotton mill workers before it burned down in January 1903. When Denver outlawed horseracing in 1908, the stables sheltered horses for the First Colorado Cavalry Regiment, which trained at Overland during World War I. A fire destroyed the stables in 1934.[26]

As automobiles gained popularity in the early 1900s, Overland Park saw men racing on the track at speeds of up to 35 miles an hour. In 1904, Dusty Daredevil reached a speed of a mile a minute on an unbanked track, a record-breaking feat at the time.

A crowd of 110,000 paid to attend the 1909 weeklong fair and exposition at Overland Park. Many expected to watch Ivy Baldwin perform stunts with his hot-air balloon, but his gas generator failed on the first day. The next day the balloon filled until it burst, disappointing onlookers. The following year spectators witnessed a historic flight, the first in Colorado, when French aviator Louis Paulhan assembled his yellow Farman biplane at Overland Park and took off toward Ruby Hill. Again, in November 1910, a three-day show featured three American barnstormers flying Wright biplanes. One stayed in the air for 20 minutes on the first day. On the second day, however, a plane's wing collapsed while its aviator was making two spiral turns over the park; he crashed on South Delaware Street and died.[27]

One thousand members of the American Federation of Motorcyclists raced on Overland's 1-mile dirt track in 1913, vying for professional and amateur honors.

Constructed in 1896, Overland was Denver's first country club. Golfers enjoyed Overland's nine-hole course out in the country near West Jewell Avenue and South Santa Fe Drive.

In addition, Colorado's National Guard trained at Overland Park in 1917. The park was renamed Camp Baldwin for the duration of the war, to honor balloonist Baldwin, who flew on several missions during World War I. After the war, the City and County of Denver bought the 160-acre tract, Rufus Clark's old homestead, and changed the name back to Overland Park.

A popular motor camp for tourists before the advent of motels, Overland Park provided a three-story clubhouse built in 1927 with a ballroom, restaurant, bathrooms, barbershop, grocery store, and laundry—all free of charge for tenters. The main entrance was on South Santa Fe Drive at West Colorado Avenue. The motor camp closed in the early 1930s and the city plowed up the racetrack to make way for a nine-hole golf course.[28]

Golfers once again strolled across the land when the new golf course opened in 1932. The popular public course expanded to 18 holes in 1957. It closed temporarily after the flood on June 16, 1965, and reopened the following June. To celebrate its 100-year history, the city tore down the tile-roofed, stucco clubhouse in 1995 and replaced it with a state-of-the-art facility containing a 16-seat bar, a restaurant seating 125, and a banquet room for 40, plus a patio overlooking the first hole and putting green. Improvements also included restrooms and a snack bar with access from the outside, a new maintenance building, and hole changes that added 122 yards to the course.[29]

Overland Neighborhood Homes and Businesses

Overland saw its first settlers in 1858, when the Lawrence Party panned the South Platte River for gold and laid out Montana City, the area's first platted township, on the river's east bank just south of West Evans Avenue. Settlers soon tore down their cabins and moved closer to the fledgling towns of Auraria and Denver City, which were competing for supremacy. Men floated logs down the river or moved them by mule and oxen to rebuild closer to the active trade centers. Only a few logs remained from the "string of shanties" along the east bank of the Platte River by the summer of 1859.[30]

In about 1860, Rufus "Potato" Clark spearheaded local agricultural efforts, homesteading the floodplain across from Ruby Hill to cultivate potatoes and other vegetables to feed prospectors and the growing towns at the Cherry Creek–South Platte River confluence.

Manufacturing came to Overland as railroads followed the river south and provided a way to bring goods to market. Trolleys also traveled south from Denver down Broadway, turning west at West Jewell Avenue to bring visitors to the popular Overland Park for which the neighborhood was named. Retail shops and businesses soon dotted South Broadway and South Santa Fe Drive and filled in during Denver's growth spurts—the gold and silver booms of the late 1800s, post-war building in the 1920s and 1950s, and Cold War defense development.

The S.W. Shattuck Chemical Company built a state-of-the-art facility at 1805 South Bannock Street and processed chemicals, including radium, from 1918 to 1969. In the 1960s, the Martin Marietta ICBM boom sprouted residence motels such as Titan Manor along South Santa Fe Drive. As traffic increased, Santa Fe Drive was widened to expressway dimensions, wiping out adjacent businesses and cutting Overland in two. With major traffic arteries and the opening of the light rail in the 1990s, the neighborhood struggled as a place to live, work, and play while thousands of vehicles streamed through daily. Diverse residences included scattered Victorian houses and the more common modest bungalows and wartime factory homes.

The Shattuck Cleanup

In the 1980s, Deborah Spaar Sanchez and her husband, Mike, a house designer and builder, looked for a lot with solar access next to green space for their home. They selected one on West Jewell Avenue, near the South Platte River, and built their passive solar home in 1984. "With the river, Overland Golf Course, and Ruby Hill, this was the second largest green space in Denver, next to City Park. We liked the wildlife along the river, especially the birds," Deborah said.[31]

Then they learned that the Shattuck Chemical Company site near their home was contaminated and had been placed on the National Priority List in the mid-1980s as a Superfund location earmarked for cleanup. The 5.9-acre site was part of the larger 6.9-acre Shattuck Redevelopment Area bounded by West Iowa Avenue, South Broadway, West Evans Avenue, and South Santa Fe Drive in the heart of the Overland neighborhood. The Environmental Protection Agency (EPA) encapsulated hazardous materials on the site and capped it in 1996–1998, covering it with a 14-foot mound of riprap (large rocks). Residents called it the Monolith.[32]

Concerned about piles of contaminated tailing from radium processing at the Shattuck site, Deborah helped spearhead a grassroots campaign to remove the contaminated materials. Deborah's roots in southwest Denver ran deep, from her pioneer grandfather's blacksmith shop on the west side to her alma mater, Abraham Lincoln High School, in Harvey Park. She thought briefly about moving but decided to stay and defend her community. "This was my home, where my life was. Why should I have to go?" she reasoned.

During 1999, she and Helene Orr spoke for many Overland neighbors who attended numerous special EPA hearings held in the neighborhood. In September

2000, at the request of Colorado Senator Wayne Allard, Deborah testified at congressional hearings in Washington, D.C. After pressure from community residents, Senator Allard, Congresswoman Diana DeGette, Governor Bill Owens, and Denver Mayor Wellington Webb, the EPA decided to clean up the site to allow for unrestricted use, which entailed removal of the Shattuck Monolith and related soils to a disposal facility out of state.

A cooperative visioning process began in December 2001 to define future land use for the Shattuck site. Input from community residents, various city agencies, and several consultants was combined to form a 20-year plan for redevelopment. In November 2006, residents and city officials celebrated completion of the Shattuck site cleanup.

The South Platte Waterway

Grant-Frontier Park marked the site of Montana City, the short-lived town founded in 1858. During Denver's centennial celebration in 1959, historian and physician Dr. Nolan Mumey built a log cabin on the Montana City site using logs retrieved previously from a dilapidated 1858 cabin and added a mining display to create Pioneer Park at West Evans Avenue by the South Platte River. The fenced park fell into disrepair after a 1960 bond issue failed to raise funds for improvements. Then, for Earth Day in 1970, Grant Junior High School science teachers Alan Wuth and Carl Crookham, along with Geoffrey Muntz and a small ecological club, began restoration activities as one of their permanent projects. They cleaned, repaired, and landscaped the neglected park and called it Frontier Park. With the approaching 1976 Colorado centennial, teachers obtained funds to beautify the park and students pitched in to clean up the grounds and chink logs on the cabin. The park was renamed Grant-Frontier Park in honor of the restoration work by Grant Junior High students and teachers. For several years, children from Denver Public Schools participated in outdoor classes and learned about history, water chemistry, gold panning, and conservation at the park.[33]

Other groups concerned about indiscriminate dumping and disgraceful misuse of the South Platte River began to formulate plans for revitalization of the Platte corridor in the Denver area in the 1970s. Trout Unlimited, the Colorado Open Space Council, and the League of Women Voters pushed for cleanup of the waterway and presented a proposal for protection of the floodplain and open spaces throughout the metro area. Memories of the 1965 flood lingered as Denver Mayor William H. McNichols formed the Platte River Development Committee and named State Senator Joe Shoemaker to head it.[34]

With $13 million in federal money, private contributions, and foundation grants, the Platte River Greenway began to realize its potential as parks, pedestrian bridges, paths, and picnic spots appeared along the river. Signs informed bicyclists and hikers about landmarks and the history of the area. Beginning at Confluence Park where Cherry Creek joins the South Platte River, development created recreational opportunities for rafters and kayakers and an informal amphitheater for outdoor entertainment. Dedicated in September 1975, Confluence Park provided a focal point for core city redevelopment.

Stretching south, other parks along the 10.5-mile Platte River Greenway include:

- Weir Gulch Marina and Park, north of West 8th Avenue
- Frog Hollow Park, south of West 8th Avenue
- Front Range and Barnum Park viewing point, near the 3rd Avenue bridge
- Valverde Park, north of West Alameda Avenue
- Habitat Park, north of West Exposition Avenue
- Vanderbilt Park, south of West Exposition Avenue
- Overland Ponds, north of West Florida Avenue
- Ruby Hill Park, south of West Florida Avenue
- Overland Park Municipal Golf Course, south of West Florida Avenue
- Pasquinel's Landing, north of West Evans Avenue
- Grant-Frontier Park, south of West Evans Avenue[35]

The greenway flourished as fish and other wildlife returned to the waterway, while roller skaters, bicyclists, and joggers found it a refuge from heavy motor traffic. To ensure continued maintenance, Shoemaker oversaw transformation of the Platte River Development Committee into the Platte River Greenway Foundation in 1976.

As the neighborhood improved, nature began moving back into Overland's Platte River Greenway and parks. Jack Unruh and his wife Eloise May live in a home that backs up to Grant-Frontier Park and the river. They said they often see coyotes, foxes, raccoons, beavers, turtles, trout, huge carp and smaller fish, diving ducks, great blue herons, great horned owls, and even bald eagles visiting the habitat.[36]

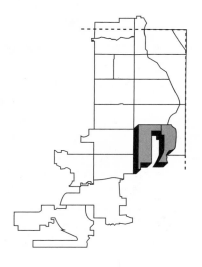

CHAPTER ELEVEN

South Platte and College View

This part agricultural/part industrial area of Denver is marked by two long-standing businesses that flourish today—Dardano's Flowerland and Robinson Brick and Tile Company (Robco). The South Platte neighborhood, annexed by Denver in 1956, is bounded by West Jewell Avenue on the north, the South Platte River on the east, West Dartmouth Avenue on the south, and South Pecos Street on the west. College View was annexed by Denver in 1962, with the boundaries of South Federal Boulevard, West Jewell Avenue, South Pecos Street, West Evans Avenue, South Zuni Street, and West Dartmouth Avenue. In both neighborhoods, community ministries and churches have been active in bringing about improvements in services and infrastructure, with Sisters and students from nearby Loretto Heights College leading the way.

Dardano's Flowerland

The son of Italian parents who immigrated to Denver in the late 1800s, Frank Dardano served in World War II and returned home to marry his longtime sweetheart, Arlene Garramone. She was the daughter of former bedding plant grower Mike Garramone, the first farmer to grow bedding plants in Denver. Frank and Arlene Dardano started truck farming in the rich soil near their home in 1946.

The young couple grew tomatoes, peppers, celery, and other vegetables on their land near West Evans Avenue and the South Platte River and sold their produce at the farmers' market. Each year they sold a greater variety of vegetables. Then Arlene began selling a few bedding plants to passersby. Soon they were selling dozens of pansies and petunias in homemade wooden boxes. The hardworking couple purchased 2 acres across the street from their farm and built a 30,000-square-foot greenhouse and 100-space parking lot.

Dardano's Flowerland, dubbed Colorado's first Supermarket Garden Center, opened April 25, 1965, with cars lined up on West Evans Avenue waiting for a parking place. Two months later, on June 16, 1965, a 12-foot wall of water swept down the South Platte River and destroyed their uninsured business, including the flowerland and greenhouses across the street. With borrowed money, they reopened the following spring. Eventually adding a 10,000-square-foot extension and a full-service flower shop, they expanded to include award-winning carnations, leaf lettuce for restaurants, and holiday poinsettias.

Loretta Dardano with her parents, Frank and Arlene Dardano, in their new store, which reopened in May 1966. The flood of 1965 destroyed their first store just two months after its original opening.

Innovators in their field, the Dardanos were the first to advertise bedding plants on billboards and the first to sponsor TV gardening shows featuring local gardeners (Matt Matteyka and Herb Gundell). At one time, they sold bedding plants from three locations and operated Dardano's Fruitland with produce from Palisade, Colorado. Frank developed a rose named Arlene Dardano to honor his wife, and in 1980 he received the Grower of the Year award from the Colorado Bedding and Pot Plant Association. Named to the Floriculture Hall of Fame, he created the Children's Miracle Rose in 1987 with Denver Children's Hospital, the Marie Osmond Foundation, and Channel 4.

Because of Frank's failing health, the Dardanos moved to Arizona in 1984. Daughter Loretta and son Frank Jr. continued to run the business with the help of their longtime employees, Herman Arellano and Richard Barnes. They remodeled the entire greenhouse in 1992, and in 1993 they arranged flowers in the chapel at Camp St. Malo for Pope John Paul II's World Youth Day celebration.

Frank died in 1996, the year the business celebrated its 50th anniversary at the same neighborhood location. After Frank's death, Arlene returned to Denver to be involved with the business once again.

Loretta said the business has changed over the years due to various factors, such as competition and rising heating bills for the greenhouses. "However, our customers can still find the city's largest selection of bedding plants and the best value for their money. And we're doing something we absolutely love— putting our hands in the soil, seeing seeds grow, and watching satisfied customers return each spring."[1]

An Area of Contrasts

In the 1950s, a shantytown existed in Arapahoe County near the Ruby Hill dump site. Scores of children played in trash and debris scattered around the tar-paper shacks and outhouses. While some homes were neat and equipped with purified city water, many others lacked city water or even wellwater. The area west of the South Platte River between West Jewell Avenue and West Evans Avenue contained dried-up, weed-covered ditches, unpaved streets, dirt sidewalks, uncovered garbage cans, and piles of weather-beaten lumber. Junk cars and car parts littered yards, few houses featured indoor plumbing, and fire danger lurked constantly.[2]

The Arapahoe County building inspector at the time, Martin T. Goodman, claimed that zoning was in place and the whole area was under building restrictions and a building code. "We condemn some of those places almost daily," he said. "City water is being piped in now and I've heard rumors of a new sub-division. The area is in a period of transition…. It will be straightened out in time."[3]

In contrast, the new Gunnison Heights subdivision, built by Burns Construction Company north of Jewell Avenue, boasted of sturdy, attractive homes with neat, grass-covered yards for children to play in.

Robinson Brick Company

One of the thriving industries near the South Platte River began as a brick yard on the prairie east of Denver. George W. Robinson, a Civil War veteran with only an eighth grade education, arrived in Denver in 1880 after working on railroad construction in Wyoming. He used his team of horses to scrape clay from the pit and to turn the mixing mills in which the clay was mixed with water. Then he threw wet clay into wooden molds, dumped them upside down on the ground, removed the molds, allowed the bricks to dry in the sun, and fired them in wood-fueled kilns. The process took about 30 days and limited pro-duction to two million bricks during the six warm months of the year.

In 1893, George's son, William B. Robinson, joined the business, which was known in the early days as Colfax Pressed Brick Company. He converted the operation to steam power and added new machines that allowed production to continue during the winter months. William's sons, William W. and F. George, joined the company in 1927 and improved quality, making bricks for many of the city's beautification projects and residential areas. The company operated from several sites until the city's growth prompted them to look southwest for more space.[4]

Brickmaking evolved from these crude procedures of the late 1800s to more sophisticated methods.

The Robinson brothers acquired land at 500 South Santa Fe Drive in 1941 and built a new plant to replace the one on West 17th

A truck used to transport bricks at Robinson Brick Co. in the 1920s.

Avenue and Clay Street, the present site of the parking lot for Invesco Field. The new plant contained one of the West's first tunnel kilns. During World War II, the plant produced pressed brick for the Rocky Mountain Arsenal and other defense uses. But after nine months, it shut down for the remainder of the war. At the request of the War Production Board, the plant started up again in January 1945 with labor from a Japanese internment camp.

Other memorable events occurred in 1945 as the owners dismantled the original South and East Brick Yards and changed the company's name to Robinson Brick and Tile Company, nicknamed Robco. William B. Robinson died in 1947. His sons continued to run the company—with F. George handling the administrative, accounting, and record-keeping duties, while William W. concentrated on sales. The plant began producing glazed brick in 1948. The new line comprised 65 percent of the company's sales by 1956. In 1968, Robco provided glazed tile for construction of the Eisenhower Tunnel at the Continental Divide.

The company's Plant 2 was constructed at South Platte River Drive and West Dartmouth Avenue in 1962. Three years later, the 1965 flood deposited about 3 feet of mud, trash, dead livestock, and even a four-room frame house at the site. After six weeks of cleanup efforts, the plant was operating again. Losses amounted to more than $1 million. "We built an earthen dike on our south boundary and arranged brick piles and sandbags on the east to protect us until the Chatfield and Mt. Carbon Dams were completed," F. George Robinson stated. Plant 1 was spared from flood damage.[5]

During the energy crisis of the 1970s, the company incorporated fuel conservation methods and reduced its rate of operation, discontinuing production of glazed tile and converting the facility to brick production. At the end of the decade, Robco completed a second kiln and dryer, raising potential production capacity from 35 million to 70 million bricks per year. William W. Robinson died early in 1983. The company announced a planned shutdown of Plant 1, which took place in September 1984. After adding a new brick-making machine to Plant 2, capacity increased to more than 100 million bricks per year. In 1985, Robco operated nine open-pit mines, produced 18 mined clays, and employed 167 workers. Five years later, it produced its one billionth brick.

F. George Robinson Jr., of the fourth generation, worked for the company during his college years and took a full-time position upon receiving his M.B.A. in May 1978. He purchased the company from his father and other family members in 1990. His company installed the country's first robotic setting machine in 1997 and developed a new Thinbrick operation the same year. Robco became the first brick manufacturer in North America to achieve the industry's highest quality standard. Robert G. Jaster joined the company in 1995 as vice president of manufacturing; he became president in 2000 and was promoted to CEO in 2003. The elder F. George Robinson, who served as chairman of the board, died in 2006 at the age of 95. The company, which celebrated its 125th anniversary in 2005, has nine masonry and design centers across the Front Range, retail stores in four states, and 500 employees nationwide.[6]

The College View Neighborhood

Located in unincorporated Arapahoe County, the College View area was platted in half-acre plots in 1897, with plenty of wells and water rights to irrigate the family gardens. Most families raised produce, mainly for their own family's use, but also to sell. Because of the goats in many of the hilltop farmyards, the College View area was often referred to as Goat Hill. While suburban housing developed rapidly to the west following World War II, College View remained a rural community.[7]

College View was annexed to Denver in 1962, with the boundaries of South Federal Boulevard, West Jewell Avenue, South Pecos Street, West Evans Avenue, South Zuni Street, and West Dartmouth Avenue. Residents of Scenic View, a small rural community located between the South Platte neighborhood and the College View neighborhood, were forced out by industrial development, and the area was annexed to Englewood.

After annexation ceased in the 1970s, builders looked to College View for lots to construct single-family residences, duplexes, and other small, multifamily units, creating a varied community of old and new homes. A strip along West Harvard Gulch was improved to provide a park with a pedestrian/bicycle path.

> *A College View Family*
> There were only scattered houses in 1953 when Charles and Mary Wilderson bought their home on West Harvard Avenue and moved from an apartment in Golden. A graduate of Kansas University, Charles worked as a mechanical engineer for the Bureau of Reclamation at the Denver Federal Center. Mary stayed home to care for their sons, Warren and Karl.
>
> "Our house was the first house on the block when it was built in 1941 by a man named Bohn. He sold it to Redeemer Lutheran Church as a parsonage for their minister. We traded an acre of ground for the house and half-acre lot," Mary said. "Houses in the area tended to be very small, almost shacks; but the yards were large. The people next door grew a tremendous garden and fruit trees

on a full acre. They also had a cow. Quite a few neighbors raised chickens and goats. I liked our big yard and I gardened extensively. I used to be called the 'Tulip Lady' because I planted tulips all around my corner yard.

"College View was considered a low-income neighborhood and made the list as a high-crime area, but I can't imagine that," Mary said. "We didn't have anything stolen and weren't concerned about safety. We trusted our neighbors. They were like family. Our kids had an 'Auntie Lundeen,' 'Grandma Pratt,' and 'Grandma Hatch,' who sat with them occasionally. Their real grandparents lived in Kansas and Oklahoma and saw them mainly at Thanksgiving and Christmas.

"The community contained a mixture of residents—some were wonderful people and some were scoundrels, but we never had any trouble. Ninety percent were homeowners when we moved in. Since the houses were spread out, I got acquainted with neighbors at College View School, where children attended from kindergarten through eighth grade. For high school they went to Sheridan Union High School, which had a board of directors for the area.

"A lot of controversy arose over the question of annexation in the early 1960s. I was in favor of annexation; however, many were opposed, especially people on the school board who would lose their influence when the area became part of Denver. After annexation in 1962, my older son attended Kunsmiller Junior High and graduated from Abraham Lincoln High School. I attended meetings at those schools and parents there did not want their children to associate with the 'scum from College View.'

"Many improvements changed the rural neighborhood because of annexation. When Burns Brentwood was developed in the 1950s, Denver secured permission to run sewer and water lines down Harvard Avenue. Residents along Harvard were allowed to hook on to Denver sewer and water if they desired. Our house was connected to sewer and water at that time, but there were still many septic tanks in the community. As part of urban renewal, sewer and water lines were completed to serve all of the area.

"The neighbor across the street had a small, inadequate house without even a septic tank. The city purchased the back half of their lot. In return for the land, Denver built a nice three-bedroom home for the family, complete with sewer, water, gas, and electricity.

Many homes didn't meet city code because they were structurally unfit, wired improperly, and lacked plumbing. People who had animals before annexation were allowed to keep them under a grandfather clause, and I still hear a rooster crow in the mornings," explained Mary, who has seen grown children move back to their childhood home after their parents died.

Mary said her life revolved around Scouts and church while her children were growing up. A charter member of Christ Congregational Church, she served as moderator, vice moderator, clerk, board chair, and Sunday school teacher. The church owned a house at the corner of West Harvard Avenue and South Zurich Street. The congregation held worship in the basement, and Sunday school classes met in the bedrooms. Charles Wilderson taught the junior high class in a building north of West Harvard Avenue. After meeting in Doull School for a year, the church built a fellowship hall and education wing in the late 1950s at 2500 South Sheridan Boulevard and added a sanctuary in the mid-1960s. Mary was also active in Church Women United and received the Church Woman of the Year award.

The Wilderson sons played on Cub Scout softball teams and earned badges in Boy Scouts. Active in Boy Scout Troop 364, Karl attained the highest rank, Eagle Scout, in 1980. Both graduated from Lincoln High School—Warren in 1968 and Karl in 1980.[8]

College View Ministry

In the mid-1960s, people at Brentwood Methodist Church on West Jewell Avenue began a study on affluence and poverty. The study revealed a poverty pocket south of West Jewell Avenue between South Federal Boulevard and the South Platte River, which included the nearby communities of College View, Scenic View, and Sheridan. By talking with residents, the church learned of the need for a convenient place to purchase low-priced clothing and household items.

Following up with considerable planning and effort, ladies from Brentwood Methodist Church opened the Community Thrift Shop on September 7, 1966, at 2420 West Evans Avenue. The organizers included Sue Albers, Vera Bruns, Marie Malone, and Eleanor Lutes. Several other churches in southwest Denver participated in the effort by donating clothing and household items to be sold and by providing volunteers to staff the store. With help from Christ the King Lutheran, Harvey Park Baptist, Harvey Park Christian, Glenn Randall Phillips Methodist, All Saints Catholic, St. Philip and St. James Episcopal, Christ Congregational, and St. Andrew Presbyterian churches, the venture proved so successful that a part-time manager was hired for a small salary the next spring.[9]

Seeing further needs in the area, ministers from southwest Denver churches formed a group called College View Ministry and hired Nancy Wolfe, a full-time social worker, as director. The Reverend Al Ossentjuct of St. Andrew Presbyterian Church was elected chairman of the board.

The Community Ministry of Southwest Denver started in the College View neighborhood in 1966 with a neighborhood thrift shop located on West Evans Avenue.

The ministry offered direct services, including emergency food, clothing, tutorial help, and summer programs. The Community Thrift Shop contributed funds to College View Ministry but remained a separate entity with its own steering committee.

About the same time that Protestants at Brentwood learned about poverty in the College View area, Sister Jean Patrice Golden recruited nuns and students from Loretto Heights College for a door-to-door survey to identify the needs of their neighbors east of Federal Boulevard. Established in 1891 as a private country school for Catholic girls, Loretto Heights College, at 3001 South Federal Boulevard, provided the inspiration for College View's name as settlers saw the college's 100-foot tower from their nearby community.[10]

Convinced that young women attending Loretto Heights should become involved in the socioeconomic problems encountered by those without a high school or college education, Sister Patrice mapped out a plan in the mid-1960s for Loretto coeds and alumnae to become College View's link with middle-class society. Although some College View residents were considered middle-class, many lacked education and vocational skills.

According to a 1965 survey, the majority of the 266 College View families were of Anglo descent and had moved to the area from the Ozarks during World War II, 10 percent of families had Spanish surnames, and 1 percent were black. Seventy percent were homeowners. For the most part, it was a community that distrusted outsiders—in fact, the community pooled its meager funds to fight annexation by Denver. The 1,244 people who lived there seldom crossed Federal Boulevard because a different class of society lived "over there."[11]

Little by little, Loretto students and alumnae broke through the class barrier as they tutored junior high youths, conducted religious education classes in homes, and helped adults who wanted a General Education Diploma (GED). After getting acquainted with residents, Sister Jean Patrice, Sister Simone Inkel, and four students—Denise Bergen, Nancy Camara, Peggy Mayhew, and Sarita Schneebeck—moved into the neighborhood in January 1967. They lived in a newly painted and repaired white frame duplex at the corner of South Zuni Street and West Iliff Avenue. One side provided living quarters with donated furniture while the other half served as a community center with a large sign proclaiming it as College View Neighborhood House. Living on a monthly income comparable to their neighbors', they initiated two new programs: tutoring for grade-school children and a sewing class for adult women.

The majority of College View residents, who were Protestant, joined the efforts of College View Ministry. They worked extensively with Wolfe, who set up her office at the Neighborhood House. Through the cooperative interfaith ministry and profits from the thrift shop, area children participated in free swimming lessons at Loretto Heights' pool, attended summer camp, played baseball, received eyeglasses and new shoes, and enjoyed a Christmas party. Although skeptical at first, adults took infants to the baby clinic, signed up for sewing lessons, and took basic education classes. Families in need also received assistance through the emergency funds set up at College View and Scenic View schools. At the time, Loretto Heights students also learned that some of the crime in the neighborhood was shoplifting by children who wanted to have what their more affluent peers possessed.[12]

The Southwest Community Center stepped in to provide leadership and direction during a period of transition after Wolfe resigned as director of College View Ministry. John Fletcher was hired as director in August 1970, and in August 1971 the organization changed its name to Community Ministry of Southwest Denver as a symbol of change from the "do-good" concept to a "we-together" emphasis. Continuing as a private organization, the ministry adopted the dual goals of providing direct services and assisting with community development from its headquarters at the Southwest Denver Community Center, 1000 South Lowell Boulevard.[13]

In August 1971, about 4,000 people came out for the Southwest Denver Community Fair, designed to open new lines of communication through fun activities and information booths from various organizations serving the area. Interagency work revolved around housing, health concerns, and youth activities, including the "crash pad" known as Glasier House.[14]

During the early 1980s, with Steve Salter as director and the Reverend Sam

Bates of Harvey Park Baptist Church as board chairman, Community Ministry supported a drive for equitable housing for citizens along South Santa Fe Drive who faced relocation due to widening of the highway. Backed by a coalition of 19 churches, Community Ministry moved its office and service center to various locations along South Federal Boulevard.[15]

Community Ministry struggled in the early 1990s. In May 1993, the ministry canceled its lease at 2430 South Federal Boulevard, terminated the paid staff, closed the food and clothing bank, and moved the office to Brentwood United Methodist Church at 1899 South Irving Street. The ministry's executive committee hired Rita Basham to manage a study on the future direction of Community Ministry. Meanwhile, on August 2, 1993, the food bank reopened (staffed by volunteers) at St. Andrew Presbyterian Church, 3096 South Sheridan Boulevard.[16]

A revitalized ministry hired Christy Ziemba as executive director in August 2000. She worked from an office at Christ Congregational Church, 2500 South Sheridan Boulevard, until the opportunity arose to consolidate Community Ministry's services in one location. With a commitment to community outreach, Garden Park Church members offered the ministry facilities for an office, food bank, and other programs. The Garden Park congregation remodeled their gymnasium at 1744 South Zuni Street and welcomed Community Ministry to its new premises in 2001.[17]

The Model Cities Program

College View was designated as a federal Model Cities Target Area in 1968 and was earmarked for the Denver Urban Renewal Neighborhood Development Program (NDP) in 1969. Prior to federal funding, Denver established an improvement district to install sanitary sewer mains at a cost of $756,000. In June 1970, Denver Urban Renewal Authority (DURA) began the NDP by extending water mains, sanitary sewers, drainage, and street design.[18]

Following requests from College View residents and from DURA, a neighborhood planner met with the College View Project Area Committee, members of the College View Civic Association, and other concerned persons from June through October 1971. Some residents voiced strong desire to maintain the status quo, while others with equally strong convictions wanted changes to improve living conditions in their community.

The planning office wanted to transform West Jewell Avenue and West Evans Avenue into one-way streets from South Federal Boulevard to the city limits on the west. A second proposal was to change West Yale Avenue to a six-lane arterial street from the South Platte River to South Wadsworth Boulevard to speed up traffic from southern Jefferson County to downtown Denver. Residents stridently opposed these two proposals, so when the planning office finally approved the Comprehensive Plan for College View on February 16, 1972, the street changes for Jewell, Evans, and Yale Avenues were omitted.

The plan described the neighborhood as 98 percent white, which included an estimated 600 Spanish-surnamed individuals. Seniors over 62 years totaled 10.5 percent of residents. Single-family dwellings numbered 702, a decrease from 877 in 1960 due to the demolition of substandard housing. Multifamily units increased during the 1960s from 8 percent to 11.3 percent. The planning office recommended 16 amendments to the Comprehensive Plan, including expansion of College View Elementary School, and construction of a new community center in the vicinity of West Harvard Avenue and South Decatur Street. Suggestions were listed for improving current street patterns and for constructing new streets to provide access to back lots for potential redevelopment.[19]

College View Elementary School

Works Progress Administration (WPA) workers built College View Elementary School at 2680 South Decatur Street in 1939. The school, part of Fort Logan District 13, added more rooms in 1944 and 1949. Students trudged up or down stairs to classrooms on different levels, ate lunch in the basement cafeteria, and darted across the street for recess on the playground.

After annexation by Denver in 1962, the school came under the auspices of the Denver Public Schools district. Although the Denver Planning Office recommended a new school for the area, the new facility was not constructed until 1995. A modern $3.6 million building houses classrooms on one level, making it handicap accessible. The 48,723-square-foot building features air conditioning, telephones and cable TV in every room, a large library, and larger administrative office space. In addition, the adjacent playground provides safer access. The school has a capacity for 440 students from kindergarten through fifth grade, plus a pre-kindergarten class. Because of neighborhood needs, it offers full-day kindergarten classes.[20]

College View Recreation Center

College View Recreation Center, at the corner of South Decatur Street and West Harvard Avenue, was planned according to accessibility by public transportation and location near a park and a school. The center was built in the mid-1970s with money from the Model Cities program, a federal program that supplied half the funding, matched with an equal amount from city and state agencies.

The center opened in January 1976 with a gymnasium, craft room, senior citizens' room, and lounge area to watch TV and play games. Besides youth sports and crafts, the center offered many programs for seniors, including monthly potlucks, day trips, billiards, and bingo.

Gil Gallegos, recreation director for 19 years, said College View was the first Denver recreation center designed with the entire neighborhood in mind. A former three-sport athlete at Manual High School, Gallegos planned, coached, and refereed basketball games, organized youth soccer and baseball teams, and set up excursions to give kids new experiences. "We kept kids off the street and turned out some good ball players," he said.[21]

A wing for seniors was added in 1983 with space for dancing, ceramics, card games, exercise, yoga, and holiday dinners. When Kunsmiller Community School was phased out in the 1980s, College View Recreation Center incorporated the "50 and Better" program into its senior activities. Although youth attendance has dropped off in recent years, the senior program has remained strong.

Gil Gallegos (left) coached girls' and boys' basketball at College View Recreation Center. This girls' team won the league championship in 1982–1983.

CHAPTER TWELVE

Harvey Park

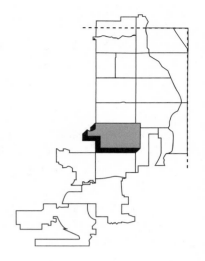

The Harvey Park neighborhood, designated by the Denver Planning Office in the early 1970s, actually consists of two subdivisions: Harvey Park, west of South Lowell Boulevard, and Burns Brentwood, to the east. The neighborhood extends from West Jewell Avenue to West Yale Avenue between South Federal Boulevard and South Sheridan Boulevard. It also includes the Sheridan Plaza, South Target Village, apartments, and houses south of West Jewell Avenue between South Sheridan Boulevard and South Harlan Street. Veterans moved into the area in the 1950s when it was new, and some original homeowners still live there along with younger Hispanic families. The neighborhood features a nice park, a recreation center, lakes, and churches, among other amenities.

Whiteman's Black and White Ranch

Much of the land that makes up Harvey Park was originally a ranch with interesting origins. Paul Whiteman, famous musician and orchestra leader, bought 160 acres of rich, rolling land on South Sheridan Boulevard, 8 miles from the heart of Denver, for his parents' retirement home in the early 1920s.

Paul's father, Wilberforce, became the music instructor for West Side High School in 1890 and went on to serve as music director of Denver Public Schools. Affectionately called The Professor, Wilberforce founded the first citywide sixth-grade choral group in the early 1900s as a benefit concert to buy shoes for needy children. He trained 100,000 student voices during his 34-year career. He also taught private pupils and directed choirs for South Broadway Christian Church, Trinity Methodist Church, and First Baptist Church.[1]

Paul's mother, Elfrida, was a well-known Denver contralto who sang in the church choirs directed by her husband. Paul's sister, Ferne, gained recognition as a musician in her own right. Ferne played operatic roles in Denver civic musicals and directed the Women's Glee Club at the University of Denver. With little interest in school, Paul jumped around West, East, North, South, and Manual High Schools and briefly went to the University of Denver. He became an accomplished violinist and left Denver in 1915 to play at the World's Fair in San Francisco.[2]

Paul hired symphony musicians and formed The Paul Whiteman Band, known for its George Gershwin theme song, "Rhapsody in Blue." The band-leader enjoyed a successful career that carried him from CBS radio shows to appearances at New York's Carnegie Hall and Metropolitan Opera House. He helped launch the career of Bing Crosby by giving him a singing job in 1929. At age 32, Paul was one of the most widely known and highest-paid professional musicians in the country. Even though he did not like jazz, Wilberforce eventually acknowledged that his son had done well with his "jazzed up" music.[3]

Margaret and Paul Whiteman celebrate with Wilberforce and Elfrida Whiteman on their golden anniversary.

Because his father was raised on a farm and had ambitions to own a farm one day, Paul developed the Black and White Ranch as the perfect retirement home for his musically gifted parents. Bordered by West Jewell Avenue, South Lowell Boulevard, West Yale Avenue, and South Sheridan Boulevard, the property featured a 13-acre lake at the center.

To reinforce the black-and-white theme, Wilberforce said at his retirement in 1924, "I'm going to raise Dutch belted cattle, the kind with a wide white stripe around their black bodies. Then I'm going to raise chickens that have black necks and tails and white bodies. And I'm going to have a couple of dogs with black spotted bodies." The ranch continued the theme with its Poland-China hogs, Holstein cattle, and Plymouth Rock chickens.[4]

A "jazz" effect was created with shingles on the roof of the two-story Dutch Colonial–style house. Constructed of wire-drawn brick, the home offered modern comforts such as electric lights and a refrigeration plant. A grand piano graced the spacious living room, and a pile of records, many of Paul's making, flanked the Victrola resting on the sunporch where the Whitemans enjoyed a view of the beautiful flower gardens.

After Elfrida's death in 1934, Wilberforce sold the ranch and moved back to Denver, realizing he was more of a musician than a farmer. He opened a voice studio, planned recitals, and arranged for students to audition in Manhattan until his death in 1939.

Paul Whiteman, meanwhile, had a son, Paul Jr., with his first wife, Vanda Hoff. Following their divorce in 1931, he married actress Margaret Livingston at the Whiteman ranch in 1933. They had two children, Margo and Richard.

Nicknamed "Pops," Paul Sr. returned to Denver for concerts at Lakeside Amusement Park in 1942, Red Rocks Amphitheater in 1954, and the dedication of Whiteman Elementary School (named for his late father) in 1956. Whenever he visited Denver, he went by the old farm site and walked the streets of southwest Denver, remembering his parents. The famed "King of Jazz" died in 1967 in New Hope, Pennsylvania, at age 77.[5]

Henri deCompiegne bought the Whiteman ranch in the spring of 1936 for approximately $40,000. The Frenchman converted the Dutch Colonial, 10-room, two-story house to a French-style dwelling of more than 20 rooms and spacious halls. Using the finest materials, deCompiegne expanded his home to more than 5,000 square feet of living area on the main floor. He put in tall double doors that opened to a vestibule adjoining a large entrance hall. The 800-square-foot living room showed off floor-length windows and a fireplace with an antique French marble mantelpiece. The master suite featured a 16-by-20-foot bedroom with fireplace, a dressing room, and six-piece baths installed in three individual rooms. An elevated dining room was served from a butler's pantry with food prepared in the adjacent kitchen. The second floor contained three bedrooms and one and one-half bathrooms. A library, a study, a family room, a large breakfast room, a sewing room, a utility room, two additional bedrooms with attached bathrooms, three more fireplaces, and a powder room completed the elegant home.[6]

Mr. and Mrs. deCompiegne owned the estate for 10 years and then sold it in 1946 to Frederick W. Bonfils, former business manager of the *Denver Post*. Bonfils and his wife lived there for two years, until May 31, 1948.

Arthur Harvey Purchases Former Black and White Ranch

Arthur "Tex" Harvey purchased the magnificent hilltop home along with 320 acres of Arapahoe County from the Bonfils' in 1948, for just over $158,000.

Two years later, Harvey bought an adjoining 160 acres, including most of the Lakeridge subdivision, for $80,000.[7]

Born in 1896, Harvey grew up in Texas on a small farm run by his father, who was also a Methodist minister. He served in both world wars and retired as an army major. Harvey ventured into the oil industry as a small stockholder in an east Texas field and drilled his first productive well in 1939. He formed the Tex-Harvey Oil Company and commuted between Texas and Colorado, tending to enterprises in both states. He raised beef cattle and chickens at his Arapahoe County farm, where he installed an underground irrigation system and built a large grain silo. His closest neighbors included banker Harold Kountze's summer residence on the west side of South Sheridan Boulevard, Dr. Henry Swan's permanent residence known as Roundtop next door, Mar Lee to the north, Brentwood and Loretto Heights College to the east, and Fort Logan Army Post to the south.

The Texas oilman opened Harvey's Food Lockers at 4320 Morrison Road. In 1960, he converted the frozen food lockers to a delicatessen called Harvey's Food Bazaar. Eighteen months later, he changed the business to a do-it-yourself dry cleaning plant with a car wash attached. He obtained two branch cleaners, one at 2165 South Sheridan Boulevard and another in Lakewood. Harvey commuted frequently to his office in Midland, Texas, leaving little time to take part in community affairs. He and his wife, Sylva, lived quietly with their three children and seldom entertained.[8]

With the ranch era fading after World War II and financial difficulties closing in, Harvey decided to sell his farm to developers. He joined Aksel Nielsen of Mortgage Investments Company and planned a new community of 1,662 homes to be called Harvey Park. Harvey kept 2 acres surrounding his large home and sold 318 acres for $30 million. The new owner petitioned Denver for annexation in March 1953.

The Harveys joined Harvey Park Baptist Church at 2112 South Patton Court, one of the first structures built around Harvey Park Lake. The church started in 1956 from a small room and evolved into a sprawling two-level complex. Then, in 1962, with their children grown and married, Tex and Sylva sold their mansion, liquidated their holdings in Denver, and moved to Texas. Harvey died in Corpus Christi at age 79. Funeral services were conducted by Pastor Sam Bates at Harvey Park Baptist Church, followed by burial at Fort Logan National Cemetery. Sylva returned to Denver and lived to be 102. They were survived by three children and 10 grandchildren.[9]

Mr. and Mrs. J. W. (Bill) Allison bought the Harvey estate on South Tennyson Way in 1962. Bill Allison was president of B.F. Allison Drilling Company.

Surrounded by more modest homes, the estate still sits quietly behind the wrought-iron gate and chain-link fence.

Burns' Brentwood Bungalows

Franklin Burns, a Denver native, joined the D.C. Burns Realty Company in 1938 as a salesman. A visionary and trendsetter, Franklin moved up to vice president a year after the death of his uncle Daniel Cochran Burns, company founder. Franklin was 28. At that time, a Burns home sold for $1,250 while the average single-family home in Denver was priced at $3,424.[10]

Daniel Cochran Burns founded his firm in 1899, recognizing the need for low-priced homes for the working class. He built and sold houses at 10 percent down long before financing was available through the Federal Housing Administration (FHA). His first low-cost homes were built in the Barnum Tract and offered an outhouse since they had no indoor plumbing. With sufficient holdings to carry him through the tough times from 1929 to 1934, he survived the Depression years. After the FHA was established in 1935, Burns Construction prospered as one of the first companies to offer FHA loans.

Following D.C.'s death, Franklin carried on the tradition of offering quality homes for the working man. He started a trend when he created Burns Brentwood, one of the first neighborhoods in the "subdivision movement." He bought a 320-acre farm in Arapahoe County from owners M. E. Clayton and Edward Selander and filed for annexation by Denver in March 1946. The land was bounded by South Federal Boulevard, South Lowell Boulevard, West Jewell Avenue, and West Yale Avenue.[11]

Burns put in utility mains and streets and built nearly 300 dream homes for veterans returning from World War II. With modern conveniences such as built-in automatic washing machines, the homes attracted young couples who desired well-constructed homes in a suburban setting. A young soldier himself, Burns conceived the idea for the development while on a weeklong furlough from the army.[12]

Until then, the plan of buying a large farm, installing utilities and streets, and obtaining city annexation had been uncommon. Burns reserved part of the acreage for a shopping center (Brentwood Shopping Center), a new Catholic parish (All Saints Catholic Church), and a Denver high school (Abraham Lincoln High School).

In 1949, Burns Construction completed more than 500 homes in the city of Denver, the most homes ever built in one year by any company in Colorado. Setting a precedent for written homeowner warranties, Burns introduced the

Homeowners Construction Warranty in honor of the company's 50th anniversary. The warranty stated his pledge to stand behind the "Burns Better-Built Bungalows."

After working in Brentwood from 1946 to 1952, the firm went on to build Gunnison Heights, Cherry Hills Vista, and Burns Aurora. Burns' enterprises branched out and by 1955 consisted of nearly 70 legal entities, including an insurance agency, an electrical equipment company, a rental company, and a savings and loan association. He was the first homebuilder inducted into the Housing Hall of Fame in 1977, due to his industry achievements in the 1940s.[13]

Veterans Move to the Area

Burns' reasonably priced housing proved popular with veterans. Basil Turner, originally from Missouri, was stationed at Lowry Field during World War II. Julia Hudson moved from Kansas to attend Barnes Business School in Denver and met Basil at a USO dance at the Rainbow Ballroom. They married in 1943 and moved with the Army Air Corps until Basil was discharged in 1945. They returned to Denver with their young daughter, Carmel, and looked for a home to buy. A fellow worker at Rigsby Truck Lines told Basil about new homes being built in southwest Denver.

"We thought that was the other side of the tracks, but were pleasantly surprised to find the attractive neighborhood of Brentwood," Julia said. "Each of us had savings bonds before we married, so we cashed them in to make the $500 down payment. We moved in as soon as the house was livable, before the garage floor and driveway were poured. Most of our neighbors were veterans, also."

In 1948, the Turners paid $8,600 for their two-bedroom frame house and garage on South Hazel Court. "I dug up the whole backyard with a spading fork so we could plant a garden. That was before I could afford a rototiller. We raised a large garden each year and always baked our own bread," said Basil, who was a mechanic and handyman as well. "I've added many improvements over the 60 years we've lived here, including a fence, front porch, patio, aluminum siding, and extended driveway." Julia worked as secretary for Hartford Steam Boiler Inspection and Insurance Company for several years before marriage.[14]

Homer and Virginia (Ginny) Grace bought their home at 2050 South Irving Street in 1947 for $8,500 through the GI Bill, which offered low-interest financing. The location was convenient for Homer's job at the Denver Federal Center. He worked for the U.S. Geological Survey, one of the government agencies to expand because of Denver's growing attraction as the nation's "Second Capital." In keeping with the times, the Grace's home telephone number was 298W.

"There was nothing south of Evans other than a large farm where the Checkers store is now at 2309 South Federal Boulevard. The farmer used to drive a team of horses through our neighborhood to Sanderson Gulch. The kids would stop playing and beg for a ride in the wagon," Ginny said. "As you can imagine, there was a passel of kids since young GIs and their families had settled in Brentwood.

"Our children were bused to Rosedale Elementary School until Johnson Elementary School opened in 1952, at 1850 South Irving Street. Brien started there as a second grader and JoAnne was in kindergarten."

An elementary school teacher, Ginny first taught at Stephen Knight in south Denver, then transferred to closer schools that opened in southwest Denver. During her 30-year career in education, she conducted classes at Gust, Schmitt, and Sabin Elementary Schools. She also taught all-day kindergarten at Westwood Elementary School when the government offered an extended learning day with an enrichment program to prepare children for reading. In addition, she taught on KRMA-TV, and she lived in Bristol, England, for a year, teaching children with speech problems through the Fulbright Exchange program.

As a testament to the community spirit in the area, Ginny claimed, "South Irving has a parkway between Jewell and Evans with a grass median down the center of the street. For years, the city did nothing to keep it up. The residents took care of it themselves, taking turns watering and mowing. It seemed like we were the stepchild of Denver, with less attention than the east side of town. In fact, we had people ask us why we would want to live on the west side of town."

Ginny never moved east—even after raising her children, even after her husband died. She lived in Brentwood for 23 years, retired from teaching, and moved to a condo in southwest Denver. Active in her late 80s, she volunteers one day a week at the Community Ministry of Southwest Denver food bank.[15]

Brentwood Churches

As families settled in Brentwood, they began to talk about churches for the area. Methodists met with the Reverend Clayton Berry to found the Brentwood Methodist Church, which held worship services and the church-school classes at Garden Home Grange Hall. The first service, on January 8, 1950, was particularly memorable because an oil heater caught fire. The following year, Berry's large garage at 1970 South King Street was remodeled as a worship center and the congregation secured title to four lots at the corner of West Jewell Avenue and South Irving Street. They broke ground in May 1952 and relied on volunteer workers from all over the city to help build the church on Saturdays and evenings.

On Christmas Sunday 1952, worshippers gathered in the unfinished building. Work continued through 1953, and Burns Construction Company and several subcontractors pitched in to finish the floors and painting of the first unit. Members organized a women's group, a Scouting program, youth groups, and a men's group. In 1955, the merchants of Brentwood Shopping Center provided uniforms for the church basketball team that practiced at Kepner Junior High School and played in the City Church League.

The congregation moved to its new sanctuary with the high-pitched roof in December 1956. Still growing and needing more church-school space, they purchased a house at 1880 South Julian Street in 1957. Two years later, when this youth house was condemned as a fire hazard, church-school classes met at Howell's Department Store in Brentwood Shopping Center. At its peak in 1966, the church showed a membership of 1,810, with a church-school enrollment of 1,059.[16]

Meanwhile, Catholics planned a new parish and purchased 5 acres north of Loretto Heights College as a site to be dedicated in honor of All Saints. The Reverend Anthony Weinzapel, pastor of St. Patrick's Parish in Fort Logan, was named as administrator. The first mass for parishioners was celebrated Christmas Day 1950 in the chapel at Loretto Heights College. Dedication ceremonies for All Saints Catholic Church, 2599 South Federal Boulevard, took place on

Preschool children visit the annual Pumpkin Patch sponsored by Brentwood United Methodist Church.

August 13, 1951. A barn donated by Safeway Stores was moved to the parish grounds in July, and volunteers began transforming it into a meeting hall. The barn was the remaining structure of a farm previously located at South Federal Boulevard and West Iliff Avenue, where a Safeway store preceded the Checker Auto Parts store at that location.

In June 1952, the Reverend Harley Schmitt directed vacation school for 140 children. Three Sisters of Loretto taught religious classes with the assistance of students from Loretto Heights College. Earlier that year, in April 1952, Schmitt had moved into the new 12-room rectory facing Federal Boulevard. A major fire destroyed the church building and furnishings on January 8, 1953, started by votive lights too close to Christmas boughs. Estimated at $80,000, the loss deeply touched the 550 parish families. Pope Pius XII sent a message of consolation to Schmitt and the parishioners, who held masses once again at Loretto Heights College. Sympathizers responded to the tragedy by donating $11,000. Children met in the parish hall and a rented tent for vacation school that summer.

The burned structure was razed and a new brick church seating 700 was completed in 1954. It proved popular; 1,565 people attended four masses held in the new building on August 22, 1954. By the end of the year, figures showed 1,200 families in the parish with 2,207 children under 18, including 1,222 under age 5. As the church grew, additional masses relieved crowded conditions, until a portion of the parish was incorporated into the new Notre Dame parish established in 1957. A school operated from 1959 through 1978, with classes conducted by Sisters of the Most Precious Blood.

Free of debt in 1967, the parish built a 1,100-seat structure facing Federal Boulevard. A 30-foot-high mosaic glass and plaster mural of *Christ the Savior*, designed by Henry de Nicola, adorned the exterior. The new church completed a campus that occupied the full block with a central playground and parking area bordered by the church, school, convent, parish hall, and rectory.[17]

The Harvey Park Subdivision

After the Harvey Park neighborhood was annexed by Denver in March 1954, contractor Lou Carey built 200 homes in a contemporary style at 1905 South Utica Street, touting the close proximity to Red Rocks Park and the mountains. This was the Harvey Park subdivision, where two- and three-bedroom brick-veneer homes sold for $12,000 to $15,000. They were the first show homes featured in the 1954 Parade of Homes, along with K. C. Ensor's brick tri-level houses in the 1900 block of South Wolcott, which were part of a 50-home project. The Ensor two- to four-bedroom homes were priced from $12,900 to $16,750. However, Thomas Hutchinson built the majority of homes in the area between 1954 and 1958. Some of the popular brick homes had as many as five bedrooms, two bathrooms, fireplaces, two-car garages, and full basements. The high-end model was listed at $17,000.[18]

In October 1954, the first residents moved to their homes along dirt roads off West Jewell Avenue on South Lowell Boulevard, South Utica Street, and South Vrain Street. Cars often got stuck in the mud and telephone service was lacking, yet families continued to pour in. Doull Elementary School, 2520 South Utica Street, was built in 1956; Kunsmiller Junior High, 2250 South Quitman Street, in 1957; and Abraham Lincoln High School, 2285 South Federal Boulevard, in 1960.

Hidden Lakes

Irrigation lakes became recreational spots for homeowners who purchased building sites near the Hidden Lake area in the late 1950s. Not far from Ward Lake (also known as Hidden Lake), the Lakeridge neighborhood developed in an area bounded by South Tennyson Way, West Yale Avenue, South Sheridan Boulevard, and Lakeridge Road. The area included a 10-acre lake surrounded by home sites—a quiet district unnoticed by travelers along West Yale Avenue. The lake got its water from a nearby irrigation ditch that diverted water from Clear Creek near Golden into the South Platte River near its confluence with Bear Creek. Its hilltop location afforded a view of the valley and mountains for the 140 families who bought property that once was part of the Harvey estate. Contractors built homes, many of which were larger and more expensive than those in the Harvey Park subdivision. Some cost as much as $50,000.

Wolcott Lake was initially a mud hole surrounded by weeds—a source of frustration for the residents who recognized its potential. Four charter members

Lakeridge residents built a private recreation area around Wolcott Reservoir in the 1950s. This aerial photo was taken about 1978.

formed the Lakeridge Association with the goal of creating a unique, joint-ownership, park-like area offering attractions and facilities for all ages.

Association members accomplished major improvements through careful planning and hard work. They drained the lake and sealed it. Then they bought used curb and gutter from the city for the cost of hauling, placed it around the lake's half-mile perimeter, and built an embankment to prevent soil erosion. They made a beach and added a gravel walk circling the lake. After many consultations with contractors, they decided to build a boat pier themselves since one of the residents was an engineer. They poured a concrete slab and concrete supports on dry land and swung them into the lake with a crane.

When the lake was finished, they cut weeds and designated sites for a playground, a tennis court, a horseshoe pit, shuffleboard, and parking. They added shade trees to the existing cottonwoods and installed picnic tables, a fireplace, a slip for sailboats, and lighting for night events. Architect Herbert Hantschel designed a pavilion that served as a center for social activities.[19]

Bob and Mary Werner moved to Lakeridge in 1968 from a contemporary board-and-batten house on South Newton Street. Their newer house on West Yale Avenue backed up to the secluded Wolcott Lake, which had been revamped into a nice recreation site a few years earlier. Bob, a city planner, and Mary, a nurse, joined the Lakeridge Association, and Bob served in various capacities on the board of directors. They raised three children—David, Sandra, and Steven—who enjoyed swimming, fishing, and boating in summer and ice skating in winter. The Werners also joined Terrace Club, where the children took swimming lessons.

"People are surprised to find out we can go sailing so close to home. Sailboats are allowed on the lake, but motorboats are not," Bob said. "Eighty families belong to the association and have use of the lake. Membership is voluntary with a $200 yearly fee."[20]

Ward Reservoir No. 5, commonly known as Riviera Lake, is located west of South Raleigh Street and south of West Evans Avenue. Hidden from sight because of its higher elevation and surrounding homes, the private lake started as an irrigation pond on the Harvey property. When Harvey began selling off land, Duke Desharm, a land developer, bought the irrigation pond, which went almost to South Sheridan Boulevard. Contractor Lou Carey, who also worked with K. C. Ensor, made a dam and started building custom homes around the lake.

Robert and Arlene Probst moved from the Barnum area to a lake home in 1958. Robert was a controller and business manager for Lakewood Fordland, and Arlene worked in real estate. They had two sons: Robert Jr. was already married, and James attended Kunsmiller Junior High School and graduated from

Abraham Lincoln High School in 1963. "We had great fun—fishing, swimming, waterskiing, having beach parties at night, and ice skating right in our backyard," James said. "When we moved in, nothing was west of Sheridan Boulevard except for Green Gables Country Club."

The residents formed a private homeowners' association for the 37 properties that backed up to the lake from West Evans to West Warren Avenue and South Raleigh Street to South Wolcott Court. "We have neighbors of various backgrounds —judges, teachers, barbers, dentists, and flower shop owners. The homeowners' association, known as the Riviera Circle Lake Club, has sponsored summer celebrations, including a boat parade, waterski exhibitions, skydivers that landed in the lake, and a fireworks show for members, their guests, and neighbors around the lake," he said.

James married Donna Riedel and after serving in the army started work at the Adolf Coors Brewery. Several years after Donna's death, he married again. When his parents died, he and his wife, Rosemary, moved back to the lake home. James retired after 37 years with Coors, and Rosemary retired from American Express. They like to spend time with their four children and four grandchildren, who enjoy the lake activities as well.[21]

Kunsmiller Junior High School

When Kunsmiller Junior High School opened in 1957, the afternoon session staff transferred from Kepner Junior High. William H. Anderson served as principal. La Rue Belcher started her teaching career at Westwood High School, then served as dean of girls for the new Kepner and Kunsmiller Junior High Schools. She was the first woman junior high principal, then the first woman senior high principal, and she served as the first woman assistant superintendent of Denver Public Schools from 1977 to 1983. "It was fun opening Kunsmiller, even though the offices were unfinished and we had to work on orange-crate desks," La Rue said. "The area grew rap-

La Rue Belcher

idly due to an influx of Martin Marietta engineers from Baltimore, who sought nearby housing. The kids were very smart. The median IQ was 126, so we offered mostly accelerated classes. We had very few normal classes," she added.[22]

Located at 2250 South Quitman Street, the school was directly south of the new park being developed along West Evans Avenue. In the mid-1970s, Connie Leberer served as president of Kunsmiller Community School, a concept that stressed year-round use of school buildings and other community facilities for educational, cultural, recreational, and social enrichment.[23]

Harvey Park Recreation Center

The lake and park named for Arthur Harvey took shape during the late 1950s, as dredging and grading got underway. By 1960, Harvey Park at West Evans Avenue and South Patton Court featured a gravel walk, picnic tables, and a playground area.

Carlo Fassi, famed trainer of Peggy Fleming, Dorothy Hamil, John Curry, and other Olympic ice skating medalists, was part owner of the Colorado Ice Arena at 5555 W. Evans Ave. during the 1970s and 1980s.

The Harvey Park Recreation Center, affiliated with the Denver Parks and Recreation Department, utilized space at nearby Kunsmiller Junior High School until the new facility was completed near the lake in 1975. Located at 2120 South Tennyson Way, the recreation center continued to work with the newly formed Kunsmiller Community School sponsored by Denver Public Schools. "They can do things we can't do, such as offering a typing class," said George Schneider, director of the recreation center. "And we offer classes they don't have—for example pottery and craft classes and weight-training programs. By coordinating programs of the two centers, we can enhance the community."[24]

The recreation center added an outdoor swimming pool for neighborhood children and adults in 1977. Twenty years later, the park, recreation center, and school grounds all received facelifts. Denver Parks and Recreation deepened the lake, expanded the wetlands around it, and added small islands to make the lake more interesting. Improvements also made it possible to use the lake as storage for irrigation. In addition, it provided fishing for local anglers.

Harvey Park Recreation Center built a new entryway, remodeled shower and locker rooms, made changes to the pool, and developed a cardiovascular fitness center. Funds from Councilman Ted Hackworth's office purchased new upholstered chairs for the lounge. In 2000, DPS replaced the old gravel field between the recreation center and the school with new grass athletic fields as a home for Kunsmiller's soccer and baseball games.

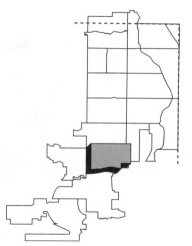

CHAPTER THIRTEEN

Harvey Park South

Starting in the late 1800s with the establishment of a Catholic girls' school, the Harvey Park South neighborhood grew in the area bounded by Yale Avenue, South Federal Boulevard, West Hampden Avenue, and South Sheridan Boulevard. More than 300 nuns lived in the area while working at the historic Loretto Heights College, and GIs moved in as subdivisions enveloped farmlands in the 1950s. Today, the long-standing Harvey Park Improvement Association works to ensure that the neighborhood remains a nice place to raise a family.

Loretto Academy/Loretto Heights College

The establishment of Loretto Heights College—now Teikyo Loretto Heights University—had a great impact on Harvey Park South. Originally, the Sisters of Loretto operated St. Mary's Academy from a two-story frame house on California Street. The Sisters journeyed west from Kentucky in 1864 to open the school at the request of Monsignor Joseph Machebeuf, Denver's first Roman Catholic bishop. The St. Mary's girls' school was so successful that it was overcrowded by the late 1880s. Mary P. Bonfils, known as Mother Pancratia, selected an area in Sheridan Heights, a sparsely settled area southwest of Denver, for a boarding school to relieve the overcrowded St. Mary's Academy. The site overlooked Denver's new military post, Fort Logan. Impressed by the magnificent hilltop view, the Catholic nuns purchased 45 acres for $16,000 and watched construction of a five-story structure during the winter of 1890–1891.[1]

On November 2, 1891, the new occupants anxiously rode 7 miles from Denver on the Circle Railway, then walked 2 miles to settle in the spacious quarters. The 20 Sisters and 51 girls spent a dark, chilly night without heat, water, or lights because the contractor had neglected to turn the utilities on. Arrival of another 19 girls brought the total to 70 students before the dedication on December 10, 1891.

Denver's noted architect F. E. Edbrooke designed the 186-room, Romanesque-style structure built with red sandstone hauled from Manitou Springs, Colorado. The 265-foot-long main hallway featured walls wainscoted with oak and a floor laid with 1-inch, colored hexagonal tiles forming snowflake designs on a white background. The hall opened into a reception area, a visiting room, recreation rooms, parlors, a study, a library, a museum, a laboratory, and classrooms. The second floor housed music rooms, the Sisters' dormitory, an infirmary, the students' dormitory and dressing rooms, restrooms, and a community room. The third and fourth floors contained study rooms, more dormitories, clothes closets, private bedrooms, and a 52-by-100-foot exhibition/lecture hall in the right wing of the fourth floor. The top of the 100-foot belfry tower was a stone-pillared observatory. A kitchen, pantries, a dining room, a calisthenics hall, and bathrooms completed the basement. A huge statue of the Virgin Mary was set in a recess over the arch at the main entrance.[2]

By the spring of 1892, 90 elementary and secondary students lived at Loretto Academy. The Sisters not only taught classes but also did cleaning and repair work, planted corn and beets, raised pigs, and tended the dairy. Sisters also nursed the sick, purchased food and cooked meals, washed and mended clothes, and kept accounts. Buggy-riding visitors to the country often noticed Sisters in their black habits working on the grounds in the late afternoon.

Students wore long dresses with leg-o'-mutton sleeves and high-topped button shoes. They took basic courses along with sewing, homemaking, and other things women were expected to learn. The first graduates, Katherine Casey and Olive Ford, received diplomas in June 1892. Mother Pancratia, unfortunately, did not attend the graduation because she had been transferred to Alabama. Casey later became a Sister of Loretto and was known as Sister Menadora.

To escape foreclosure during the Silver Panic of 1893, Mother Praxedes Carty spoke to the property's mortgage holders in Milwaukee. She boldly stated, "Gentlemen, if you take the property, you'll have to take the Sisters with it." She won her fight to save the school, and the loan was extended. Because of her drive and initiative in securing the future of Loretto Academy, Mother Carty was elected mother general of the Sisters of Loretto, a position she held for 26 years.

Sister Bartholomew, postmaster when the Loretto post office was established on September 28, 1896, climbed into a one-seated rig and traveled to Littleton each day to pick up mail. Sister Florence Marie, a later Loretto postmaster, remembered the time a practical joker sent 100 baby chicks to one of the students. The student willingly paid the postage but then wondered what to

*Teikyo Loretto Heights University started in 1891 as
Loretto Academy, a school for Catholic girls.*

do with the "peeping orphans." A kind person finally bought them all. Croaking frogs, earmarked for the biology department, often arrived at the post office as well.[3]

In 1903, founder Mother Pancratia returned as mother superior. She started plans for a separate chapel building, which was finished in 1911 and featured an auditorium on the lower level. The Rose Window of the Mater Dolorosa and six other beautiful stained-glass windows from the renowned Myer firm of Munich, Germany, were installed in the chapel. Mother Pancratia died October 12, 1915, and was buried in the private cemetery on campus.

College classes were added to Loretto Academy in 1918, and the Teacher Education Program began in 1926 to prepare women for a lifelong career. In 1930, despite the Great Depression, the school added a new classroom building called Pancratia Hall and continued to operate as both a high school and a college until the number of college students surpassed the high school enrollment.

In 1941, the high school closed and Loretto Heights became a four-year college. A nursing program was instituted in cooperation with St. Anthony's Hospital in Denver and Penrose Hospital in Colorado Springs. Pancratia Hall became a student residence, and enrollment escalated. A big building expansion occurred in the 1950s with the addition of Machebeuf Hall, a center for the performing arts, a library, and Walsh Hall. Marian Hall opened in 1960 with 250 beds and enrollment jumped to 812. By 1968, Loretto Heights College (LHC) offered living quarters for 725 students while the rest lived off-campus. LHC also built a swimming pool, a cover for the pool, and a small biology lab during the 1960s.

Things improved for the school when Denver annexed the neighborhood. "It was a big thing when we were annexed to Denver in 1958. We had a water tower for years, but life was much easier with city water," said Sister Mary Ann Coyle, an LHC chemistry teacher for 20 years.[4]

Over the years, the school gained a reputation as one of the better Catholic colleges for women. Known as a safe refuge for daughters of respectable Catholic parents, it drew mostly upper-middle-class women. Society changed drastically in the 1960s, and so did Loretto Heights College. Vatican II, an ecumenical council of the church put together by Pope John XXIII in 1962 to help renew and update the church, made a difference in many lives, including those in southwest Denver.

Mary Luke Tobin, Sister of Loretto and president of the Loretto community for 12 years, was 1 of 15 women from different parts of the Roman Catholic world to audit the Vatican II sessions in 1964. As president of the Leadership Conference of Women Religious from 1964 to 1967, she was the only woman from the United States chosen to attend Vatican II.

Sister Patricia Jean Manion, a 42-year-old Roman Catholic nun, assumed the presidency of Loretto Heights College in October 1967, after earning a Ph.D. in higher education at the University of Denver. Known as P.J., the blue-eyed, brown-haired Sister shed her long black habit and black veil. In addition, responding to changes in society, she instituted surprising reforms at the 77-year-old Catholic girls' school operated by the Sisters of Loretto.

In February 1968, P.J. announced that LHC would become a Catholic-oriented independent liberal arts women's college governed by a lay board of trustees. Sisters would be hired and paid for their work the same as other faculty members. In addition, they would give up their residential quarters and live off-campus like other teachers. Further, the college would change its format of classes and its grading system to allow for a more flexible, experimental curriculum. Loretto's specialties of teaching, nursing, and English would be retained, but graduate studies would be dropped and a humanities major added. Sisters moved from the college grounds to nearby houses in the Harvey Park or Bear Valley neighborhoods. Some took up residence at the Loretto Center at 4000 South Wadsworth Boulevard.

With the independent spirit of the founding order and the backing of her mother superior, fellow Sisters, a civilian faculty, and most of the 916 students,

P.J. forged ahead. "This isn't going to be an ivory tower any longer," she said. "It's a complex, changing, confusing world and students must be educated to meet the challenge of the future."[5]

Keeping up with progressive innovations, the college began admitting men in 1970 and started the University Without Walls (UWW) program for nontraditional students in 1971. Stanley and Rita Jacques were the first husband and wife to graduate from LHC after the college became coeducational. As registered nurses, both completed the school's specially tailored program for RNs. In 1978, a business program was established, with an emphasis on entrepreneurship and small business.

Financial problems plagued the college in the 1980s and the board sought ways to survive. Talks with Father David Clark, president of Regis University, resulted in a cooperative venture to move three academic programs to Regis—nursing, University Without Walls (UWW), and dance. Nursing became the foundation for the Regis School for Health Care Professions, and UWW was incorporated into the Regis School for Professional Studies.

Teikyo Loretto Heights University

Loretto Heights College closed in 1988 and the Teikyo University Group purchased the facilities in 1990. The Teikyo University Group was founded by Dr. Shoichi Okinaga as part of his effort to educate citizens of the world without prejudice. Dr. Okinaga had previously started nearly 30 institutions, with campuses in Japan, Germany, Great Britain, the Netherlands, and the United States. Today, Teikyo Loretto Heights offers an international learning experience focused on careers in the global economy.[6]

In keeping with the Japanese tradition of honoring ancestors, the new owners made improvements to the small graveyard behind "Old Main," where 62 Sisters of Loretto are buried. More than 300 Sisters of Loretto lived and worked at LHC during its history. Thirty-seven died there. Sister Frances O'Leary died in 1898 and was the first Sister to be buried in the campus cemetery. The deceased include notable administrators, faculty, and auxiliary staff.

Plans for a multischool center similar to the Auraria campus surfaced in 2003 as the university opened its 76-acre facility to other schools. Southwest Early College (SEC), a DPS charter school to prepare freshmen and sophomores for college, leased space in 2004. SEC also offers community college courses for high school juniors and seniors led by instructors from Community College of Denver (CCD). In addition to the Southwest Campus of CCD, the facility includes offices of AmeriCorps and the Language Training Center.[7]

Fair Hill / Hillcroft

Located west of Loretto Heights College, a farm called Fair Hill commanded a four-way view of the city, valley, and mountains. It sported well-kept gardens, nice buildings, and an orchard of cherry, plum, pear, and apple trees. John Flower, prominent Denverite and son-in-law of philathropist J. K. Mullen, owned the property and constructed a large barn for riding horses. The next owner, a U.S. Navy commander named McCarthy, added tennis courts but moved from the area for health reasons and turned the farm over to caretakers. The property deteriorated as barns were torn down and used for firewood and vandals broke floors and windows.

In 1942, Herbert C. Stebbins traded a house in Park Hill for the run-down acreage. Stebbins' daughter, Linda, said it took years to restore the place, which **they** named Hillcroft. "The main house started as a one-room cabin, probably in the 1860s. Each owner built on additional rooms, which made it a rambling house with no particular plan. A feed store, drugstore, and candy store were scattered among the farmlands stretching north to Alameda. Corn and hay fields spread southward to Fort Logan. My father was an insurance man, not a farmer, so our caretaker did the farming. We kept horses, cows, sheep, ducks, and geese. Pheasants, quail, squirrels, and even deer roamed the grounds. Of course, we had some porcupines, skunks, and snakes, too," she said.[8]

After World War II, civilization began closing in around the farm, bringing many problems such as illegal hunting, vandalism, and trash dumping on the 69 acres. A popular hangout for local youth, the unoccupied buildings, including a milk house, three-story barn, and two-story shed, were completely wrecked. In 1952, Herbert Stebbins made a deal with Loretto Heights College to buy the property upon his death.

Loretto Heights College sold 15 acres south of West Amherst Avenue and east of South Lowell Boulevard to the city for a neighborhood park in 1977. Park planners talked about preserving the Stebbins barn for a recreation or nature center, but the barn was destroyed a year later in an arson fire. Loretto Heights Park was developed south of West Amherst Avenue on the hilltop between South Lowell Boulevard and South Irving Street, with a playground and picnic area looking southward to Pikes Peak.

Subdivisions Move In

During the late 1950s, farmland gave way to subdivisions sprawling south as contractors marked off streets, surveyed lots, dug basements, and put up homes almost overnight. Young families with children moved in. Most of the men were in their 20s or early 30s, many with college educations. They often mortgaged their automobiles to pay closing costs on the houses, financed with GI loans.[9]

Couples usually owned meager furnishings, including bedroom furniture, a crib, a used sofa and chairs, a card table to eat from, and a television set for low-cost entertainment. Dyed sheets hung at the windows and throw rugs decorated the wood floors. With the energy of youth, they put up fences, planted trees, and seeded lawns and gardens. The Harvey Park community soon filled the vacant land bounded by West Yale Avenue, South Federal Boulevard, West Hampden Avenue, and South Sheridan Boulevard and eventually became known as Harvey Park South. The entire Harvey Park community gained a reputation as one of the well-kept areas in Denver and a good place to raise children.

The Harvey Park Improvement Association

Founded in 1956, the Harvey Park Improvement Association (HPIA) served as the prototype for many other neighborhood organizations to follow. The group, spearheaded by attorney Jerry Stapp, organized to enhance the development of Harvey Park and to protect against unfair taxation. With the strong backing of Harvey Park's more than 4,000 residents, HPIA campaigned for schools, libraries, parks, streetlights, and safety signals. Residents demanded better fire and police protection, resulting in Fire Station 25 at South Raleigh Street and West Harvard Avenue and the District 4 Police Station at 2929 West Florida Avenue, which later moved to 2100 South Clay Street.[10]

Young couples also started churches, Scout troops for boys and girls, and other youth activities such as the unique Keen Teen Canteen, headed by Glen and Jane Smith and financed by the community until it became self-sustaining.

Tenacious citizens fought for a branch library for more than five years, gathering 14,000 signatures on a petition in one week. People sent telegrams to the mayor, jammed the switchboard with telephone calls, and even stormed city council chambers in person when the issue came up for a vote. Despite their efforts, residents had to settle for neighborhood libraries at Athmar Park and Bear Valley Shopping Center until the city finally opened the Chalmers Hadley Branch Library at West Jewell Avenue and South Grove Street in June 1964.

The School Situation

Schools failed to keep ahead of the influx of families in southwest Denver, so many children attended split sessions for most of their school years. Sabin Elementary School was built in 1958 and added extra rooms in 1960 and

1962. Located at 3050 South Vrain Street, the school bore the name of Mary Sabin, a Denver teacher, and her sister, Dr. Florence R. Sabin. Children went on to Kunsmiller Junior High, which was built in 1957 and bursting with 1,500 students in morning classes and another 1,500 in afternoon classes until an addition in 1963 helped alleviate the crowded situation. Abraham Lincoln High School, built in 1960 at 2285 South Federal Boulevard, was also forced to provide split sessions when students moved up to the secondary level.

The 1966 opening of the new John F. Kennedy School in Bear Valley relieved the crowding at Lincoln, but junior high and senior high students still attended staggered sessions at Kennedy until it became exclusively a senior high school in 1975.

The Bear Valley Neighborhood Library operated from the Bear Valley Shopping Center until the permanent building opened in 1971.

Some of Harvey Park's children went to Horace Mann Junior High in north Denver because of court-ordered busing. The busing affected the neighborhood, as some families decided to send their children to private schools while others moved to communities where their children could walk to school. Denver's school enrollment declined while that of the nearby Jefferson County school system increased during the 1960s, 1970s, and 1980s.[11]

The Bear Valley Neighborhood Library

Nowhere was a neighborhood library more successful than in the Harvey Park/Bear Valley area. The Bear Valley Library operated from the Bear Valley Shopping Center until its permanent building opened at 5171 West Dartmouth Avenue in 1971. Anderson Barker Rinker Architects designed the distinctive contemporary structure with rounded lines and oblong windows. Architect Virginia DuBrucq created a welcoming interior for the anxious patrons who had campaigned for a branch library for more than five years.

The Bear Valley Shopping Center

The Bear Valley Shopping Center opened on April 1, 1958, at 3100 South Sheridan Boulevard near the Hutchinson Homes subdivision in Harvey Park. Miller's Supermarket and Duckwall's Variety Store were among the 22 businesses drawing shoppers from the new neighborhood. Officers for the Bear Valley Merchant's Association included Dave Allinger of Allinger Photo Studio, John Gallagher of Gallagher Party and Gift Shop, Tom O'Rourke of Bear Valley Bank, and Ruth Cruth of Bear Valley Liquor Store.

Stores such as May D&F (later becoming Foley's and then Macy's) and Fashion Bar (which is no longer in Denver) moved out of the mall in the late 1980s. Burlington Coat Factory took over the vacant May D&F building, and a Super Saver Cinema was added in hopes of revitalizing the 30-year-old center. In 1994, during the mall's second redevelopment, King Soopers built a new store and moved from the west side of South Sheridan Boulevard. The movie theater was razed in 1999 to make way for a new Home Depot store, which opened in June 2000. The neighborhood drug and hardware stores closed when the larger chain stores went in, but the new businesses did draw patrons to the center that once faced demolition.[12]

Neighborhood Leaders

Ted and Doris Hackworth bought their first house, on South Green Court in Burns Brentwood, in 1952. Both were graduates of Denver high schools and Ted had served in the Air Force. After they married on December 31, 1947, Doris worked at Texas Oil Company while Ted studied at the University of Denver. On the night of his final test, a snowstorm delayed his trip home. "We didn't have a telephone, so I couldn't call Doris to tell her I would be late. The closest phone was at a booth at the end of our block at West Vassar Avenue. I spent part of the night at my grandmother's and arrived home at 3 a.m."

The Hackworths added a room on their frame house to accommodate their growing family of one son and two daughters. The children attended Gust Elementary School, which opened in 1955. The school added the east wing the following year and another addition in 1961 to provide for its burgeoning enrollment. Ted worked for Pitney Bowes and sold automobiles for Courtesy Cars.

In 1964, the family moved to a new brick home built by Hutchinson Homes on West Linvale Place. They became involved with the Harvey Park Improvement Association, a group formed to protect the value of the neighborhood, and Doris was the organization's secretary for 23 years.

Ted was elected to the Denver School Board in 1972 and served through 1978. Elected to city council in 1979, he represented District 2 for 24 years. During his tenure, he saw the city expand south and west. Boundary disputes and zoning issues were common. Well known in the community, Ted attended every monthly neighborhood association meeting in his district. He and his longtime aide, Sue Mitchell, saved money from their city council budget to purchase special equipment to help city agencies better serve people. "We bought a raft and suits for the fire department, digital cameras for the police department to document property damage, three computers, and a laser printer for citizen use at Bear Valley Library, among other items," he said.

Hackworth's office provided discretionary funds for playground equipment and landscaping projects at several Denver schools. When Hackworth retired in August 2003 because of term limits, the Denver Board of Education recognized his efforts by naming the athletic fields at Sabin Elementary School in his honor. A sign was erected at the dedication on September 18, 2003.[13]

Jeanne Faatz replaced Hackworth on city council in the fall of 2003. Prior to her election, she managed the Governor's School to Career Program. A Harvey Park resident since 1968, Faatz formerly taught junior high/senior high students at Cherry Creek schools and college classes at Regis University and Metro State College. She and her husband, Clyde, had two daughters while living in Harvey Park.

"We noted a difference in the atmosphere on this side of town," said Faatz. "We didn't want to keep up with the Joneses and we found southwest Denver less expensive, less pretentious, more laid-back, and not so competitive."

Active in community organizations including HPIA, Faatz entered politics in 1978, when she ran for the Colorado House of Representatives and won. She served 10 terms (20 years) in the House of Representatives. In 1991, she was selected to be assistant majority leader, the highest-ranking majority position held by a woman. Faatz said distinct areas within southwest Denver presented challenges as a multicounty district. Other political jurisdictions in House District 1 included parts of Jefferson County, Arapahoe County, Englewood, and Littleton, creating confusion over mailing issues and safety concerns.

When Faatz ran for city council in 2003 she was the only Republican elected. She said the people in southwest Denver have a strong work ethic. "Most are homeowners with a major investment in their home. They are quite conservative. We find this in voter performance, taxation, spending, and economic views. Savers themselves, they don't appreciate extravagance. They are interested in the quality of their neighborhoods, public safety, and keeping government influence under control."[14]

The Terrace Club

In 1957, a lack of recreational facilities in the newly developing Harvey Park area prompted neighbors Carol Harris and Eugene and Sue Bishop to work toward the goal of building a community swim club. "We hung hand-drawn posters in store windows and made phone calls to solicit interest," Harris said. "We held home meetings and eventually formed an enthusiastic board of directors, many of whom signed $10,000 personal notes to guarantee a construction loan."

Harris continued: "After incorporating in 1958, we purchased 10 acres near South Knox Court and West Hampden Avenue, part of it a hilltop plateau with an unobstructed view of the valley and mountain range, the remainder a lower pasture with a small house and barn. In June 1960, nearly 300 member families celebrated the official opening of the Terrace Club, which boasted an Olympic-size swimming pool with high and low diving boards, a large kiddie pool, and a snack bar. In later years, the club added a gazebo and playground to the hilltop and in 1972 built five lighted tennis courts on the lower level and hired a tennis pro."[15]

Terrace Club provided swimming lessons, Red Cross certification, diving lessons, dances, and parties for a 400-member Teen Club, plus fireworks, fashion

Harvey Park citizens organized the Terrace Club for neighborhood children in the 1950s. With 300 member families, the club offered swimming and tennis lessons, teen socials, and family activities for decades before closing in 2005.

shows, and barbecues. Members served on the board, published a newsletter, spruced up the grounds, repaired broken pipes and boilers, chaperoned teen activities, and cheered at local swim meets. As Terrace Club children grew up, some moved away and some mothers went to work. Other swimming facilities competed for new members and expenses escalated. Unable to shoulder the costs any longer, Terrace Club owners sold the property to a developer in 2005, ending an institution that had served its members for more than 40 years.

Bear Creek Park

Bicyclists, dog walkers, picnickers, nature lovers, and cross-country skiers flock to Bear Creek Park, which was developed on land given to the city by the J. K. Mullen family in 1960. The only Denver city park to feature flora native to the foothill zone, Bear Creek Park stretches along both sides of Bear Creek and spans the creek with a footbridge. The north entrance, at South Raleigh Street and West Hampden Avenue, leads to the picnic area, baseball diamonds, and playground featuring a large slide shaped like a sombrero. The south entrance, at West Kenyon Road, half a mile west of South Lowell Boulevard, provides access to a less-developed natural refuge for birds and wildlife. A bike path links the park with Bear Valley Park west of South Sheridan Boulevard.[16]

CHAPTER FOURTEEN

Fort Logan

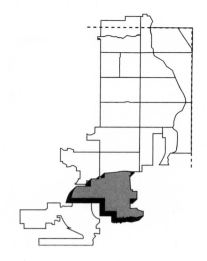

The Fort Logan neighborhood is named for a fort that was established in the 1800s. Located out in the country, 9 miles from Denver, at what is now South Lowell Boulevard and West Quincy Avenue, it was developed as Fort Logan Military Post in the late 1880s. Notables such as later President Dwight D. Eisenhower passed through in the first part of the next century. When the fort closed after World War II, the land was sold to developers or deeded to the city. Today, the area is marked by the still-busy Fort Logan Post Cemetery, the Colorado Mental Health Institute at Fort Logan and its agencies (which use the original red brick buildings from the fort), and the well-respected, coed prep school, J. K. Mullen High School. One Victorian building from the original Fort Logan is on the State Register of Historic Places, and the former parade ground now hosts local soccer games. The neighborhood has irregular boundaries but generally extends between West Hampden Avenue and West Belleview Avenue from South Federal Boulevard to South Pierce Street.

Fort Logan Military Post

In 1870, the arrival of the "iron horse" concluded the pioneer era in Denver. At the time, Congress recognized the economic advantage of abandoning small military posts in favor of larger forces near railroads because rail moved troops faster than horses and mules in times of emergency. Numerous small posts were abandoned since most Native tribes had moved to reservations and fewer cavalry garrisons were needed to protect white settlers moving out West. Meanwhile, Denver's Chamber of Commerce pressed Congress for a new military fort, not only for citizens' protection but also for the social events it would provide. In 1887, President Grover Cleveland signed a bill to establish the fort and appropriated $100,000 for construction of the necessary buildings, quarters, barracks, and stables. Lt. Gen. Philip H. Sheridan was authorized to select the site from 11 proposed by the Denver committee. Many local citizens preferred a tract of land adjacent to Sloan's Lake so they could easily attend military band concerts, dances, and parades.[1]

To their dismay, Sheridan selected a location 9 miles southwest of Denver, called the Johnson Tract, on the Morrison branch of the South Park Railroad. He chose the site because of the rail spur, a "never-failing stream of pure, clear water" (from Bear Creek), a plateau fitting for a parade ground, and good views of the mountains and plains. Some thought, "General Sheridan's object in placing it there was to prevent, as far as possible, the soldiers from coming into the city and spending their money in dissipation." Although disappointed in the location, individuals and businesses rallied and donated money to pur-

Soldiers at Fort Logan Army Post in 1917.

chase land for the 640-acre outpost. The War Department temporarily referred to it as the Camp Near the City of Denver, while Denver citizens informally called it Sheridan Post or Fort Sheridan.[2]

The first soldiers, 22 from the U.S. Army's 18th Infantry, came 206 miles from Fort Hays, Kansas, in late October 1887. The men pitched 25 tents on the banks of Bear Creek and set up cookstoves to fix hearty meals of bacon, hardtack with bacon gravy and onions, canned vegetables, fried potatoes, and black coffee. Sibley stoves provided heat against the snow and wind. More troops arrived by train from Fort Leavenworth a few days later with two army wagons and 12 mules. Among them was the wife of a sergeant, apparently the first woman on the post and its first laundress. After camping mistakenly for several days on a nearby ranch, they made permanent camp on October 31, 1887, at the military reservation in the area of present-day South Lowell Boulevard and West Quincy Avenue.

In need of better facilities, soldiers built temporary barracks, which were completed on December 24, in time for Christmas. A guardhouse was finished on New Year's Eve. The following year, the first quartermaster, Capt. Lafayette E. Campbell, laid out plans for the grounds featuring a large oval area for parades.

Frank Grodavent, a civilian architect, designed permanent buildings and the Corps of Engineers started construction in July 1888.

An interesting story led to the official name of Fort Logan, which was decided on in April 1889. Another military post being established about the same time near Chicago was originally known as Fort Logan in honor of John Alexander Logan, Civil War hero and statesman from Illinois. When Gen. Sheridan lay near death, however, he was made a four-star general and requested that the Chicago fort be named for him. So the Chicago military post was named after Sheridan, and Denver's post was designated as Fort Logan. Logan, who had risen to the rank of major general with volunteer troops in the Civil War, had visited Colorado several times. He served as first commander of the Grand Army of the Republic (GAR) and started Decoration Day (later called Memorial Day) when he asked GAR members to decorate graves of soldiers with flowers on May 30, 1868.[3]

Starting in 1888, a Denver & Rio Grande train nicknamed Uncle Sam transported soldiers and civilians from Denver to Fort Logan and Littleton. In 1889, Fort Laramie closed and most of the 7th Infantry under the command of Col. Henry C. Merriam transferred to Fort Logan. One of the units included a brass band that played in parades and celebrations. The musicians played "over the shoulder-type horns" with backward-facing bells so the troops at the rear of the formation could hear the music and keep step with the beat.[4]

Gen. Sheridan's influence lived on through the town of Sheridan, named for him, and a major street called Sheridan Boulevard. First called Petersburg after Peter Magnes, the "Father of the Sugar Beet Industry," the town of Sheridan incorporated in 1890, including the settlements of Sheridan Park, Military Park, Logantown, and Petersburg. Loretto Academy opened the following year as a girls' high school on the hill overlooking Fort Logan.[5]

In December 1890, Col. Merriam and six companies from Fort Logan left the train depot to help quell a Sioux uprising in South Dakota. Because of delays in crossing the icy Missouri River, they were not involved in what became known as the Massacre at Wounded Knee.

In 1894, the self-contained post of Fort Logan included accommodations for 28 officers, two cavalry troops, eight infantry companies, a headquarters staff, and a band that practiced in a frame bandstand. The hospital had room for 40 patients. Three stables could house 70 mules and horses. The fort also featured a commissary, post office, bake house (bakery), icehouse, guardhouse, coal yard, greenhouse and nursery, dead house (morgue), pump house, sewer system, oval parade ground, and roadways.[6]

The officers lived well in red brick, Victorian-style homes facing the 32-acre, horseshoe-shaped parade ground. The commanding officer's quarters were at the apex, flanked by two roomy residences for field officers. Grassy lawns and shrubs surrounded the homes, which had wine cellars in the basements, brick window wells, and sandstone sidewalks leading to front porches. The field officers' quarters (designated later as a historic landmark) featured large reception hall, parlor, fireplaces, sitting room, dining room, butler's pantry, kitchen, food pantry, and bathroom. Six bedrooms with closets and a bathroom were located on the second floor. The attic contained bedrooms for servants, and laundry facilities were in the basement. All the buildings had central heating and indoor plumbing. Kerosene lamps provided light until electricity was installed in 1904.

Occupants typically included the officer, his wife, children, and four live-in servants—butler, cook, upstairs maid, and downstairs maid. The officers, not the army, paid the servants' wages. The army did provide two enlisted servants, usually a yard man and a chauffeur who lived in the barracks for enlisted men.

Six two-story brick barracks housed the infantry, with one company in each building. The first floor of each contained a barbershop, a library and reading room, a dining room, a kitchen, and bathrooms. On the second floor, a row of neat single beds lined each side of the large, airy dormitories. Every Friday, the men hung all the bedding outside for airing. A private earned only $13 a month, but the army furnished food and clothing as well as comfortable accommodations.[7]

Life for the ordinary soldier was not easy. On summer days, all units were on the rifle range by 5:30 a.m. and often practiced firing until noon. The men

Fort Logan's 9th Company occupied these barracks in 1915. Infantrymen hung bedding out to air every Friday.

performed signal drills with flags plus tedious heliograph and telegraph drills. Those who wanted to learn "the three Rs" attended classes three hours a day for eight months of the year. Some, in fact, were ordered to study because of their "gross ignorance." Soldiers also endured practice marches to areas east of Englewood, to Palmer Lake, and even to Colorado Springs as part of their training. In the early years, the post canteen provided a place for soldiers to relax with snacks, soft drinks, and beer. Later, temperance efforts convinced the army that alcoholic beverages should be prohibited on the post. Saloons, however, sprang up nearby to attract soldiers on payday.

Five companies were dispatched to Denver on March 15, 1894, to protect public property during Governor Waite's siege of city hall, and to Trinidad on July 2, to protect property and mail held up on the railroad during the Pullman Strike. Many said the Air Force originated at Fort Logan when a Signal Corps observation balloon arrived in 1894 along with 28-year-old Ivy Baldwin, who enlisted as a sergeant to handle the balloon. After the balloon was destroyed by a strong wind, Sgt. Baldwin and his wife made a replacement balloon that was sent to Cuba when the Spanish-American War started in 1898.

In preparation for Cuba, infantrymen put two changes of cotton underwear, socks, soap, towels, and a mess kit in a knapsack and rolled it in a pack with a blanket, tent, canteen, tin cup, and rubber poncho. Each man strapped on a belt holding 100 rounds of ammunition and carried a Krag-Jorgensen rifle. The troops, including officers, wore brown canvas leggings, rough blue-woolen shirts, and campaign hats. They kissed wives and sweethearts goodbye and boarded the train while the band played "Auld Lang Syne."

The 16-car freight train was loaded with army wagons, two hospital ambulances, 40 draft mules, and 10 horses for the commanding and staff officers, plus baggage, an extra 16,000 rounds of ammunition, and 30 days of regulation rations—bacon, potatoes, flour, pork, canned tomatoes, beans, onions, coffee, sugar, salt, pepper, baking powder, soap, and candles. Everyone cheered as the train pulled out. Other Fort Logan soldiers were stationed in the Philippines during the war. Wives and children stayed at the fort, while women without children moved in with parents until the "cruel war was over."[8]

Baldwin's balloon was shot down in Cuba, retrieved, and returned to the United States, ending Fort Logan's early era of flight. Baldwin, who performed as a wire-walker at Elitch Gardens and Eldorado Canyon, left the army in 1901. He went on to fly airplanes and performed high-wire acts until the age of 84.[9]

After soldiers returned from the war, social life at the post kicked into high gear as young officers and their idle, fun-loving wives eagerly planned dances, teas, and parties. They laid out a golf course, constructed tennis courts, and started several card clubs. Evening parties were almost a nightly occurrence, some at the luxurious quarters of Capt. Allaire, a society bachelor as well as an army officer. He invited couples to chaperone house parties, where he introduced society girls to West Pointers and other single men from the barracks. It was said that every society girl, along with the students at Loretto Heights College, dreamed of being asked to a Fort Logan house party. One of the wives, a graduate of the Chicago Conservatory of Music, performed frequently on both piano and organ.[10]

Gen. Arthur MacArthur served as commanding officer in 1901–1902, while his son, Douglas, studied at West Point. Douglas MacArthur went on to become a national hero in World War II.

Although the post bought an additional 340 acres in 1908 to store water and gain space for drills, the facility was reduced to a recruit depot in 1909 and remained so through World War I. Then on February 24, 1922, it was reinstated as a training facility. However, manpower included only about 300 or 400 soldiers, compared with earlier numbers of 700 to 800. Maj. Dwight D. Eisenhower reported for recruiting duty at Fort Logan in 1924 before heading to the Command and General Staff School in Leavenworth, Kansas. His wife, Mamie, enjoyed the temporary assignment because her parents lived in Denver.

Buildings at Fort Logan deteriorated during the 1920s, and dirt roads leading to it were almost impassable in wet weather. Denver newspapers called for repairs, referring to it as "Fort Forgotten." Improvements began in the 1930s when Works Progress Administration (WPA) funds enabled the rehabilitation of old buildings plus construction of new duplexes for noncommissioned officers and frame barracks for training purposes. The Civilian Conservation Corps (CCC) used the site for its headquarters and supplies.

The facility became a subpost of Lowry Air Base from 1941 to 1946, training clerks for the Air Corps and later serving as a 326-bed convalescent center. During World War II, it was a War Department Processing Center for soldiers entering and separating from the army. German prisoners of war were held on the grounds for several months. At its height during World War II, Fort Logan housed more than 5,500 persons as an inclusive community with more than 200 buildings on 973 acres. The fire department even had 50 men and five trucks.[11]

The fort was declared surplus when the war ended, and it closed in 1946. Much of the land was transferred to adjacent districts for schools and parks or sold to private developers. The Denver Housing Authority leased the frame barracks to help relieve the housing shortage. About 577 acres, including most of the buildings and facilities, were transferred to the Veterans Administration, which used the hospital until a new VA hospital opened in Denver in 1951.

After the VA relinquished control, various interest groups made proposals to use the land for veterans' housing, a rehabilitation center, and a TB hospital for the Indian Bureau. The Martin Company occupied some buildings for about two years.

The Colorado Mental Health Institute at Fort Logan

A new era began in 1960, when 236 acres were deeded to the State of Colorado for the Fort Logan Mental Health Center, to be operated by the newly created Department of Institutions. The property was annexed by Denver, and new buildings were constructed to serve the needs of a modern, community-oriented treatment facility for psychiatric and alcoholic patients. The first patients moved in on July 17, 1961. Some of the clinical staff lived in the original red brick duplexes. Other buildings became office facilities for the mental health center, additional state agencies, and educational and human service organizations. The large parade ground attracted numerous youth soccer groups from the metro area.[12]

Friends of Historic Fort Logan organized in 1990 as a not-for-profit corporation to promote preservation projects and educational activities at the facility, now called the Colorado Mental Health Institute at Fort Logan. The group was responsible for restoring the one remaining Field Officers' quarters, listed on the State Register of Historic Places. The flagpole, cannon, and many original buildings remain as a reminder of the fort's former significance. The water tower was torn down in the 1960s.[13]

In January 2005, Marva Livingston Hammons, executive director of the Colorado Department of Human Services, announced plans for a homeless shelter for families on the Fort Logan campus, a joint venture of state and city agencies to renovate an empty building and provide housing for approximately 11 families.[14]

Fort Logan National Cemetery

The Fort Logan post created a cemetery on June 28, 1889, with the burial of Mabel Peterkin, daughter of Pvt. Peterkin, Company E of the 18th Infantry. The original 3.2-acre cemetery was near the northwest corner of the military facility. Since the Fort Logan post commander could authorize burials of other than military personnel, it is believed that several trappers, cowboys, and possibly a few Native Americans were buried there. Post burials numbered 367 persons, including one German POW. A group burial occurred in 1947 when eight bodies were recovered from an earlier plane crash.[15]

Congress established Fort Logan as a national cemetery on March 10, 1950. The cemetery contained the grave of Juanita Davis, wife of Herndon R. Davis. Mr. Davis painted the famous face on the barroom floor at the Teller House in Central City. Two Congressional Medal of Honor recipients from the Vietnam War were interred at Fort Logan. A third Medal of Honor recipient, a Civil War Union soldier, is remembered with a marker in a memorial section. In addition, two memorial sections honor more than 700 veterans whose bodies were not recovered or who were buried at sea.[16]

The 214-acre cemetery, located south of West Hampden Avenue between South Lowell Boulevard and South Sheridan Boulevard, holds ceremonies every Memorial Day to honor American servicemen and women who died for their country. The Avenue of Flags along the main drive features burial flags that were presented to the next of kin following a veteran's committal service and donated later to the cemetery for display. Additionally, flags from all 50 states fly from different sites around the grounds. A rock wall flanks the central flagpole near the 6-acre Veteran's Lake, the assembly point for all special events. A tree-lined memorial walkway extends along the centrally located Memorial Lake.[17]

Because of the cemetery's age, veterans of the Civil War, the Spanish-American War, the Indian Wars, World War I, World War II, and the Gulf Wars are interred there, as well as those from conflicts in Korea, Vietnam, Bosnia, and Afghanistan. The cemetery contains a variety of grave markers, but most are the regulation upright marble headstones.

In 2003, Fort Logan National Cemetery began a multiyear project to develop 64 additional acres, construct a new administration building, renovate the old administration building as a public information facility, and provide new landscaping. In 2005, the cemetery had 69,023 gravesites (86,090 interments) and held an average of 15 funerals per weekday—more than 3,000 per year. The total burial capacity is 150,000.[18]

The J. K. Mullen Home for Boys and J. K. Mullen High School

John K. Mullen was 9 when his family left a famine in Ireland and moved to New York. At 14, he quit school to work in a flour mill to supplement the family's income. He arrived in Denver in 1871 as a 19-year-old looking for new opportunities. A journeyman miller, he found a job with Merchant's Mills in west Denver. With hard work and wise money management, he moved upward financially and socially and ultimately amassed a fortune, which he shared with the people of Denver.

John Mullen

Catherine Mullen

Originally from Ireland also, Catherine came to Colorado with her widowed mother. She met John while they were both teaching Sunday school classes at St. Mary's Catholic Church in Denver. She, too, had compassion for poor and needy persons because of her work at the mission church in Central City before moving to Denver. With similar interests in church and a desire to help others, John and Catherine enjoyed a successful marriage and became leading benefactors for many Denver facilities.

John and Catherine Mullen had often talked about establishing an orphanage for boys, "to feed them, house them, clothe them properly, and give them the benefit of a good Christian education." After Catherine's death in 1924, Mullen sought advice from Father Edward J. Flanagan, who operated Boys Town in Omaha, Nebraska. With encouragement from Flanagan, Mullen contacted the Christian Brothers of New Orleans–Santa Fe Province to run the proposed school. Mullen died before the school opened, but he and his wife had established a long-term, nonprofit organization to fund "religious, charitable, benevolent, and educational purposes" extending after their lifetime.[19]

Representatives from the John K. and Catherine S. Mullen Benevolent Foundation completed negotiations in 1931. Meanwhile, 17 boys and three Christian Brothers lived temporarily at Regis College until the Mullen Foundation found an appropriate site for the orphanage.

Mullen's descendants considered 50 possible sites and finally purchased the Shirley Dairy Farm straddling Bear Creek on 420 acres south of Loretto Heights College. Col. D. C. Dodge, a wealthy landowner, had operated the farm as a hobby until his death. A group of farmers then rented the property but allowed the buildings to deteriorate. The Mullen Foundation bought the farm in January 1932 and started renovations.

The first students were 10- to 15-year-olds from St. Vincent's and St. Clara's orphanages. The staff included Brother Basil Mejean, director (principal); Brother Adrien Irenee; and A. Victor. They moved into their quarters at the J. K. Mullen Home for Boys at 3601 South Lowell Boulevard on April 8, 1932. The boys occupied a single building, which served as a school, dormitory, chapel, kitchen, dining room, and residence for the Christian Brothers. The farmhouse was transformed into a dormitory with lavatory, showers, and storage during the summer of 1933. Forty boys were admitted that fall. Fifty boys lived there in 1934 and the staff added Adrian Anthony, Adrian Michael, Anacletus Joseph, Angel Lucien, and Anthony Gabriel. Brother Charles Crouzet became director.[20]

Brother Lucien, an artist of French origin, built a grotto in the hillside north of the farm, carving it out of solid rock to duplicate a shrine in Lourdes, France. He lined the grotto with cement and installed electric lights in the cave to make it more visible. Lucien diverted water from a ditch to form two waterfalls and planted shrubs near the opening. Inside, he placed two statues, one of the Virgin Mary and one of Bernadette, who was later canonized for her visions of the Virgin Mary. The Mullen Home Grotto of Our Lady of Lourdes was blessed by Archbishop Urban J. Vehr on Sunday, April 28, 1935, following a procession by Denver Catholics who walked the half-mile trail from the home to the shrine. The shrine provided a solemn site for meditation and special celebrations. A tall cross, lighted at night, stood atop the hill and could be seen for miles.

The pupils kept to a rigid schedule, rising at 6:05 a.m. and assembling for prayer and mass before breakfast. They milked cows twice a day, did housework, cleaned barns, cared for animals, took classes, studied, and still participated in band and athletics. It was not unusual for many to change clothes five times on certain days—twice to milk, once for class, once for band, and once for a sport. Occasionally, they went on picnics or took mountain trips.[21]

In 1936, the Mullen Foundation purchased the 480-acre Wolcott Farm adjacent to the dairy farm to raise feed for livestock. The boys and farmworkers helped the Christian Brothers operate a successful dairy farm that produced about 500 tons of alfalfa annually, plus thousands of bushels of wheat, barley, oats, and corn, on their 900 acres. By 1938, the Mullen Home had a chapel, classrooms, dormitories, a gymnasium, cattle and poultry sheds, a tool house, a dairy house, and a greenhouse. The boys raised championship horses and participated in 4-H.[22]

The first graduates received diplomas in 1936: Wilfred Martin, Ernest Ponickvar, and Robert Pitt. Following graduation, Martin enlisted in the U.S. Army and flew B-29 bombers during World War II. He earned the Distinguished Flying Cross and retired as a lieutenant colonel. Ponickvar joined the Christian Brothers and taught classes at Mullen. Pitt stayed on the Mullen Home farm and worked with the dairy herd.

Brother Lucien started a band, which received superior ratings in all categories of competitions with larger schools in 1939. Thirty-two of the 40 students played in the band. Most band members played football, basketball, and baseball as well. Students made the first football uniforms themselves, covering their pads with brown coveralls. The Mullen Mustangs, coached by 1941 graduate

In 1932, the Mullen family bought the Shirley Dairy Farm, which straddled Bear Creek, as the location for the J. K. Mullen Home for Boys.

Sam Jarvis, won the Catholic League football championship in 1943. They battled Pueblo for the Catholic State Championship in 1950 and ended in a 13–13 tie. Cheerleaders from Holy Family High School supported the football team during the 1940s and 1950s.

The basketball team won the Catholic League championship in 1945 and shared the title with St. Francis High School in 1950. The Mullen boxing team established a winning tradition in 1938 with Denver policeman Dick Brown and his brother, Dan, as volunteer coaches. Athletic success was largely attributed to the boys' healthy lifestyle and plenty of milk.[23]

Times were changing in 1950s as the farm era began to fade. Two barracks were moved to the Mullen Home from Fort Logan in January 1950 to provide additional classrooms and space for woodworking and mechanics. Ten graduates brought the number of alumnae to 100. John McGregor, class salutatorian, joined the religious order of the Society of Mary and was the first alumnus ordained as a priest. In September, day students and paying boarders joined the student body, bringing the enrollment to 70. Tuition was $80 for the year, including book rental. The year 1950 proved rough, as a fire in October took the lives of two farmworkers and destroyed the bunkhouse where they lived, and another fire demolished the gymnasium the next month.

In 1953, the school changed its name from the J. K. Mullen Home for Boys to J. K. Mullen High School. Boosters, students, and faculty financed and built a new football stadium north of Bear Creek and carried bleachers to the field, making it ready for the 1954 season. The dairy cows, known for their quality milk, were sold in 1955 to the Carnation Milk Company, which bought the entire herd. Denver annexed the property in 1958, and seniors graduated in City Auditorium with students from all the Denver Catholic high schools.

When housing developments popped up north of Mullen, residents realized the need for better access to and from their homes. The old dirt road, first known as Sheridan Avenue and later as Hampden Avenue, was widened and paved in 1960, becoming US Highway 285. The highway cut through Mullen property, isolating the football field and grotto from the campus. The school built another football stadium to the west and dedicated it in October 1960. Mullen gave some of its land to Denver for a park along Bear Creek and sold some property to developers. Enrollment declined that year due to an increase in tuition costs and the opening of Abraham Lincoln High School on South Federal Boulevard.

Eighty-two seniors graduated in June 1966, the last class that included orphans and paying boarders. From 1966 to 1989, Mullen operated as a day school for boys only. The Christian Brothers of New Orleans–Santa Fe Province negotiated for two years with the Mullen Foundation to purchase the school and property. Meanwhile, Brother Bernard Kinneavy, the first director of development, headed a $500,000 fundraising campaign. The Christian Brothers' purchase of the school and 41 acres south of Hampden Avenue was finalized in September 1980 with the stipulation that the school's name always remain the same. The Mullen Foundation retained 30 acres, including land used at one time by the Southwest Denver Little League for baseball diamonds.[24]

In 1989, the school admitted female students for the first time in its 60-year history. Michelle Poffel was the first girl to enroll. The arrival of girls boosted dwindling school spirit and increased attendance at sporting events and school shows. The young women also heightened the need for additional restrooms and sports programs. For several years, Mullen leased almost 2 acres from the Fort Logan National Cemetery for soccer and lacrosse fields. In exchange for use of the land, they agreed to put in grass and a sprinkler system. They had to give up the fields in 2003 when Fort Logan needed the property for expansion because of the increased number of veterans' deaths.

Over the years, Mullen has evolved from a training school for orphaned boys into one of Colorado's most respected coeducational prep schools. The campus has expanded from a few farm buildings to a modern facility with the newest equipment, due to fundraising campaigns launched in the 1990s. An annual Mardi Gras event raises money for scholarships, since 25 percent of the 1,000-member student body needs help with tuition. "The school continues the Lasallian tradition, which promotes social justice," said Karen Scharf, development director. "As a graduation requirement, students devote 60 hours of community service at area hospitals, soup kitchens, canned food drives, mission projects, and similar activities."[25]

Scharf said the lake on the school property lost water when the Westbridge homes were built west of Mullen in the late 1990s, so the school bought water rights to the McBroom ditch and put in water lines to feed into the pond and irrigate the campus. There is less wildlife, but students still see Canada geese, squirrels, skunks, and spotted owls. Hawks and eagles nest outside Partners Hall, the only original building on the grounds.

A former teacher and coach, Vincent Creco, who served 22 years as an administrator in Jefferson County, was chosen as the first lay principal in 1993. Linda Brady became the first female principal in 2002. Although Brother Kinneavy died in 2001, his influence lives on. The football stadium was renamed Brother Bernard Kinneavy Stadium after the man who started the tradition of having freshmen form an "M" on the field during halftime at the homecoming game.

Cut off from the campus, the deteriorating grotto near US Highway 285 and South Knox Court was demolished in 1996. Known only to former students, longtime residents, and youth who hung out there, the grotto gave way to development when Village Homes bought the property and built 61 homes on the terraced hill. Fifteen U-Stor-It sheds went up where the old football field was located.[26] The Westbridge subdivision, designed for single families, was constructed in 1998, offering 200 moderately priced homes off West Kenyon Avenue, just west of J. K. Mullen High School.

Norgren's Pinehurst Farm and Country Club

After six years of ranching near Rifle, Colorado, Carl Norgren and his wife Juliet moved to Denver in 1925. An engineer who grew up on a cattle ranch in South Dakota, Carl worked from home, making and selling a small hose coupling he invented. Two years later, he developed the Norgren Oil Fog Lubricator, destined for international success. The business struggled through the Depression years and was finally sold to a Chicago holding company. In 1932, the Norgrens reclaimed the business and paid off their creditors. They built a manufacturing plant, which expanded over the next 12 years.

"When we moved onto Pinehurst Farm, in 1947, we expected to live there all of our lives," Carl Norgren related. He said the farm had a nice log home, perfect for his family, and a lovely lake stocked with rainbow trout. "We put in a swimming pool and had a beautiful garden. The farm buildings were sufficiently removed to ensure peace, quiet, and tranquility. The whole family was joyously happy."[27]

The Norgrens and their three sons raised Hereford cattle on their 320 acres south of West Hampden Avenue and west of South Sheridan Boulevard. Meanwhile, Carl's successful manufacturing company moved to a new factory and office building in Englewood. During World War II, the company provided hose assemblies and lubricators for shipyards, aircraft plants, and army arsenals. In 1956, Carl created an international operations department to serve the growing European markets.[28]

Small farms stretched south and west of Denver, but after World War II fewer people were interested in farming. Farmers were almost desperate to sell their land. "I was offered almost every farm for miles around for comparatively nothing if I would just assume the taxes and pay the interest on a loan," Carl said. In the 1950s, industry began to expand and developers eyed the land for houses and shopping centers. "Land values boomed. Farm labor disappeared. Farming became a real problem. Farmers dispersed their herds of cattle, until we were the last ones left in our area."[29]

With the manufacturing business booming and farming faltering, the Norgren's explored other uses for their farm. Their three sons were grown and they rambled around in the huge Pinehurst home, named for its stately pine trees. They finally decided to preserve the rolling country by building a golf course. The sport was becoming popular, and the Norgrens wanted to establish an affordable country club for middle-income families. They cut down many pine trees for two courses: an 18-hole and a 9-hole. Carl wanted to put in 36 holes, but there was not enough space, so he built the only 27-hole course in Denver. He also wanted to build houses in the $30,000 range—fancy, but not as high-scale as the Cherry Creek district.

On June 25, 1960, Carl hit the first golf ball to start play on a course designed by J. Press Maxwell. The spacious clubhouse, covering 1.25 acres under one roof, was completed in December on the hilltop at 6225 West Quincy Avenue. The 1,200 members paid $300 to join and $12 monthly dues. Don January was the first golf pro. Pinehurst was annexed by Denver in December 1969, after four years of boundary disputes with Jefferson County. The old barn remained to house maintenance equipment, and the windmill survives to remind golfers of the course's farm history. The log house was eventually surrounded by homes in Pinehurst Estates at South Sheridan Boulevard and West Mansfield Avenue.

The Pines/Bow Mar Heights

In 1951, realtor Walter Koelbel completed 289 houses north of West Quincy Avenue and east of South Sheridan Boulevard. Known as The Pines, the community featured a wide boulevard built to resemble the 6th Avenue Parkway close to downtown Denver.

The area called Bow Mar—named after two nearby lakes, Bowles and Marston—was developed in the 1950s with large ranch-style homes on sizable lots south of The Pines. Bow Mar Heights nestled between the two. Bow Mar Heights was annexed by Denver in 1958, but Bow Mar remained a separate entity, with Lloyd King (of King Soopers fame) as mayor. King started plans to build one of his King Soopers stores on South Sheridan Boulevard and West Dartmouth Avenue.[30]

Marie Stearns Perlman moved to Bow Mar Heights in 1963 with her husband, Larry, who worked at the Air Force Finance Center, and their three sons. They bought a five-bedroom, two-bath, brick ranch-style home with a two-car garage. They wanted a new house, close to schools, in a quiet neighborhood with a low crime rate.

"We were un-annexed and then re-annexed because Arapahoe County protested the tax-base loss. After the re-annexation, this area was forced to pay Arapahoe County taxes for a while, even though we were in Denver County," Marie said.

Marie loved gardening and set about planting flowers and vegetables in her big backyard on West Radcliffe Avenue. "Our house was built on the old Fort Logan training ground, where soldiers did maneuvers. I had to use a pickax to dig holes for my iris roots, because the ground was packed so hard from tramping feet and heavy artillery," she explained. "The neighborhood was quieter after we got rid of the nearby Englewood Speedway and Centennial Race Track."[31]

Stock cars had raced on the track at the Englewood Speedway, at South Federal Boulevard and West Oxford Avenue, since 1950, before the land was developed as the Sheridan Industrial Park and the Sherwood Business Park. Centennial Race Track, a horse track at South Federal Boulevard and West Belleview Avenue, operated from 1950 to 1983. Although approximately 100 horses drowned when the South Platte River flooded in 1965, the track opened for the season a month later, with a delay of only four days. Horseracing declined in popularity after the Mile High Kennel Club opened lower-priced dog races, so the racetrack was torn down. The site was developed as the Centennial Downs apartment, condominium, and office complex and the Centennial Golf Course in Littleton.

Denver annexed land for Centennial Estates and Centennial Acres in the early 1960s. Homeowners campaigned for community services and were pleased when their efforts resulted in a fire station and park along West Quincy Avenue and South Quitman Street in 1972. Mary S. Kaiser Elementary School, built at 4500 South Quitman Street in 1974, was named after a longtime teacher. With a neighborhood school nearby, many residents were unhappy to see their young children bused across town in the 1970s in an effort to racially integrate Denver schools.

Unusual Homes

In 1910, Frederick O. Vaille bought land for a summer home at 3999 South Sheridan Boulevard. Vaille was president of Denver's first telephone company. He built a two-story log house, designed by Temple H. Buell, which was connected to a log addition by a crossing wing featuring elaborate carving. The house was purchased by the Carl Norgren family in 1947 and later became part of Pinecrest Estates, with an address on South Chase Way.

John and Eleanor Campbell—a former gambler and a Las Vegas showgirl —ran a successful business purchasing items from estate sales and selling them at their six Red Barn Furniture stores. On the edge of Pinehurst Country Club, next door to the Vaille/Norgren house, the Campbells transformed their 16,000-square-foot, Italian Renaissance–style home to resemble a Japanese temple, complete with torii, the traditional gateway entrance to a Shinto shrine. They lived in a trailer during the 18-month construction period, while Eleanor, inspired by a *National Geographic* article on Japanese shrines, served as the architect, interior and landscape designer, general contractor, and construction supervisor. When finished, the 16,000-square-foot, $1 million home contained a 2,800-square-foot master bedroom suite and a roofed gallery with glass floor overlooking an indoor-outdoor swimming pool. The gardens included a teahouse surrounded by a moat.[32] Several stories revolved around the house. One was that Juan San Frisco Cortez, son-in-law of the Campbells, ran a tin gold–mining scam by entertaining prospective clients at the luxurious home and introducing the Campbells as caretakers. Another was that actor Peter Fonda stayed at the home and helped hide Easter eggs. Rumors circulated in 1976 that Elvis Presley, the famous singer, was interested in buying the house. Purportedly, the deal fell through because he could not build a security fence around the property due to zoning restrictions.[33]

The Michael Shinn home on South Zenobia Street won the House of the Year award from *American Home* magazine in 1974 for its ranch-style design, natural exterior, privacy from neighbors, and conveniences for entertaining. *American Home* magazine, the Denver Home Builders' Association, and Public Service Company of Colorado asked a panel of 42 homemakers to help plan the perfect dream house. Built by Koelbel and Co., Inc., and landscaped by Gerald F. Kessler, the 2,200-square-foot home accommodated 100 people for parties.[34] In 1992, Pinehurst was designated as the site for the Parade of Homes.

The Southwest Family YMCA

The Southwest Family YMCA opened at its new location on West Kenyon Avenue and South Sheridan Boulevard in 1981, after operating for four years from an office in the Bear Valley Shopping Center. The branch had sprouted from the 20th Street YMCA, founded in 1938. It moved to a house at West 6th Avenue and Kalamath Street in 1942 and called itself the Westside YMCA. Moving farther south, it operated from Prince of Peace Church, 2025 West Mississippi Avenue, and a location on Santa Fe Drive before moving to a small house at 2680 West Mexico Avenue in 1952. Many programs were carried out in nearby parks and schools until a new building and pool were constructed in 1959. At that point, the name changed to Southwest Family YMCA.[35]

As the city spread out and other agencies provided more services, the directors decided to relocate again. The YMCA sold the facilities to the city in 1977 (for the Athmar Park Recreation Center) and conducted its activities in southwest Denver schools and churches while looking for a permanent home. After considering several sites, the board of managers, chaired by Hartman Axley, negotiated a long-term use agreement with the city for 5.5 acres in Bear Creek Park, north of Fort Logan National Cemetery.

Generous donations exceeded the YMCA's goal for the first phase of construction. The new facility featured a six-lane swimming pool, locker rooms, a weight room, six handball-racquetball courts, offices, and meeting rooms. Expansion continued to mark the 1980s as the YMCA built a gymnasium and a running track, added fitness equipment, and developed youth athletic fields.

Twenty-five years later, the YMCA serves a more diverse population. "We have 4,000 to 4,500 members and nearly 50 percent of them are seniors, many who participate in the Silver Sneakers program sponsored by Kaiser and Secure Horizons health plans," said Linda James, director. "The bike path along Bear Creek is convenient for people who like to run. Our only limitation is parking space, and we're working on an agreement with the city to expand one parking lot."[36]

CHAPTER FIFTEEN

Bear Valley

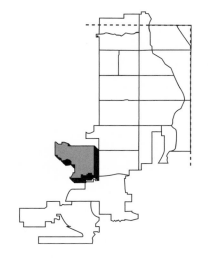

A well-known neighborhood in southwest Denver, Bear Valley is home to the Molly Brown Summer House, on the National Register of Historic Places, and Bear Valley Park, stretching along Bear Creek. The area south of Lakewood's Thraemoor district was annexed by Denver in 1960 and is roughly bounded by West Hampden Avenue to the south, West Yale Avenue to the north, South Sheridan Boulevard to the east, and South Wadsworth Boulevard to the west. Among other prominent residents, the late *Rocky Mountain News* columnist Gene Amole lived in the area with his family.

The Molly Brown Summer House

J.J. and Margaret (Molly) Brown, one of the famous couples who gained wealth from Leadville silver mines, moved to Denver's Capitol Hill in 1894. Three years later, they built a summer home in the country near Bear Creek. Seeking acceptance into high society's "Sacred 36," Margaret staged lavish parties in her Victorian home at 1340 Pennsylvania Street and also invited weekend guests to their country residence. Perhaps as an added attempt to impress Denver's wealthy citizens, Margaret supervised construction of a Foursquare-style, two-story red brick house at what is now 2690 South Wadsworth Boulevard. In doing so, she set the trend among Denver's affluent to build country homes and develop the rural area southwest of the city.[1]

The 10-room house, called Avoca Lodge, overlooked the fertile valley along Bear Creek. The setting inspired the name, taken from Thomas Moore's poem "The Meeting of the Waters." The poem's last verse reads:

Sweet vale of Avoca! How calm could I rest
In thy bosom of shade, with the friends I love best,
Where the storms that we feel in this cold world should cease,
And our hearts, like thy waters, be mingled in peace.[2]

Guests took the train from Denver to the railway station near present-day West Hampden Avenue and South Pierce Street, where the Browns' servants picked them up in a horse-drawn carriage. Visitors enjoyed the beautiful grounds graced by maple, apple, apricot, and cherry trees; flourishing rosebushes and other flowers; plus a large water fountain supplied by an artesian well. Yale was not a street then, and terraced lawns stretched south to the creek. During parties, music flowed from the loft of the red brick barn as dancers waltzed on the oak dance floor. Margaret, in expensive gowns complementing her red hair, mingled with her refined guests while J. J., who did not like big parties, hung out with stable hands in the horse barn.

J.J. and Margaret (Molly) Brown and their children, Helen and Lawrence.

J. J. raised fine horses, cows, and chickens on the 240-acre ranch along with wheat, oats, alfalfa, and barley. East of the house, a shed insulated with hay bales and refrigerated with blocks of ice held processed chicken, which J. J. sold to downtown restaurants. Milking took place in the dairy barn near Bear Creek. The farm supplied fish from a large lake along with fresh milk, butter, fruit, and poultry for meals at the Browns' city home.[3]

Shortly after completion of the main rectangular house, a one-story addition was built onto it. The front porch wrapped around to the south side, ending at the projecting bay, while the rear porch extended along the south wall of the addition. Both porches featured a wooden railing in a chinoiserie pattern. A sandstone cornerstone was inscribed "J.J. Brown, 1897."

Doors and frames, floors, and woodwork were constructed of hand-grained golden oak. The main portion of the house had a library and two sitting rooms, one on the north side and one on the south side, which held a bay window. The library housed a fireplace similar to a green-tiled fireplace in the Pennsylvania Street home, except this one featured sky-blue ceramic tiles designed with columbines and hummingbirds. Four bedrooms on the second floor provided sufficient space for the Browns and their two children, Lawrence and Elizabeth (called Helen), who were about 12 and 10 years old at the time Avoca Lodge was built.

In January 1906, at the time their marriage was floundering, the Browns sold 200 acres surrounding the house. After a legal separation in 1909, the Browns went their separate ways—J.J. to mining properties in Arizona, Utah, and California, and Margaret to East Coast resorts and European cities. Margaret, actually known as Maggie most of her life, gained international fame as a survivor of the tragic event of April 15, 1912, when the *Titanic* sank off the Newfoundland coast. Dubbed "The Unsinkable Mrs. Brown" by newspaper reporters, Margaret nursed sick survivors, took messages from the dying, and aided frightened women immigrants who lost their husbands. She helped raise more than $10,000 for destitute victims of the tragedy.

The Browns sold their summer home in 1918 to Benjamin F. Simpson, who sold it the same year to Louise C. Donley. In 1922, J.J. died; Margaret died 10 years later in New York City. According to Kristen Iversen's book, *Molly Brown: Unraveling the Myth*, details of Margaret's personality and life were exaggerated over the years by journalists, politicians, and movie producers. Her fame as "Molly Brown" began in the 1960s with a Broadway musical titled *The Unsinkable Molly Brown*. Composer Meredith Wilson admitted changing Maggie's name to Molly because it was easier for singers to enunciate. A movie version of the Broadway play starred Debbie Reynolds as Molly Brown.[4]

The current owner of the Molly Brown Summer House, Jane Garland, said, "My parents, Robert and Rose Fehlmann, bought the property in 1928, when Wadsworth was a dirt road." Jane grew up on the farm, where she and her three siblings helped their parents in the garden. Robert, a gardener, grew lettuce, tomatoes, peas, beans, carrots, cantaloupe, radishes, celery, and cabbages. He took fresh items every day to Denargo Market at Speer Boulevard and Colfax Avenue. Growers vied for first in line to get attention from grocers, who picked out produce for their stores. "I went with my father many times," Jane said. "We got up at 4 a.m. The market opened at 5 a.m. and we were usually home by 7:30 a.m."

The Fehlmann children planted tomatoes in "hotbeds." They gathered cattails from the surrounding area, cut and dried them at home, laid them out on a wooden loom, tied them together with jute twine, and made mats to cover the hotbeds. "We had acres of sash [glass windows] to cover in the evenings and open in the mornings. It took constant maintenance to protect the plants from hail. Father was very inventive. He developed a way to transfer the

The Fehlmann sisters, Ferne Kurtz and Jane Garland, along with Jane's daughter, Mary Rose Shearer, care for the historic Molly Brown Summer House originally called Avoca Lodge.

seedlings into the fields. His farming methods changed during World War II because help was scarce. Women and older men did the work, and he also hired part-time Chinese and Japanese workers for share farming. The Japanese farmers were sadly sent to an internment camp in California," Jane said.

"Money was tight during the war. Once, Father had to dump a whole load of cantaloupe in back because he couldn't sell it. Since produce was difficult to sell, the farm changed to raising animals. We had hundreds of sheep, turkeys, geese, and chickens. We sold eggs, butter, anything to keep money coming in. Mother hand-dressed geese for customers who had them blessed for Thanksgiving and Christmas dinners. Then the farm was put into crops and father hired people to plant hay and corn. When planters refused to do less than 500 acres, the farm went to pastureland and we boarded horses.

"About 1952 or 1953, near the end of my father's life, the farm was subdivided for residential sites. Some of the property known as the Fehlmann subdivision was sold for The Village complex in the mid-1960s. After Father's death, my mother, my sister Ferne, and I tried to take care of the pastureland, walking irrigation ditches to regulate the water. When mother became more fragile after a series of strokes, she was bedridden. She stayed in the house until four weeks before her death in 1980 at age 94."

Jane knew there were bees in the chimney, but when honey began trickling down the upstairs walls, she realized the problem was serious. She located a beekeeper to remove the hive and a mason who would repair the buttered brick chimney after the hive was removed. The chimney stood 7 feet into the attic and covered two stories for a total of 15–20 feet and had five stacks inside that fed several rooms. The beekeeper found a solid mass of honeycombs, some of which were at least 60 years old.

J.J. and Margaret Brown built their summer house, Avoca Lodge, in 1897. The historic house, now at 2690 S. Wadsworth Blvd., is open for special events by reservation.

Growing up in the historic house, Garland heard stories about the Browns from former carriage drivers, cooks, and upstairs maids who occasionally stopped in and shared the noon meal. She said they referred to the Browns as "Maggie and Jiggs" from a popular comic strip.

Jane graduated from Bear Creek High School, attended the University of Denver, and taught preschool and junior high students during her 33-year career as a teacher for Denver Public Schools. She recalled several families who built homes in the area over the years. The Fred Schnell family owned land south of the Fehlmanns' property. The McManns built a country home in what is now Forest Glen on the west side of South Wadsworth Boulevard, north of Yale Avenue. In the 1920s, the Kountze family of Colorado National Bank built a house in what is now Thraemoor.

Vernon Z. Taylor, connected with Helena Rubinstein cosmetics, bought dry ground from Fehlmann to protect his property from encroachment. The very private family entertained Princess Anne at their home called Stroube, which reportedly contained 100 rooms. Henry Swan, vice president of U.S. National Bank, built a white house with a round turret. His son, Henry Swan II, became professor of surgery at Colorado General Hospital. An internationally recognized heart physician, Swan was the first surgeon to perform a successful open-heart surgery in the early 1950s.

Over the years, 37 of the farm's remaining 40 acres were sold to farmers and developers. Several outbuildings, including a foreman's house, were removed from the farm. The property was annexed by Denver in 1966 during a period of rapid growth, and the large buttered brick barn with its polished hardwood floor was torn down to make way for a water main. The house was listed on the National Register of Historic Places in 1990.

Jane and her sister, Ferne Kurtz, cared for the family farm, making repairs and improvements as needed within financial limitations. After renting the house to other businesses, Jane and her daughter, Mary Rose Shearer (who goes by Momo), managed a women's boutique, known as Persnickety's, for several years. Then in 2006, Jane and Mary Rose redecorated the house and opened it for luncheons, tours, and special events to keep the Molly Brown heritage alive. Mary Rose also puts together gourmet gift baskets featuring goodies and gifts for individuals, businesses, and corporations.[5]

The Duke Family Farm

Cressie Duke, who was born in Iowa in 1880, came to Denver at age 18 and worked as a clerk for the Daniels and Fisher department store (the D&F of May

D&F, the predecessor to Foley's and Macy's in Denver). The young woman went back to Iowa, married Clifford W. Duke, and returned to Colorado. Clifford was a member of the school board at Bear Creek, where their children attended school. Cressie wrote Grange Insurance and served as secretary-treasurer of the Jefferson County Farm Loan Association for 20 years. In 1916, Cressie and Clifford Duke moved with their three children into a two-story, three-bedroom farmhouse, which they remodeled once. Built in 1885 on 120 acres that ran along South Sheridan Boulevard from Hampden .75 miles north and 0.25 miles east, the house was about a block north of Bear Creek.

The Duke family raised anywhere from 1,000 to 5,000 turkeys on the farm at 3077 South Sheridan Boulevard and sold them all over Denver. In addition to turkeys, the Dukes milked 20 dairy cows and maintained a hog lot. The Dukes had a contract with the Fort Logan Military Post to get the fort's garbage as food for the hogs. They also raised feed crops such as barley and silage corn. For a short time, they grew sugar beets and took them to a sugar beet dump on South Pierce Street, south of West Hampden Avenue, to await transport to a sugar factory. "My father even tried to raise his own tobacco," said Richard H. Duke, youngest son of the family. "But it seemed that worms would appear just when the tobacco was ripe."[6]

After Clifford's death in 1937, Cressie farmed the land herself until 1945 and then leased it. A hired man helped them for 23 years. Cressie lived to be nearly 97, enjoying picnics at her cabin near Bailey and activities with church friends and family. She died in 1977.

The Dukes' older son, Vernon, graduated from the University of Colorado (CU) in 1928. He worked for KOA in Denver for eight years and then the National Broadcasting Company in New York for 37. A pioneer in the television industry, he helped produce the first color television shows and received the 1966 Herbert T. Kalmus Gold Medal Award from the Society of Motion Picture and Television Engineers. He held 15 U.S. patent grants and was honored with CU's Distinguished Engineers Award.

The Dukes' younger son, Richard, graduated from the University of Colorado Law School; he was admitted to the Bar Association in 1941. Before practicing law, Richard spent three-and-a-half years in the army and served for 18 months in Italy as a weather forecaster. He then practiced law from an office on South Sheridan Boulevard, where he noted that old U.S. quartermaster spoons from Fort Logan were dug up when the bicycle shop on West Dartmouth Avenue was being built. The Dukes' daughter, Mildred, moved to Vancouver, Washington, where her husband practiced veterinary medicine.

Over the years, the Duke family sold land to developers for residential dwellings and rented land for businesses, including a Conoco service station, a King Soopers grocery store, a McDonald's restaurant, and the First National Bank of Bear Valley, which later became Wells Fargo Bank. During the 1970s, they loaned land to the Southwest Denver Little League Association for baseball fields and to the Boy Scouts of America for the West District Camporee. A whole generation of bicycle riders grew up on the dirt piles near the old farmhouse, which was demolished in 1978. The land stood vacant until 2000, when the Dukes sold their last piece of property for construction of 350 units called the Bear Valley Park Apartments.[7]

More Development

Bear Valley was annexed by the city in 1960, with 470 acres zoned for single-family residences. The large plot, bounded by West Hampden Avenue on the south, West Yale Avenue on the north, South Sheridan Boulevard on the east, and South Lamar Street on the west, contained only three houses. Aksel Nielsen was president of Mortgage Investment Company, the prime investment firm for the proposed development.[8]

Twenty-two custom builders put up quality homes of various types—three-bedroom ranches, tri-levels, and colonials. The homes ranged in price from $16,000 to $30,000. Residents were mostly in their 20s and 30s and held jobs as policemen, salesmen, state and federal employees, junior executives, and attorneys. They were concerned about the lack of schools, since their children were bused to University Park Elementary School and Kunsmiller Junior High. Older students provided their own transportation to Abraham Lincoln High School. Merle Jackson, a supervisor at Martin Company, served as the first chairman of the Bear Valley Improvement Association to head the drive for neighborhood amenities.[9]

The Bear Valley West subdivision was added in 1962, consisting of the area from South Lamar Street west to South Wadsworth Avenue, between West Yale Avenue and a jagged line south of West Dartmouth Avenue. Other annexations took place through the 1960s and early 1970s, including Bear Valley Church of Christ at West Yale Avenue and South Lamar Street in 1963 and various parcels of land along West Kenyon Avenue between South Sheridan Boulevard and South Harlan Street.

Denver encountered many boundary disputes with Jefferson County, even though annexations ceased after passage of the Poundstone Amendment in 1973. Some areas were annexed and de-annexed repeatedly.

Bear Valley Park

A long, narrow strip of land designated as Bear Valley Park follows Bear Creek along West Dartmouth Avenue from South Sheridan Boulevard west to South Wadsworth Boulevard. The Bear Valley Improvement Association (BVIA) applied for Community Development Agency funds through the Neighborhood Small Project program in 1980 to improve the park. Rick Nuanes, BVIA vice president, coordinated a work weekend that attracted 35 men, women, and children to install playground equipment purchased with the grant. The association also used grant money for tennis court backboards and soccer field goals, a bulletin board, bike racks, trash containers, picnic tables, and benches.

BVIA received another grant in 1981, which funded equipment for a challenge course along the bike path, the second phase of improvements. Frank Clark, BVIA president, headed the project, assisted by Larry Lindauer and members of Boy Scout Troop 498, who helped with planning and labor.[10]

Seven Springs: The New Bear Valley

A "new" Bear Valley neighborhood sprang up on the south side of Bear Creek, appealing to young families who wanted safe, clean streets, neat parks, Denver services, and lower taxes than the suburbs—the same benefits that attracted earlier residents of "old" Bear Valley on the north side of Bear Creek. About 80 homes nestled quietly in the semirural neighborhood known as Seven Springs.[11]

In 1981, city traffic engineers suggested construction of a vehicular bridge crossing Bear Creek at South Fenton Street to provide better emergency access for the new residents on the south side of Bear Creek. However, residents on the north side objected due to the possibilities of increased traffic, damage to the park area and wildlife, danger to joggers on the bike path, and concern for schoolchildren. A task force including city engineers, residents from Bear Valley and Harvey Park, and Councilman Ted Hackworth held several community meetings and looked at various alternatives before scrapping the plan.[12]

Phil and Joyce Neufeld bought a lot in 1991 and built a four-bedroom, two-story home in the Seven Springs neighborhood. The land, once owned by Hans Nielsen, was originally a landfill for Gates Rubber Company. "We had to get two soil samples when we built our house, one before the basement was dug and another before the foundation was poured, because there were layers of trash and pieces of rubber all over the area," Joyce said.

Phil, a computer programmer, and Joyce, a church administrator, raised three children, Corina, Andy, and Bryan, who had to take the bus to their school across Bear Creek. "We thought the quiet, secluded neighborhood was great," Joyce admitted, "but there is only one way in and one way out, which makes a longer response time for emergency vehicles. And we have to drive 3 miles to the high school 7 blocks away. A footbridge crossing Bear Creek at West Dartmouth Avenue and South Lamar Street was installed around 2001, making easier access for the students that walk to Traylor Elementary School, Henry Middle School, and John F. Kennedy High School."

Active in the Seven Springs Neighborhood Association, Joyce said the community has grown to 120 single-family residences, including 3 blocks of custom-built homes in the area bounded by West Dartmouth Avenue on the north, South Ivan Way on the east, West Hampden Avenue on the south, and South Newland Street on the west. Several apartment and condominium complexes were built along West Hampden Avenue, such as Water's Edge (formerly Peachtree II), Hunter's Ridge, and Seven Springs Condominiums. The Bear Valley Condominiums along the south side of Bear Creek were built for 110 residents in 2003.[13]

The Bear Creek Swim and Tennis Club

Families west of South Sheridan Boulevard organized the Bear Creek Swim and Tennis Club about the same time Harvey Park residents founded the Terrace Club swimming pool to the east. The Bear Creek member-owned facility, built in a secluded area north of the frontage road along West Hampden Avenue at South Pierce Street, featured a 25-meter swimming pool, a diving tank, a baby pool, tennis courts, an expansive grass area, barbecue grills, and a sand volleyball pit for picnics and parties. The private club offered competitive swim and dive teams for juniors, swimming and diving lessons, family swim nights, club and league tennis play for adults and juniors, professional tennis instruction, and various social events throughout the summer.[14]

"We joined the swim club after moving to the neighborhood in 1972," said Tony Bilello, who lives with his wife, Carol, on South Gray Street. "Our three girls, Jeanne, Jennifer, and Susan, took swim lessons," added Carol. "If Tony took the car to work, the girls and I walked across the creek to get to the club, since there weren't foot bridges at that time and we only had one car. Every Fourth of July we took a picnic lunch and celebrated at the club with inner tube races, egg-throwing contests, and other fun events."[15] The club, now more than 40 years old, continues to offer a limited number of family and empty-nester memberships.

Schools

Traylor Elementary School, 2900 South Ivan Way, was built in 1968 and named after Frank A. Traylor, a Board of Education member. Built in 1966, John F. Kennedy High School, at 2855 South Lamar Street, initially served both junior and senior high students with staggered sessions until Henry Junior High School opened at 3005 South Golden Way in 1975. The new school was named for Arthur S. Henry, the school district attorney. Kennedy then went to normal hours for high school students only. Traylor and Greenlee Elementary Schools in Lincoln Park were paired for racial integration during the 1970s, and high school students from northeast Denver were bused to Kennedy.

John F. Kennedy High School, named for the 35th president of the United States, offered a unique aeronautics class featuring a Link GAT-1 general-aviation trainer simulating the cockpit of a single-engine airplane. Thomas Cross, a licensed pilot and class instructor, said that, to his knowledge, Kennedy was the only high

John F. Kennedy High School was on the edge of town when it opened in 1966, serving both junior and senior high students for its first nine years.

school in the world with a Link trainer in the late 1970s. The Link trainer, purchased with National Defense Education Act funds, was available to other Denver high school students on a rotating schedule for simulated flight training.[16]

Another first-of-its-kind class involved a cattle-feeding project designed to impart knowledge of animal growth. Kennedy zoology and botany students built corrals and a pole shelter for four cows that were boarded near the school on South Wadsworth Boulevard. Students fed the animals on their own time and tracked their progress before selling them at market value. Biology teachers Craig Secord and Lynn Williams supervised the project.[17]

Prominent Residents

Residents of Bear Valley included athletes, journalists, and politicians, to name a few. The following is a look into the lives of some prominent citizens of Bear Valley.

The Haggertys

Janet and Patrick "Pat" Haggerty had a home built on South Depew Street in 1962. Two weeks after they moved into their new house, a housewarming gift arrived—their adopted baby, Kelly Jo. They had already adopted Patrick Andrew, Jr. two years earlier.

Patrick Sr. played baseball, basketball, and football at Denver's North High School and baseball at the University of Northern Colorado, where he met Janet. Both graduated as physical education (PE)

Patrick Haggerty

teachers. In 1947, Haggerty signed a pro baseball contract with the Detroit Tigers and played for five years in the Tigers' minor league system. In 1953, he wore the Denver Bears uniform as one of the few local athletes who played for the minor league hometown team. A PE teacher for 35 years, he taught at Valverde Elementary School before going to Abraham Lincoln High School when it opened in 1960. He also coached the Lincoln varsity baseball team for 29 years.

In addition, Patrick officiated at football games, working his way up from high school to college games and then to the National Football League (NFL), where he established a sterling reputation as a fair and efficient official respected by both coaches and players. For 26 out of 28 seasons, he received a playoff assignment as head referee with the NFL and was selected to officiate at three Super Bowls—in 1979, 1982, and 1985.

"The whole family went to the Super Bowl in Miami," said daughter Kelly. "It was quite exciting." Remembering other happy times with her family, Kelly, a 1980 graduate of John F. Kennedy High School, mentioned camping trips, vacations in California, and hiking near their cabin at Estes Park—the cabin her grandfather bought from a bootlegger for $100. "We had lots of football parties and Fourth of July celebrations and shared good times with our friends and next-door neighbors, the Gene Amole family."[18]

Kelly's mother, Janet, died of cancer in 1988 at age 59, and her father, Pat, died of cancer in 1994 at age 67. Kelly, who had a successful acupuncture practice, returned to the family home and stayed until her marriage in 2005. Pat Jr., once a batboy for his father's baseball teams at Lincoln High School, accepted a plaque at his father's induction into the Colorado Sports Hall of Fame on March 8, 2005.

The Amoles

Gene Amole and his wife, Patricia (Trish), raised four children—Tustin, Brett, Jon, and Susan—in their Bear Valley home on South Depew Street. A Denver native, Gene was active in commercial broadcasting since 1942. His radio career began with KMYR, following military service with Gen. George Patton in World War II. After a couple of stints as a foreign correspondent, Gene became involved with television production when Denver first started programming. He wrote and produced programs for Channels 2, 4, 6, 7, and 9. He won the prestigious George Foster Peabody Award for *Panorama*, one of the programs he wrote and narrated. A pioneer in TV news broadcasting, Gene hosted one of the industry's first talk programs.[19]

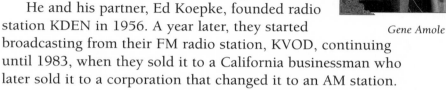

Gene Amole

He and his partner, Ed Koepke, founded radio station KDEN in 1956. A year later, they started broadcasting from their FM radio station, KVOD, continuing until 1983, when they sold it to a California businessman who later sold it to a corporation that changed it to an AM station.

While serving as president for Southwest Denver Little League baseball, Gene organized 500 children into teams that were formed by a draft. "If I had it to do over again, I would have stayed on the sidelines and let them organize their own teams and own play," he said later.[20]

Gene started as a columnist for the *Rocky Mountain News* in December 1977, declaring himself to be an "implacable foe of malignant bureaucracy" in his first column titled "Morning." His columns were published in four books: *Morning*, 1983; *Amole Again*, 1985; *Amole One More Time*, 1998; and *The Last Chapter: Gene Amole on Dying*, which chronicled his deteriorating health and ended with his death in May 2002. During his lifetime, Gene received numerous awards for his contributions to radio, television, and journalism.

A few months before his death, Gene attended a special ceremony recognizing his civic efforts. Mayor Wellington Webb proclaimed the day, December 20, 2001, as Gene Amole Day in Denver. As a tribute, the city changed the name of Elati Street between West 15th Avenue and West Colfax Avenue to Gene Amole Way, thereby creating a new address for the *Rocky Mountain News* at 100 Gene Amole Way. (The former address was 400 West Colfax Avenue.)

The Kyles

When Lyle and Ruedene Kyle moved to Denver, they looked for a home close to the mountains. They bought a home by a well-known builder, Hutchinson, in the southern section of Harvey Park, where they lived

Lyle C. Kyle

for 15 years with their four children: Ann, Larry, Kurt, and Kevin. "People were in our economic stratum and we didn't have to worry about keeping up with the Joneses," they said. However, in 1973, when they wanted a larger home with a two-car garage, they moved to a custom home in Bear Valley, where they had friends.

Respected and well-liked by politicians of both parties, Lyle served 27 years as Director of Colorado's Legislative Council and worked with five governors: Steve McNichols, John Love, John Vanderhoof, Dick Lamm, and Roy Romer. Lyle hired and managed the staff who researched information for state legislators and staffed the committees of the legislature. He was responsible for publishing the "blue book" of pros and cons on ballot issues for voters. "We printed 5,000 copies in 1958 and had to beg people to take them. Now [in 2005] they're so popular, they're mailed to every home," he said. In 1968, he was elected to chair the National Conference of State Legislators and got acquainted with people of other states. He also chaired the State Board of Equalization for 15 years.

As active members of Harvey Park Christian Church, the Kyles have held numerous positions, including board chair, elder, deacon, and Sunday school teacher. They both enjoy singing in the choir and sometimes sing duets. Lyle was the lead in the Men's Quartet, which entertained at many events, and he continues to sing at weddings and funerals.

When their boys were on split sessions at Kennedy Junior-Senior High School, Ruedene folded newspapers for three routes, so they could deliver the evening edition of the *Denver Post* after school. Lyle served as cubmaster for Cub Scouts and as treasurer for the Southwest Denver Little League.

In April 1983, the state legislators surprised Lyle with a celebration for his 25 years of service and paid tribute to his integrity, expertise, diligence, and impartiality. Following his retirement in December 1985, Lyle served as president of the Colorado Public Expenditure Council for four years. He now finds pleasure in his gardening hobby and raises a large crop of tomatoes each year.[21]

CHAPTER SIXTEEN

Marston

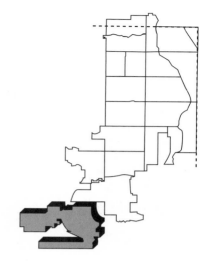

$\mathcal{T}$he development of Marston—almost in the foothills, roughly from West Quincy Avenue to West Sumac Avenue (north of West Bowles Avenue) and South Sheridan Boulevard to South Kipling Street—is marked by the development of reservoirs and water companies. The neighborhood's primary draw today is the thriving subdivision of Grant Ranch, with its numerous water features and Raccoon Creek Golf Course. Various cities and counties battled over annexing the valuable ranch property. Much of the neighborhood, however, ended up with Denver addresses and reflects the character of southwest Denver.

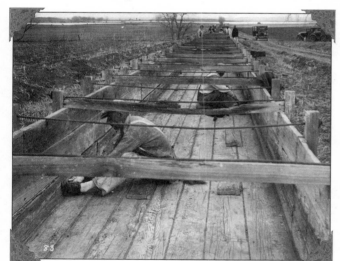

Workers install a flume at Marston Reservoir near West Quincy Avenue and South Wadsworth Boulevard around 1931.

Marston Lake and the Water Companies

Following the railroad's arrival in 1870, Denver's population swelled to nearly 6,000, and the need for water increased. Denver City Water Company, founded by Col. James Archer, brought the first domestic water service to the young city in 1872. Until then, citizens had depended upon wells for potable water and a string of ditches for irrigation. Prominent businessmen David Moffat, Walter Cheesman, and Daniel Witter served on the water company's

top left: Pipe molds, 90 inches in diameter, for Marston Water Treatment plant, 1924.
top right: Mr. Lowther and Mr. Cross sit on an intake pipe during construction, May 4, 1925.
above: Employees of Look Joint Pipe Company load concrete pipe.

board of directors. Evidently, they had a disagreement with Archer, so they formed a rival company called Citizen's Water Company.[1]

Citizen's Water Company organized in 1889 and purchased Marston Lake, a large natural basin out in the country beyond Fort Logan. Headed by Moffat, Citizen's Water Company built embankments, transformed the basin into an immense storage reservoir, erected a large filtration plant, and connected it with two water mains leading to the city. Because of intense competition with Denver City Water Company, Citizen's canceled all fees and supplied customers with free water for about two years. However, neither firm prospered and the rivalry ended in 1894, when the two merged into the Denver Union Water Company with Walter Cheesman as president and David Moffat as treasurer.

Located about 10 miles southwest of the capitol building, Marston Reservoir stretched half a mile long and a third-mile wide. The embankments were raised 12 feet in 1897 and the lake area increased to 1 square mile with a storage capacity of 2.5 billion gallons. After raising the embankments another 16 feet one year later, the reservoir contained more than 8 billion gallons of water.[2]

Meanwhile, forward-looking leaders began planning a dam on the South Fork of the South Platte River as a larger source of water for the burgeoning metropolis. Construction began in 1898 on a dam near Deckers, using granite blocks quarried from the area. Named for Walter Cheesman, Cheesman Dam was completed in 1905 as a major component of Denver's water system to follow. Denver voters approved the purchase of the water system for $13,970,000 in 1918 and placed it under the control of the Board of Water Commissioners.[3]

A vital link in the Denver water system, the Marston Water Treatment Plant, at 6100 West Quincy Avenue, was built in 1925 beside Marston Reservoir. One of three major treatment plants, the full-processing facility treats water from the South Platte River, Blue River, and Bear Creek. A clear water reservoir was added in 1961, and new rapid sand facilities were constructed in 1967, bringing the plant's treatment capacity to 200 million gallons per day. A micro-strainer facility also increased the treatment capacity, and the plant expanded again in 1991 with pre-treatment facilities. The Quality Control Laboratory for chemical and biological testing was established in 1969, with additions in 1976 and 1986 to enhance the laboratory's testing capability. Marston's laboratory currently conducts about 80,000 tests each year for a wide range of possible water pollutants.[4]

Plant Supervisor Garth Rygh said Marston's present water treatment capacity is 250 million gallons per day. The Moffat Water Treatment Plant has capacity for 185 million gallons per day, while Foothills Water Treatment Plant lists a capacity of 280 million gallons per day. Overall, Denver Water serves more than a million people, including the city and county of Denver and nearly 40 percent of the suburbs.

The American Water Works Association

Farther west, the American Water Works Association (AWWA) established its headquarters more than a century ago on a 3-acre site at 6666 West Quincy Avenue. AWWA, a nonprofit scientific and educational society, was organized in 1881 to improve water for people worldwide. Members are mostly managers, engineers, and other employees of utilities that supply drinking water to people in the United States, Canada, and Mexico.[5]

The present office building, constructed in 1977, surrounds an open courtyard with a recirculating fountain. Donyelle Alexander, association services representative for six years, said AWWA has approximately 56,500 members whose purpose is to assure safe drinking water for all people.

Grant Ranch

Fast-forward to the 1990s, when water plans are in place and land is plentiful. Marty camped out for three nights as the seventh in line for a new home in the Grant Ranch subdivision. A Denver fireman, Mamigonian was required to live within the city limits at that time, so the original Denver addresses in Grant Ranch were coveted. (Denver voters, however, overturned the residency requirement in November 1998, four months after he moved to his new house in Heron Estates, one of the 22 villages that make up the Grant Ranch community.) Marty, a graduate of John F. Kennedy High School, and his wife, Kristy, preferred to live in southwest Denver. They lived in the Bear Valley Seven Springs neighborhood for seven years. Then, with three growing sons, they looked for a larger home. "These were the first new homes in the southwest part of town," he said. "A lot of Denver police officers, attorneys, judges, and other city employees moved to this area also."

Marty had a second job with Edelweiss Realty, and Kristy opened a candle shop a few years later. "We don't participate in all the social activities, because we are busy with our jobs and our sons' lacrosse and wrestling matches," they said. "However, we like the Village Center, which has a swimming pool and tennis courts, the large greenbelt area, and the Fall Migration festivities."[6]

Neighbors Dan and Donna McNulty also stood in line to sign up for a new home in Grant Ranch. "About 30 of us were in line to buy dirt. None of us knew prices; we just wanted a new home in the southwest Denver city limits," she said. Dan was a motorcycle officer with the Denver Police Department. Donna became active with the homeowners' association and was eventually hired as office/event manager for the Grant Ranch Village Center, operated by the homeowners' association (HOA).

The Grant Ranch Master Homeowners Association sponsored holiday socials, recreational activities, self-improvement opportunities, Easter egg hunts, Fourth of July barbecues, swim meets, sailing regattas, yoga, and art classes. "The annual Fall Migration Festival started as part of a grant proposal requiring a community event," Donna explained. "It was a way to bring residents together to say goodbye to the birds who leave for the winter. Funds from the grant will help build the nature park and learning gardens in the isthmus between Bowles Reservoir and Marston Reservoir. The nature park will feature a diversified habitat for cottontail rabbits, red fox, and pelicans, plus a rookery for blue herons."[7]

Several of the villages were constructed on the shoreline of Bowles Reservoir with access to private boat docks and beaches. The HOA maintains a recreational lease of 172-acre surface rights on Bowles Reservoir No. 1. Residents can use their own non-motorized boats or rowboats, canoes, and pedal boats provided by the Village Center, which also offers an Olympic-size outdoor swimming pool, spa, tennis courts, and large lakeside clubhouse for community and private events. Homeowners can fish on a catch-and-release basis or observe a variety of waterfowl and other birds on nearby lakes. Grant B and Grant C Reservoirs are part of the 18-hole Raccoon Creek Golf Course, located adjacent to Grant Ranch just south of Bowles Reservoir No. 1.

The reservoirs that mark Grant Ranch today all started as natural water holes. The remainder of this chapter will take a look back at when the area actually served as a ranch and realte how it developed into today's popular neighborhood.

Grant Ranch's Original Owner

Colorado's third governor originally owned the land now known as Grant Ranch. James B. Grant came to Colorado in the late 1870s as a mining engineer. Originally from Alabama, Grant and an uncle started a smelter in Leadville. It was moved to Denver and became the Omaha and Grant Smelting Company. Grant, who was also a real estate and water rights speculator, bought a number of properties southwest of Denver, developed the water rights, and sold some of the property as irrigated farmland. Grant Ranch extended roughly from West Bowles Avenue to West Belleview Avenue between South Sheridan Boulevard and South Kipling Street. He kept the land as a cattle ranch and a hunting and shooting club, but he never lived on the grounds.

James B. Grant, governor of Colorado from 1883 to 1885.

Involved in civic affairs, Grant served as vice president of Denver National Bank and president of the Denver School Board. He was elected governor of Colorado and served from 1883 to 1885. In 1902, Grant built a mansion at 770 Pennsylvania Avenue, now known as the Grant-Humphreys Mansion, and lived there until his death in 1911. Today, the mansion is owned by the Colorado Historical Society and may be rented for weddings, corporate events, and celebrations.[8]

Selling Off the Ranch

In 1917, Grant's widow sold Grant Ranch to Mary Baker, who built most of the ranch buildings in the 1920s. When Baker died, her son George inherited the property and struggled unsuccessfully to keep it during the Depression years. After foreclosure, the property was purchased by the family of James Grant's nephew, whose descendants still own a portion of the original ranch.

Mary Belle and Edwin (Ned) Grant with Susan, Patrick, and Newell, winter 1946.

One of the descendants, Edwin (Ned) Grant, and his wife, Mary Belle, built a house and raised their children on the ranch. A son, Newell, remembers riding horses, shooting ducks on the lake, and waiting for the school bus on unpaved West Bowles Avenue. From the 1930s through the 1970s, the Grants operated the ranch, raising milk cows, hogs, sheep, horses, wheat, corn, and even sugar beets. They showed calves at the National Western Stock Show and raised horses that raced at Centennial Race Track. Granville, a well-known horse in the late 1930s, ended up at the ranch after his racing career halted because of an injury. Another famous horse named Seabiscuit trained against Granville, but the two horses did not compete in the same races.[9]

Several municipalities attempted to annex Grant Ranch over the years. In the early 1970s, Denver annexed the property. Jefferson County filed a lawsuit contesting the annexation. The ensuing court battles ended in the Colorado Supreme Court, which decided in favor of Denver. Denver's second attempt to annex a different part of Grant Ranch proved unsuccessful after the appellate court found the second annexation to be invalid. Lakewood annexed a strip of land in the 1980s, so Grant Ranch was then under three jurisdictions.

During 1983–1984, the Grant family built the Raccoon Creek Golf Course, remodeling the ranch house as the new clubhouse. They maintained the ranch atmosphere by leaving the original farm buildings and the brown granary along the entrance road. The golf course was opened for public play in both the city and county of Denver and Jefferson County.

Although still involved in the community, the Grant family sold the land to Simeon Residential Properties in the early 1990s. Simeon put in roads, water lines, sewers, and then sold parcels of land to several homebuilders. Planners envisioned small villages with single-family residences, townhouses, and condominiums where single professionals, young couples, growing families, and empty-nesters would be neighbors. About 130 of the 493 acres in the Denver part of Grant Ranch were dedicated to open space for activities such as picnics, Frisbee, softball, and soccer.

Newell Grant is active on the board of directors of the Joseph W. Bowles Reservoir Company, owner and operator of the Bowles Reservoir. He served as board president in 2005. The reservoir company, along with Bowles Avenue, was named for Joseph Bowles, a pioneer with property along the South Platte River. Newell's brother, Pat Grant, is president and CEO of Denver's National Western Stock Show.

Schools Move In

As Grant Ranch developed with various home styles and prices, it attracted people of diverse racial backgrounds and numerous choices for recreation and education. Denver's Grant Ranch School, for pupils in early childhood classes through eighth grade, opened at 5400 South Jay Circle on August 20, 2001. The state-of-the-art facility, with its distinctive clock tower, featured more than 35 classrooms, a gymnasium containing boys' and girls' locker rooms, a huge cafeteria, and several computer rooms. Because of new boundaries, the school drew students from the Grant Ranch and Park West communities, including those previously bused to Sabin and Kaiser Elementary Schools and Henry Middle School. High schoolers were directed to John F. Kennedy High School.

Jefferson County's Blue Heron K–6 Elementary School opened in the fall of 2002, not far from the Denver school. Knowledge Beginnings (formerly called Meritor Academy), an early learning center for infants through private kindergarten located on Grant Ranch Boulevard, offers another choice for parents, as well as open enrollment in Littleton Public Schools. "We think it's good to have opportunities to place our children in schools that best suit their needs," a parent said.[10]

Other Marston Communities

The Marston neighborhood, with its irregular boundaries, includes Grant Ranch and a portion of the Raccoon Creek Golf Course, roughly the area defined by South Sheridan Boulevard on the east, Sumac Street on the south, West Quincy Avenue on the north, and South Wadsworth Boulevard on the west. The Marston neighborhood includes two communities west of South Wadsworth Boulevard, Autumn Run and Park West.

The Autumn Run community extends from South Wadsworth Boulevard to South Estes Street between West Crestline Avenue and South Cross Drive, behind Southwest Plaza Shopping Mall, which was once part of James Grant's ranch. The Park West community comprises homes from South Wadsworth Boulevard to South Kipling Street between West Quincy Avenue and West Belleview Avenue, except for a strip along West Quincy Avenue between South Carr Street and South Kipling Street.

When the school was built, homeowners in these older communities voiced legitimate concerns and arguments against locating the new Denver elementary school in the Grant Ranch community. Park West homeowners said their community had been waiting for a school for at least 20 years, since houses were built in the late 1970s. In spite of protests from the Park West/Autumn Run Homeowners Association, the Denver school board voted to build the new elementary school in Grant Ranch.[11]

Denver Thrives

Denver's appearance has changed over the years as the growing metropolis developed everything from libraries, museums, live theater, art galleries, and a symphony orchestra to several professional sports teams and modern technological centers —all of which attract people of refinement and distinction. U.S. presidents, world leaders, and religious dignitaries, including the pope, have experienced Denver's hospitality. Clearly, Denver has moved beyond its earlier reputation as a cow town to claim its current status as "Queen City of the Plains." And the people of southwest Denver can be proud of their contributions to its rich history.

Modern skyscrapers frame the Voorhies Memorial entrance leading from downtown Denver to Civic Center in 2005. Locals and tourists still enjoy the city's central gathering space, which was developed in the early 1900s.

Notes

CHAPTER 1: *Westside Beginnings*

1. Jerome C. Smiley, *History of Denver* (Denver, Colorado: Times-Sun Publishing, 1901), p. 234.

2. Ibid., pp. 323–324.

3. Hank Fellerman, "Southwest Denver's Civil War Camp: Camp Weld," *Denver Herald-Dispatch*, March 20, 1997, pp. 1, 3.

4. Isabella L. Bird, *A Lady's Life in the Rocky Mountains* (Norman, Oklahoma: University of Oklahoma Press, 1960), p. 138.

5. Phil Goodstein, *Denver Streets: Names, Numbers, Locations, Logic* (Denver, Colorado: New Social Publications, 1994), p. 7.

CHAPTER 2: *Civic Center*

1. William C. Jones and Kenton Forrest, *Denver: A Pictorial History* (Boulder, Colorado: Pruett Publishing Co., Second Edition, 1985), p. 105.

2. Sally Davis and Betty Baldwin, *Denver Dwellings and Descendants* (Denver, Colorado: Sage Books, 1963), pp. 29–34.

3. Thomas J. Noel, *Mile High City: An Illustrated History of Denver* (Denver, Colorado: Heritage Media Corporation, 1997), pp. 52–53.

4. Thomas J. Noel, *Buildings of Colorado* (New York, New York: Oxford University Press, 1997), p. 45.

5. Jones and Forrest, p. 110.

6. David Kent Ballast, *The Denver Chronicle: From a Golden Past to a Mile-High Future* (Houston, Texas: Gulf Publishing Company, 1995), pp. 56–60.

7. Phil Goodstein, *DIA and Other Scams,* Volume Two of *Denver in Our Time* (Denver, Colorado: New Social Publications, 2000), pp. 351–353.

8. Ibid., pp. 354–355.

9. Noel, *Buildings of Colorado*, p. 46.

10. Ibid., pp. 46–48.

11. "Night Lights Bathe the City and County in a Warm Holiday Glow," *Denver Herald-Dispatch*, December 2004.

12. Noel, p. 48.

13. Ibid., pp. 48–49.

14. Civic Center District Plan, "History of Civic Center," City and County of Denver, Planning and Development Office, June 23, 1998, p. 38.

15. Goodstein, p. 254.

16. Ibid., p. 255.

17. Jones and Forrest, p. 257.

18. Denver Art Museum brochure, 2005.

19. Goodstein, pp. 254–255.

20. Ibid., pp. 255–256.

21. Kristi Arellano, "Golden Triangle's King," *Denver Post*, February 29, 2004, pp. 1K, 3K.

22. Ibid.

23. Noel, p. 44.

24. "A Taste of Colorado 2005," *Denver Post*, September 1, 2005, p. 10F.

CHAPTER 3: *Lincoln Park*

1. Lyle W. Dorsett and Michael McCarthy, *The Queen City: A History of Denver* (Boulder, Colorado: Pruett Publishing Company, 1986), p. 1.

2. "Westside Neighborhood Plan," City and County of Denver, Planning and Development Office, p. 2.

3. Jerome C. Smiley, *History of Denver* (Denver, Colorado: Times-Sun Publishing, 1901), p. 735.

4. Ibid., p. 738.

5. Gene Vervalin, *West Denver: The Story of an American High School* (Boulder, Colorado: EHV Publications, 1985), pp. 9–10.

6. Emily M. Marrs, *The Lost History of West* (Denver, Colorado: West High School, 1941), pp. II–10.

7. Bill Barker and Jackie Lewin, *Denver! An Insider's Look at the High, Wide, and Handsome City* (Garden City, New York: Doubleday and Company, 1972), p. 49.

8. Michael Paglia, "Architectural Profile," prepared by the Modern Architecture League for the DPS Historic Preservation Project, Landmark Designation Application, West High School, 1992, p. 4.

9. Interview with Pearle Cameron, September 21, 1999.

10. "History," West High School Singing Christmas Tree Program (Denver, Colorado: West High School, 1995).

11. "West High Named a 'School of Excellence,'" *Denver Herald-Dispatch*, November 2, 2000, p. 16.

12. Don Etter, *The Denver Park and Parkway System*, prepared for the Colorado Historical Society, August 1986, pp. 59–61.

13. Smiley, pp. 542–545.

14. Louise Boyd, "History of Colorado Training School," Denver Public Library, Western History Department Clipping File.

15. "Nurses' Residence Opened in Connection with the Denver General Hospital," *The City and County of Denver Municipal Facts*, January/February 1928, p. 9.

16. Phil Goodstein, *Denver in Our Time,* Volume One: *Big Money in the Big City* (Denver, Colorado: New Social Publications, 1999), pp. 18–21.

17. *Rocky Mountain News*, April 20, 1970, Denver Public Library, Western History Department Clipping File.

18. *Rocky Mountain News*, May 15, 1996, Denver Public Library, Western History Department Clipping File.

19. Laura Glatfelter, "Profile: Dr. Patricia A. Gabow: A Visionary in City Health Care," *Colorado Woman News*, April 2003, pp. 12–13.

20. Ibid., p. 13.

21. Rev. C. J. Darley, "Historical Sketch of St. Joseph's Parish, Denver, Colorado, 1883–1934," p. 1.

22. Gene Fowler, *A Solo in Tom-Toms* (New York, New York: Viking Press, 1946), p. 115.

23. Mary Voelz Chandler, "Denver's Historic Churches Find a Partner," *Rocky Mountain News*, Art & Architecture column, January 2, 2000.

24. William J. Convery III, *Pride of the Rockies: The Life of Colorado's Premier Irish Patron, John Kernan Mullen* (Boulder, Colorado: University Press of Colorado, 2000), pp. 3–87.

25. Ibid., pp. 217–227.

26. Thomas J. Noel, *Colorado Catholicism and the Archdiocese of Denver, 1857–1989* (Niwot, Colorado: University Press of Colorado, 1989), p. 345.

27. Rosemary Fetter, "A Walking Tour of Ninth Street Historic Park," Auraria Communications, 1997.

28. Frances Melrose, "3 Buildings Marked for History," *Rocky Mountain News*, June 2, 1983, p. 29.

29. Phil Goodstein, *Denver Streets: Names, Numbers, Locations, Logic* (Denver, Colorado: New Social Publications, 1994), p. 83.

30. Al Nakkula, "Closing of Byers Branch Library Fought," *Rocky Mountain News*, March 12, 1957, p. 17.

31. Memo from Henry G. Shearhouse, Jr. to Members of the Library Commission, May 6, 1956.

32. "'Historic' Status Stirs Row," *Denver Post*, Denver Public Library, Western History Department Clipping File.

33. "Westside Neighborhood Plan," City and County of Denver, Planning and Development Office, p. 4.

34. "Baker and La Alma/Lincoln Park Neighborhoods Tour, League of Women Voters," June 6, 1982, p. 17.

35. Patricia Callahan, "DHA's North Lincoln Park Is National Model," *Denver Post*, April 6, 1997, pp. 1B, 5B.

CHAPTER 4: *Baker*

1. Nancy L. Widmann, *The Baker Historic District* (Denver, Colorado: Historic Denver, Inc., 1999), p. 68.

2. Widmann, p. 6.

3. National Register of Historical Places Inventory Nomination Form, Item No. 8, p. 1.

4. Ibid., p. 4.

5. Widmann, p. 93.

6. *Colorado History NOW*, Colorado Historical Society, December 2001, p. 10.

7. Interview with Doretta Philpot, August 27, 2003.

CHAPTER 5: *Sun Valley, West Colfax, and Villa Park*

1. "Neighborhood Narrative," City and County of Denver, Planning and Development Office, 1998.

2. Ida Libert Uchill, *Pioneers, Peddlers, and Tsadikum: The Story of Jews in Colorado* (Boulder, Colorado: University Press of Colorado, Third Edition, 2000), pp. 94, 226–227.

3. "Denver Municipal Facts," Rude Recreation Center Files, 1921.

4. Frances Melrose, "Jerome Park Rich in Charm, Neighborly Pride," *Rocky Mountain News*, February 13, 2000, p. 23D.

5. "Neighborhood Narrative."

6. Interview with Jerry Garcia, February 17, 2006.

7. Interview with Edgar "Nick" Nichols Jr., November 23, 2005.

8. Mariah McGuire, "Human Services Center Prepares to Open in 1999," *Denver Herald-Dispatch*, pp. 1, 12.

9. "Neighborhood Narrative."

10. Phil Goodstein, *Denver in Our Time*, Volume One: *Big Money in the Big City* (Denver, Colorado: New Social Publications, 1999), pp. 279–281.

11. Ruth Eloise Wiberg, *Rediscovering Northwest Denver: Its History, Its People, Its Landmarks* (Denver, Colorado: Bradford Printing Company, 1976), pp. 155–157.

12. Uchill, pp. 200–201.

13. Wiberg, pp. 156–157.

14. Ibid.

15. Robert Autobee, *If You Stick With Barnum* (Colorado Historical Society, 1993), pp. 5–6.

16. Ibid., p. 9.

17. Jerome C. Smiley, *History of Denver* (Denver, Colorado: Times-Sun Publishing, 1901), pp. 756–757.

18. "Villa Park Neighborhood Plan," City and County of Denver, Planning and Development Office, April 29, 1991, pp. 4–5.

CHAPTER 6: *Barnum and Barnum West*

1. Robert Autobee, *If You Stick With Barnum* (Colorado Historical Society, 1993), p. 9.

2. Victoria Cooper, "Exploding Denver's P.T. Barnum Myths," *Rocky Mountain News*, Lifestyles section, October 9, 1990, p. 34.

3. Phil Goodstein, *Denver Streets: Names, Numbers, Locations, Logic* (Denver, Colorado: New Social Publications, 1994), pp. 34–36.

4. Cooper, p. 34.

5. Autobee, pp. 9–10.

6. Ibid., p. 62.

7. Ibid., p. 11.

8. Ibid., p. 15.

9. Ibid., p. 11.

10. Roscoe Fleming, "William Norman Bowman," *Rocky Mountain News*, October 25, 1941, Denver Public Library, Western History Department Clipping File.

11. National Register of Historic Places, Statement of Significance, August 1986, Section 8, p. 2.

12. "The Red Brick Savio House Completes 'Mission Impossible,'" *Denver Herald-Dispatch*, July 18, 2002, pp. 1, 6.

13. Interview with Ivan Rosenberg, 1995.

14. "Quentin Rosenberg Passes Away at 75," *Denver Herald-Dispatch*, August 7, 1997, pp. 1, 3.

15. "Community Cry Is Heard! We're Back!" *Denver Herald-Dispatch*, July 26, 2001, p. 1.

16. Autobee, p. 19.

17. "Reminiscences of Mrs. Leopold," *Denver Herald-Dispatch Southwest Denver Progress Edition*, April 22, 1965, pp. 9–10.

18. Interview with Waldon and Dorothy Brose Garlington, January 7, 1998.

19. Interview with Bill Jeffs, May 1997.

20. Autobee, pp. 21–22.

21. Ibid., p. 25.

22. Ibid., p. 26.

23. Ibid., p. 32.

24. Ibid., p. 33.

25. "Longtime Barnum Resident Moves, Missed by Many," *Denver Herald-Dispatch*, June 5, 2003, p. 7.

26. Autobee, pp. 37–38.

27. Ibid., p. 38.

28. Ibid., pp. 57–58.

29. Socrates Apergis, "Tribute to My Father, Anthony Apergis," *Denver Herald-Dispatch*, October 12, 2000, pp. 1, 10.

30. Mike Kirkpatrick, "Federal Heating Up the Neighborhood," *Denver Herald-Dispatch*, January 27, 2000.

31. "Barnum Lake: Forgotten Project?" *Denver Herald-Dispatch*, October 3, 1996, p. 3, and "Barnum Lake Gets Facelift," *Denver Herald-Dispatch,* January 22, 1998, p. 7.

32. Hank Fellerman, "Local Landmark Moving to Lakewood," *Denver Herald-Dispatch,* January 15, 1998, p. 1.

33. Autobee, p. 61.

CHAPTER 7: *Valverde and Athmar Park*

1. Landmark Designation Application, February 20, 1997.

2. Ibid.

3. Registration Statement, City and County of Denver, Department of Zoning Administration, December 21, 1955.

4. Interview with Jeanne Amen, September 27, 2000.

5. "Valverde Neighborhood Plan," City and County of Denver, Planning and Development Office, May 1991, p. 4.

6. "Athmar Park Neighborhood Perimeter Plan," Denver Community Planning and Development Agency, September 6, 2000, p. 18.

7. "Valverde Neighborhood Plan," p. 5.

8. Jerome C. Smiley, *History of Denver* (Denver, Colorado: Times-Sun Publishing, 1901), pp. 884–885.

9. Jennifer A. Darr, "Valverde Elementary Celebrates 75th Anniversary," *Denver Herald-Dispatch*, March 11, 1999, p. 7.

10. E. J. Clark, M.D., "Valverde and Her Celery Industry," *The City and County of Denver Municipal Facts*, October 11, 1913.

11. "Valverde Neighborhood Plan," p. 5.

12. Clark.

13. Ibid.

14. "Valverde Neighborhood Plan," p. 5.

15. "Hangman's Tree," *Denver Herald-Dispatch Southwest Denver Progress Edition*, April 22, 1965, p. 4.

16. "History in a Nugget of Valverde Elementary School," by Kay Mills, Program Chairman, undated report, Valverde Elementary School file.

17. Darr. p.7.

18. Internet site, http://www.archives.state.co.us.

19. Interview with Karen Gowans, September 27, 2000.

20. "Valverde Neighborhood Plan," p. 13.

21. Ibid., p. 35.

22. Ibid., p. 5.

23. Ibid.

24. "Athmar Park Neighborhood Perimeter Plan," Denver Community Planning and Development Agency, September 6, 2000, p. 20.

25. "St. Rose of Lima Celebrates 75 Years," *Denver Herald-Dispatch*, August 12, 1999.

26. Daniel Williams, "Valverde to Hold Reunion Picnic 29th," *Denver Herald-Dispatch*, July 5, 2001, pp. 1, 26.

27. "Valverde Neighborhood Plan," p. 6.

28. Ibid., pp. 16, 43.

29. Ibid., p. 34.

30. Hank Fellerman, "West Denver Jail Site Cancelled," *Denver Herald-Dispatch*, July 10, 1997, p. 1.

31. "Athmar Park Neighborhood Perimeter Plan," p. 18.

32. Ibid., pp. 18, 20.

33. Ibid.

34. Ibid.

35. Frances Melrose, "When New Homes Featured Bomb Shelters," *Rocky Mountain News*, October 12, 1997.

36. "Athmar Park Neighborhood Perimeter Plan," p. 28.

37. "Athmar Park Residents Enjoy Area's Diversity," *Denver Post*, January 10, 1993, p. 1H.

38. Sharon R. Catlett, "Saigon Educator's Escape to U.S. Buffered by Years of Education," *Denver Post*, Neighbors Central section, April 8, 1981, p. 4.

39. "Asian Market Expanding," *Denver Herald-Dispatch*, June 10, 1999, pp. 1, 19.

40. "Alameda Business Projects Under Way," *Denver Herald-Dispatch*, August 26, 2004, p. 9.

CHAPTER 8: *Westwood*

1. Willets Farm Map 1899, Denver Public Library, Western History Department.

2. "School History," *The Crusader Yearbook*, Garden Home High School, 1940.

3. Betty Baker, "Westwood Elementary School—Then and Now," undated report.

4. Sam Lusky, "New Annexations to City Being Planned, Is Report," *Rocky Mountain News*, October 15, 1944.

5. "Attempt Biggest Grab to Date," *Englewood Enterprise*, December 14, 1944, Denver Public Library, Western History Department Clipping File.

6. "Westwood School Scandal," *Denver Herald-Dispatch Southwest Denver Progress Edition*, April 22, 1965, pp. 9a–10a.

7. Ibid.

8. Interview with Charles Allen, April 25, 1996.

9. Interview with Wanda Bradley Chase, January 19, 1996.

10. Interview with Bill Mahana, October 20, 1999.

11. Interview with Lue Setta Mahana, October 20, 1999.

12. Interview with La Rue White Belcher, September 8, 1999.

13. Alex Murphree, "Wilford H. Woody," *Denver Post*, March 24, 1947.

14. Interview with Lena Lovato Archuleta, October 6, 2003.

15. "Center Has Come Long Way," *Denver Herald-Dispatch Supplement—Southwest Community Center*, March 4, 1976, p. 2.

16. "Westwood Community Complex Is Center of Beauty and Practicality," *Denver Herald-Dispatch Supplement—Southwest Community Center*, March 4, 1976, p. 4.

17. Interview with Jan Marie Belle, November 11, 2003.

18. "SWIC Celebrates 10 Years of Community Service," *Denver Herald-Dispatch*, August 20, 1998, pp. 8, 9.

19. "SWIC History Part II 1987–1988," *Denver Herald-Dispatch*, August 27, 1998, pp. 8, 9.

20. Ibid.

21. "Community 'Unity' Bolstered by New Westwood Family Health Center," *Denver Herald-Dispatch*, July 17, 2003, p. 24.

22. Eric N. Bowen, "Indian Center Graduates Its Final Class," *Denver Herald-Dispatch*, March 21, 1996, pp. 1, 3.

23. Charles Leckenby, "American Indian School to Open Doors Again," *Denver Herald-Dispatch*, April 11, 1996, p. 1.

24. Letitia Foisset, "Indian Center Appoints Executive Director," *Denver Herald-Dispatch*, February 24, 2000, p. 4.

25. Interview with Bill Mattocks, October 6, 2005.

26. "Thank You, Cathy," *Denver Herald-Dispatch*, May 23, 1996, p. 27.

27. Mariah McGuire, "Landmark to Be Bulldozed for Street Widening," *Denver Herald-Dispatch*, June 24, 1998, pp. 1, 8.

28. Olivia DiFeterici, "T-Wa Inn: Denver's First Remains No. 1 in Vietnamese Cuisine," *Denver Herald-Dispatch*, November 13, 2003, p. 12.

29. Michael Holzmeister, "Property to Be Mix of Commercial, Residential Buildings," *Denver Herald-Dispatch*, March 30, 2000, p. 7.

CHAPTER 9: *Mar Lee*

1. "Fred Jackson, Pioneer SW Denverite, Passes Away at 82," *Denver Herald-Dispatch*, April 11, 1996, p. 5.

2. Interview with Ruth Jackson, May 8, 1996.

3. "Harry Davis, Lawyer, Dies," *Denver Post*, September 8, 1968, p. 22.

4. Interview with Richard Kolacny, February 24, 2006.

5. Interview with Elroy Adams, February 27, 2006.

6. Interview with Jerry and Debbie Smith, September 3, 2005.

7. "Garden Home Grange #407," Colorado State Grange History, 1874–1975 (Westminster, Colorado: North Suburban Printing and Publishing, 1975), pp. 191–193.

8. Interview with Dorothy Ridgely, January 16, 2006.

9. Interview with Louis and Waneta Cuhel, Jeanette Simons, and Linda Intrery, April 21, 2005.

10. Ibid.

11. Denver City Directory, 1960.

12. Interview with Candis Holmes Pilosi, November 2, 2002.

13. "Lutheran High School Completes Successful Decade," *Denver Herald-Dispatch Southwest Denver Progress Edition*, April 22, 1965, p. 21a.

14. "The Saga of Harvey Park," *Denver Herald-Dispatch Southwest Denver Progress Edition*, April 22, 1965, p. 38.

15. Interview with Steve and Peggy Hildmann, February 23, 2004.

16. Eddie Britt, "Neighborhood Mobilizes Battle Heading to Governor," *Denver Herald-Dispatch*, November 23, 2000, p. 7.

17. "Mar Lee Fight Against State Agency Leads to Governor," *Denver Herald-Dispatch*, November 9, 2000, pp. 1, 8, 19.

CHAPTER 10: *Ruby Hill and Overland*

1. "Paper Now King," *Rocky Mountain News*, August 23, 1891, p. 1, Denver Public Library, Western History Department Clipping File.

2. "Manchester," *Rocky Mountain News*, May 27, 1892, Denver Public Library, Western History Department Clipping File.

3. "New Paper Combination," *Denver Times*, January 24, 1901, Denver Public Library, Western History Department Clipping File.

4. William Logan, "Some Hearts Hang Heavy as Tall Landmark Tumbles," *Rocky Mountain News*, March 29, 1964, p. 8, Denver Public Library, Western History Department Clipping File.

5. Ibid.

6. "Southwest Denver Neighborhood Tour, League of Women Voters," 1977, Denver Public Library, Western History Department.

7. "Ruby Hill Fires Called Nuisance," *Rocky Mountain News*, April 19, 1946, Denver Public Library, Western History Department Clipping File.

8. Geoffrey L. Muntz and Alan S. Wuth, *A Path Through Time: A Guide to the Platte River Greenway* (Frederick, Colorado: Jende-Hagan Bookcorp, 1983), pp. 16–18.

9. Gene Amole, "About the Author," *Morning* (Denver, Colorado: Denver Publishing Company, 1983), back page.

10. Gene Amole, "Diary of Dying," *Rocky Mountain News*, December 6, 2001.

11. "Ruby Hill Park Master Plan," City and County of Denver, Department of Parks and Recreation, April 27, 2004, p. 5.

12. Millie Van Wyke, *The Town of South Denver* (Boulder, Colorado: Pruett Publishing Company), 1991, p. 107.

13. "Ruby Hill Park Master Plan," Appendix C.

14. Jan Marie Belle, "Neighborhood Organizations Celebrate Traffic Changes," *Denver Herald-Dispatch*, June 17, 2004, p. 5.

15. "Ruby Hill Park Master Plan," p. 34.

16. "The Cotton Mill," *Denver Republican*, June 4, 1890, Denver Public Library, Western History Department Clipping File.

17. "Benjamin Lindsey: Colorado's Little Giant," *Colorado History NOW* (Colorado Historical Society, July 2003), p. 3.

18. "Not Enough Unskilled Workers in Colorado to Maintain Textile Industries, He Says," *Denver Republican*, October 10, 1901, Denver Public Library, Western History Department Clipping File.

19. "Many on Verge of Starvation," *Denver Republican*, December 8, 1903, Denver Public Library, Western History Department Clipping File.

20. "David Moffat Helps to Relieve Suffering at Overland Mills," *Denver Republican*, December 10, 1903, Denver Public Library, Western History Department Clipping File.

21. Ibid.

22. "Plan Reopening of Cotton Mills," *Denver Republican*, March 16, 1904, Denver Public Library, Western History Department Clipping File.

23. John Rebchook, "Old Industrial Building Made History," *Rocky Mountain News*, July 11, 1995.

24. Ibid.

25. Van Wyke, pp. 25, 26, 107, 108.

26. Ibid., p. 109.

27. Ibid., pp. 109, 110.

28. Ibid., pp. 111, 112.

29. Todd Phipers, "Overland Gets New Look at 100," *Denver Post*, June 22, 1995, p. 6D.

30. Van Wyke, pp. 129, 130.

31. Interview with Deborah Sanchez, January 20, 2006.

32. "Shattuck District Plan: An Economic Feasibility Plan for the Redevelopment of the Shattuck Superfund Site and Context," Prepared for the City and County of Denver Community Planning and Development Agency and Mayor's Office of Economic Development and International Trade, Adopted by Denver City Council February 2003, p. 7.

33. Van Wyke, pp. 8–9.

34. Phil Goodstein, *Denver in Our Time,* Volume One: *Big Money in the Big City* (Denver, Colorado: New Social Publications, 1999), p. 401.

35. Muntz and Wuth, pp. 9, 21, 31.

36. Interview with Jack Unruh, January 24, 2006.

CHAPTER 11: *South Platte and College View*

1. Interview with Loretta Dardano, June 2, 2005.

2. Bill Miller, "Just a Row of Shanties in Denver Town," *Rocky Mountain News*, December 27, 1954, Denver Public Library, Western History Department Clipping File.

3. Ibid.

4. F. George Robinson Sr., "Outline of Robinson Brick Company History," May 9, 1985.

5. Ibid.

6. "Celebrating 125 Years of Excellence," Robinson Brick Company publication, 2005.

7. "College View Plan," City and County of Denver, Planning and Development Office, Neighborhood Planning Program, June 1972.

8. Interview with Mary Wilderson, May 6, 2004.

9. "Background of the Community Ministry Thrift Shop," March 1968, Files of Community Ministry of Southwest Denver.

10. "Protestant Women, Nuns Join in Helping Low-Income Area," *Denver Post Zone 2*, July 5, 1967, p. 23.

11. "College View . . . a Place . . . a Mood . . . a Challenge," by Louise Bartko, Loretto Heights College.

12. Ibid.

13. "History," undated paper, Files of Community Ministry of Southwest Denver.

14. "Youth Council Community Project," August 12, 1971, Files of Community Ministry of Southwest Denver.

15. "Sharings," May 1981, Files of Community Ministry of Southwest Denver, pp. 1–3.

16. "News Release," May 25, 1993, Files of Community Ministry of Southwest Denver.

17. Interview with Christy Ziemba, March 1, 2005.

18. "College View Plan."

19. Ibid.

20. Peter Lisowski, "$3.6 Million College View Elementary Set to Open," *Denver Herald-Dispatch*, August 3, 1995, p. 1.

21. Interview with Gil Gallegos, January 17, 2007.

CHAPTER 12: *Harvey Park*

1. Harry F. Shuart, "Wilberforce Whiteman Quits Schools as Music Instructor to Become Farmer," *Denver Post*, May 18, 1924, Denver Public Library, Western History Department Clipping File.
2. Frances Melrose article, *Rocky Mountain News*, November 27, 1983.
3. Thomas A. DeLong, *Pops: Paul Whiteman, King of Jazz* (Piscataway, New Jersey: New Century Publishers, 1983), pp. 75, 130.
4. Shuart.
5. Melrose.
6. Barbara Sievers article, *Denver Post Zone 2*, June 27, 1962, p. 19.
7. "A Look at the Past," *Denver Herald-Dispatch*, November 27, 1997, p. 3.
8. Sievers.
9. "Arthur Harvey," *Denver Post*, March 24, 1976, p. 32.
10. Thomas J. Noel, *Mile High City: An Illustrated History of Denver* (Denver, Colorado: Heritage Media Corporation, 1997), p. 206.
11. "Denver Petitions to Annex Part of Arapahoe County," *Denver Post*, March 8, 1946, Denver Public Library, Western History Department Clipping File.
12. Noel, pp. 207–209.
13. Ibid.
14. Interview with Basil and Julia Turner, June 5, 2005.
15. Interview with Ginny Grace, March 1, 2005.
16. "Brentwood UMC 50th Anniversary 1950–2000," Brentwood United Methodist Church, pp. 1–6.
17. "All Saints," Booklet by All Saints Church, September 22, 1961, pp. 1–20.
18. "$9 Million Homes Project Started in Harvey Park," *Denver Post*, September 9, 1954, p. 1.
19. "Lakeridge Typical of S.W. Denver Residents," *Denver Herald-Dispatch Southwest Denver Progress Edition*, April 22, 1965, p. 3a.
20. Interview with Bob Werner, January 2006.
21. Interview with James Probst, January 2006.
22. Interview with La Rue Belcher, September 8, 1999.
23. Sharon R. Catlett, "Kunsmiller Community Center Concept Becomes a Reality," *Denver Post Zone 3*, October 15, 1975, p. 2.
24. Sharon R. Catlett, "Harvey Park Center's Utilizing New Facilities," *Denver Post Zone 3*, October 22, 1975, p. 14.

CHAPTER 13: *Harvey Park South*

1. "Historic American Buildings Survey Inventory," National Register of Historic Places, May 1968.
2. Ibid.
3. Lois Cress, "Every Day's New for Postmaster," *Denver Post*, Denver Public Library, Western History Department Clipping File.
4. Interview with Sister Mary Ann Coyle, August 8, 2000.
5. Olga Curtis, "Sister P.J. at Loretto," *Denver Post Empire* magazine, February 4, 1968, pp. 11–14, Denver Public Library, Western History Department Clipping File.
6. "Teikyo Loretto Heights University Celebrates 5-Year Anniversary," *Denver Herald-Dispatch*, November 30, 1995, p. 6.
7. Manny Gonzales, "Charter School to Join Teikyo Campus," *Denver Post*, March 15, 2004, p. 2B.
8. Interview with Linda Stebbins, 1977.
9. "The Saga of Harvey Park," *Denver Herald-Dispatch Southwest Denver Progress Edition*, April 22, 1965, p. 38.
10. Ibid., p. 40.
11. Phil Goodstein, *DIA and Other Scams,* Volume Two of *Denver in Our Time* (Denver, Colorado: New Social Publications, 2000), p. 112.
12. "The Saga of Harvey Park."
13. Interview with Ted and Doris Hackworth, June 22, 2004.
14. Interview with Jeanne Faatz, May 12, 2004.
15. Interview with Carol Harris, June 2, 2005.
16. "Southwest Denver Neighborhood Tour," Bear Creek Park, League of Women Voters, 1977, Denver Public Library, Western History Department.

CHAPTER 14: *Fort Logan*

1. Earl McCoy, *From Infantry to Air Corps: History of Fort Logan* (Boulder, Colorado: The Denver Westerners Roundup, November/December 1986), pp. 4–5.
2. Ibid., p. 6.
3. Evan Edwards, "Historical Background of Fort Logan, Colorado," Paper presented to Denver Westerners, August 25, 1962.
4. "Friends of Historic Fort Logan," Newsletter, Winter 1999, p. 2.
5. William Bright, *Colorado Place Names* (Boulder, Colorado: Johnson Books, 2004), p. 162.
6. Edwards.
7. "Typical Day at Fort Logan," *Colorado Sun*, January 10, 1892, Denver Public Library, Western History Department Clipping File.
8. "Fighting Seventh Departs for Cuba," *Rocky Mountain News*, April 21, 1898, Denver Public Library, Western History Department Clipping File.
9. McCoy, pp. 9–11.
10. *Denver Times*, November 17, 1901, Denver Public Library, Western History Department Clipping File.
11. Edwards.
12. "Colorado Mental Health Institute at Fort Logan," Brochure.
13. "Friends of Historic Fort Logan," Brochure.
14. "New Fort Logan Homeless Shelter for Families Is in Need of Donations," *Denver Herald-Dispatch*, January 27, 2005, p. 6.

15. Edwards.

16. Talk by Earl McCoy, Bear Valley Library, October 6, 1995.

17. "Fort Logan National Cemetery," *Denver Herald-Dispatch*, May 25, 1995, p. 1.

18. "Fort Logan National Cemetery," National Cemetery Administration of Veteran's Affairs, Brochure, 2006.

19. William J. Convery III, *Pride of the Rockies: The Life of Colorado's Premier Irish Patron, John Kernan Mullen* (Boulder, Colorado: University Press of Colorado, 2000), pp. 205–211.

20. Brother Bernard Kinneavy, F.S.C., *The History of J. K. Mullen High School* (Denver, Colorado), pp. 6–8.

21. Ibid.

22. Thomas J. Noel, *Catholicism and the Archdiocese of Denver, 1857–1989* (Niwot, Colorado: University Press of Colorado, 1989), p. 133.

23. Kinneavy, p. 9.

24. Ibid., p. 49.

25. Interview with Karen Scharf, June 16, 2004.

26. Charlie Leckenby, "'The Cave' Area Construction Begins," *Denver Herald-Dispatch*, May 9, 1996, p. 1.

27. Carl A. Norgren, *As I Was Saying* (Boulder, Colorado: Johnson Publishing Conpany, 1965), pp. 22–23.

28. Thomas J. Noel, *Mile High City: An Illustrated History of Denver* (Denver, Colorado: Heritage Media Corporation, 1997), pp. 308–309.

29. Norgren.

30. Talk by Jim Prochaska, Kaiser Elementary School, November 15, 1995.

31. Interview with Marie Stearns Perlman, July 24, 2002.

32. Thomas J. Noel, *Buildings of Colorado* (New York, New York: Oxford University Press, 1997), pp. 130–131.

33. Prochaska.

34. "Southwest Denver Neighborhood Tour, League of Women Voters," 1977, Denver Public Library, Western History Department.

35. "History of the Southwest Family YMCA," Fact Sheet.

36. Interview with Linda James, August 19, 2005.

CHAPTER 15: *Bear Valley*

1. National Register of Historical Places, No. 8, Statement of Significance, pp. 1–3.

2. Thomas Moore, "The Meeting of the Waters," poem.

3. LeRoy Standish, "Molly Brown Memories," *Sentinel and Transcript Newspapers*, August 22, 2002, p. 4.

4. Kristen Iversen, *Molly Brown: Unraveling the Myth* (Boulder, Colorado: Johnson Books, 1999), pp. 52–57.

5. Interview with Jane Garland, March 9, 1998.

6. "Interview with Mr. Richard Duke," *Centennial-Bicentennial Bear Valley 1776–1876/1976–USA, Littleton Independent, 1976*, pp. 10–11.

7. Sharon R. Catlett, "Illegal Dumping Creates Nuisance in Bear Valley," *Denver Post Central Zone*, July 1, 1981, p. 3.

8. "Council Annexes 470 Acres Despite Annexation Warning," *Rocky Mountain News*, October 11, 1960, p. 8.

9. Ellison Smith, "Bear Valley: A Political Mushroom," *Denver Post*, May 9, 1963, p. 88.

10. Sharon R. Catlett, "Barnum, Bear Valley Use Sweat, Agency Funds for Improvements," *Denver Post Central Zone*, June 10, 1981, p. 7.

11. Thomas Graf, "'Graying' Enclave's Just Fine," *Denver Post*, December 8, 1985, p. 30.

12. Sharon R. Catlett, "Input Is Sought on Bridge Plan," *Denver Post Central Zone*, January 7, 1981, p. 14.

13. Interview with Joyce Neufeld, January 5, 2006.

14. "Bear Creek Swim and Tennis Club Hosts Free Open House May 22," Denver Herald-Dispatch, May 12, 2005, p. 14.

15. Interview with Tony and Carol Bilello, January 2006.

16. Sharon R. Catlett, "Students 'Fly' in Kennedy Classroom," *Denver Post Zone 2*, June 1975, p. 20.

17. Sharon R. Catlett, "JFK Biology Students Feed 4 Head of Cattle," *Denver Post Zone 2*, June 23, 1976, p. 16.

18. Interview with Kelly Haggerty, June 17, 2004.

19. Gene Amole, "About the Author," *Morning* (Denver, Colorado: Denver Publishing Company, 1983), back page.

20. "Amole's Diary of Dying," *Rocky Mountain News*, January 31, 2002.

21. Interview with Lyle and Ruedene Kyle, November 30, 2005.

CHAPTER 16: *Marston*

1. Jerome C. Smiley, *History of Denver* (Denver, Colorado: Times-Sun Publishing, 1901), pp. 794–795.

2. Ibid., pp. 801–802.

3. William C. Jones and Kenton Forrest, *Denver: A Pictorial History* (Boulder, Colorado: Pruett Publishing Company, Second Edition, 1985), p. 136.

4. "Marston Treatment Plant," Denver Water, 1600 W. 12th Ave., Denver, CO, 80204, 2006.

5. "Southwest Denver Neighborhood Tour," League of Women Voters, 1977, Denver Public Library, Western History Department.

6. Interview with Marty and Kristy Mamigonian, October 10, 2005.

7. Interview with Donna McNulty, December 7, 2005.

8. Wilbur Fiske Stone, *History of Colorado* (Chicago, Illinois: SJ Clarke, 1918–1919).

9. Interview with Newell Grant, December 7, 2005.

10. "Grant Ranch Elementary," *Denver Herald-Dispatch*, March 1, 2001, pp. 1, 3.

11. Mike Kirkpatrick, "Controversy Continues Over Proposed Location of New School," *Denver Herald-Dispatch*, February 17, 2000, pp. 1, 15.

Photo Credits

Cover: J. K. Mullen High School (left); Permission of Newell M. Grant (center); J. K. Mullen High School (bottom)

Title Page Courtesy, Colorado Historical Society, George D. Wakely, CHS.X4777

Page 7 Denver Public Library Western History Collection, X-8480

Page 8 Courtesy, Colorado Historical Society, Neg. No. F.799

Page 10 Courtesy, Colorado Historical Society, F 34671

Page 12 Denver Public Library, Western History Collection, X-18291

Page 13 Denver Public Library, Western History Collection, Charles D. Kirkland, X-25044

Page 15 Denver Public Library, Western History Collection, Jennings and Russell, X-26104

Page 17 Denver Public Library, Western History Collection, X-28214

Page 18 Dorothy Brose Garlington

Page 23 Denver Public Library, Western History Collection, X-29804

Page 24 Denver Public Library, Western History Collection, George L. Beam, GB-7469

Page 25 Denver Public Library, Western History Collection, X-28846

Page 26 Denver Public Library, Western History Collection, Z-2348

Page 29 Denver Public library Western History Collection, Louis Charles McClure, MCC-2966

Page 31 Sharon Catlett

Page 33 Courtesy, Colorado Historical Society, F36701

Page 35 Denver Public Library, Western History Collection, X-28572

Page 42 Denver Public Library, Western History Collection, Harry Mellon Rhoads, Rh-1038

Page 44 Denver Public Library, Western History Collection, MCC-3673

Page 46 Denver Public Schools

Page 47 Denver Public Library, Western History Collection, Barbara S. Norgren, X-25528

Page 49 Courtesy, Colorado Historical Society, Brown-Byers Studio

Page 51 Lindell Catlett

Page 52 Denver Public Schools

Page 55 Courtesy, Colorado Historical Society, CHS.X7230

Page 59 Lindell Catlett

Page 60 Denver Public Schools

Page 61 Denver Public Schools

Page 65 Sharon Catlett

Page 68 Ivan Rosenberg Family

Page 71 Dorothy Brose Garlington

Page 75 Sharon Catlett

Page 81 Denver Public Library, Western History Collection, Louis Charles McClure, MCC-2722

Page 83 Courtesy, Colorado Historical Society, Charles S. Lillybridge, CHS-L1014, CHS-L1063, CHS-L1792

Page 86 Duane Howell, The Denver Post

Page 87 Duane Howell, The Denver Post

Page 95 Denver Public Schools

Page 99 Wayne Frank, Janet Merrifield Steele

Page 102 Lena Archuleta

Page 104 Southwest Denver Improvement Council

Page 106 Southwest Denver Improvement Council

Page 107 Southwest Denver Improvement Council

Page 107 Southwest Denver Improvement Council

Page 111 Anthony Merelli

Page 114 Ruth Jackson

Page 117 Richard Kolacny

Page 118 Elroy Adams

Page 121 Waneta Cuhel

Page 122 Waneta Cuhel

Page 123 Sharon Catlett

Page 129 Courtesy, Colorado Historical Society, Buckwalter CHS. B347

Page 132 Denver Public Library, Western History Collection, X-20702

Page 136 Denver Public Library, Western History Collection, X-19871

Page 142 Ira Kay Sealy, *The Denver Post*

Page 144 Denver Public Library, Western History Collection, X-23912

Page 144 Robinson Brick Company

Page 149 Community Ministry

Page 153 Gil Gallegos, College View Recreation Center

Page 155 Courtesy, Colorado Historical Society, Denver Post Historical Collection 86-296-4657

Page 161 Brentwood United Methodist Church

Page 163 Lakeridge Association

Page 165 La Rue Belcher

Page 166 Irwin Steiner

Page 169 Loretto Heights College Records, Archives and Special Collections, Regis University

Page 174 Denver Public Library, Western History Collection, X-28015

Page 177 Terrace Club

Page 180 Denver Public Library Western History Collection, George L. Beam, GB-7560

Page 182 Courtesy, Colorado Historical Society, George L. Beam, CHS.X7034

Page 187 Courtesy, Colorado Historical Society, F16203

Page 187 J. K. Mullen Foundation

Page 189 J.K. Mullen High School

Page 197 Courtesy, Colorado Historical Society, F4099

Page 199 Mary Rose Shearer

Page 199 Christopher Catlett

Page 205 Denver Public Schools

Page 206 Kelly Haggerty

Page 207 Dean Krakel, Rocky Mountain News

Page 208 Ed Maker, The Denver Post

Page 209 Denver Public Library, Western History Collection, X-23981

Page 210 Denver Water

Page 213 Courtesy, Colorado Historical Society

Page 214 Permission of Newell M. Grant

Page 217 Millie Van Wyke

Index